Inside Hamas

ALSO BY
Zaki Chehab

Inside the Reisistance

INSIDE HAMAS

The Untold Story
of
the Militant Islamic Movement

ZAKI CHEHAB

NATION
BOOKS

WWW.NATIONBOOKS.ORG

INSIDE HAMAS:
The Untold Story of the Militant Islamic Movement

Copyright © Zaki Chehab 2007

Published by
Nation Books
An Imprint of Avalon Publishing Group, Inc.
245 West 17th Street, 11th Floor
New York, NY 10011

Nation Books is a copublishing venture of the Nation Institute and Avalon
Publishing Group, Incorporated.

AVALON
publishing group incorporated

Library of Congress Cataloging-in-Publication Data is available.

ISBN-13: 978-1-56025-968-8
ISBN-10: 1-56025-968-X

9 8 7 6 5 4 3 2

Printed in the United States of America
Distributed by Publishers Group West

Contents

Preface

Tense with anticipation after clearing my luggage with the Jordanian customs, I braced myself for the border crossing ahead. On that sunny May morning in 1998, as I approached Israel for the first time, I was preparing for the inevitable grilling in light of my Palestinian heritage. I boarded one of the ageing buses which ferry passengers at regular intervals between the Jordanian side of the border and the Israeli checkpoint. Glancing around at my fellow passengers as we travelled across no man's land – the narrow King Hussein Bridge separating Jordan from the Israeli border – I noted that the majority of my fellow travellers were Palestinians like me.

Young Israeli soldiers supervised by Israeli intelligence took turns asking the purpose of my journey. As the interrogation wore on, it sunk in that, despite the fact that I was standing in the land of my forefathers, it was I who was the stranger. As I was body-searched, the questions continued. Whom was I going to see? Was I carrying any weapons? Where was I born? I was born in Tyre, just a few miles from Israel's border with south Lebanon. They appeared suspicious of my answers and asked me to wait in the interrogation room while they excused themselves to a side room to confer. Nothing in their attitude reflected the triumph of the signed Oslo Peace Accords, negotiated over a five-year period and which seemed to herald the end of decades of bloodshed, hatred and wars. I was finally given permission to enter Israel, not because of my Palestinian background, but thanks to my British passport.

As I emerged on the Israeli side of the border, my first thought was to wonder what ancient secrets the craggy hillsides must hold about this beautiful but troubled land. Driving towards Jerusalem, the often repeated stories of my parents and grandparents as they described their homeland unfolded in front of my eyes. I no longer felt a stranger as the scenery, until now just a mental picture, rolled past the windows. But beyond the fields of my parents' memory were the Jewish settlements. Row upon row of white houses with red rooftops spread along the hilltops like mushrooms, a man-made blot on the natural landscape.

It was with a sense of unreality that I finally arrived in Jerusalem. I had chosen to stay at the American Colony Hotel because it was in East Jerusalem, the Palestinian side of the city. My colleagues had recommended this well-known refuge for foreign correspondents so that I would not feel out of place in the Holy City. I immediately set out to experience Jerusalem with Mohammed Salhab, an old friend who lives within the ancient city walls. He owns an antique shop not far from Al Aqsa mosque, which was top of my list of sites to visit. The third holiest shrine for Muslims worldwide, its modest silver-black dome is almost eclipsed by the golden dome of the Mosque of Omar that dominates the panoramic view of old Jerusalem.

We were soon walking through the narrow alleys lined with tiny shops crammed with spices, brass antiques, silverware and wooden souvenirs. Palestinians dressed in their traditional *galabieh* robes with black-and-white chequered *kofiehs* jostled with guidebook-carrying tourists and Orthodox Jews wearing their distinctive black hats and floor-sweeping coats. A sense of *déjà vu* again washed over me, as these scenes were reminiscent of those described to me so many years ago as a child in Lebanon.

It was Friday, the Muslim holiday, and thousands of Palestinians, young and old, men and woman, had challenged the Israeli measures restricting them from praying at Al Aqsa. As we moved slowly through the crowded alleyways, Mohammed surprised me by picking up every clean newspaper or piece of cardboard he spotted on the ground. As we approached the gate which opened into the mosque's courtyard, I was taken aback by the scale of the Israeli military presence: soldiers and police were checking every person who entered. It was then that I learned the purpose of the papers Mohammed had been conscientiously gathering. He spread them on the ground of the courtyard as makeshift prayer mats. Thousands of us would be praying outdoors as every inch of the Mosque's prayer hall was already covered with kneeling worshippers. I thought of my mother and father, whose dream it has always been to pray in the very place I was sitting. So strong is this longing that on the wall of our home back in Burj El Shamali camp in Lebanon there is a three-dimensional model of the Al Aqsa mosque complex and its iconic golden dome. They have not been allowed to visit the country since they fled in 1948. Mohammed, who is married to an English lady and is not very observant in his practice of Islam, explained to me the profound feeling he and many Palestinians like him experience, which brings them here each Friday. It is their way of expressing, at least once a week, that Jerusalem is theirs too and the Israelis cannot ignore them.

My first visit to the Holy Land was to last one month. It was not just a personal pilgrimage; I had been following the Palestinian cause and its leaders around the world for decades. With the signing of the Oslo Accords in 1993, these leaders had come home and were trying to build their state. For five years, after he had returned from exile in Tunis, the Palestinian leader Yasser Arafat encouraged me to visit him at his headquarters in Ramallah and Gaza. Similarly, during telephone interviews I conducted with them from London, Sheik Ahmed Yassin, Hamas' spiritual leader and Dr Abdul Aziz Al Rantisi, a Hamas firebrand and leader, would urge me to come to Gaza. I also wanted to see Mahmoud Abbas, the Palestinian president who was at that time heading the Palestinian negotiating team with Israel. Abbas did his best to convince me to visit my parents' home town in the Galilee, but this was one journey I was not ready to make. I could not go there before a just peace had been achieved.

Shortly after my arrival in Jerusalem, Arafat invited me for lunch in his Ramallah headquarters, housed in the former British mandate headquarters which later became those of the Israeli administration in the West Bank. Arafat had made himself very much at home, styling his office in a similar fashion to every other headquarters he had made in exile. A poster of Al Aqsa mosque was behind a desk piled high with papers and faxes, and there was a large table that at every meal would accommodate a number of advisers, petitioners and visitors. Arafat's expression of happiness was unforgettable as he kissed and hugged me warmly and greeted me: 'Welcome to Palestine!'

After lunch we sat and talked in private. He was about to leave for Saudi Arabia for an audience with the late King Fahad, and he asked if I would wait in Gaza until his return forty-eight hours later. It was an experience for me to observe the crowds of Palestinian women who would gather next to his office overlooking Gaza beach to ask for financial assistance or help of other kinds. Arafat was childlike in expressing his enthusiasm for all things Gazan. Born and raised in Gaza, he would say to me things like 'Isn't Gaza's fish the best you have ever tasted in your life?'

I finally came face to face with Sheikh Ahmed Yassin and Dr Abdul Aziz Al Rantisi, the most influential figure in the Hamas movement at that time and second in command during the Yassin era. When I had only been able to talk to them over the telephone, they had been guarded in their answers but now, on the ground, as I sat in their homes and talked about their plans and goals, they were much more frank and gave me an insight into the underground political organization they were developing.

At the end of my month in the West Bank, Gaza and Israel, I returned to Lebanon. In one day, I travelled through three countries, crossing from Jerusalem to Jordan via the Allenby Bridge and then flying from Amman to Beirut that same afternoon. On the plane back to the Lebanese capital, I reflected on how the reverse journey would be the ultimate dream for my mother Fatima, who today is still living in the refugee camp in southern Lebanon where she was forced to flee to from her village in the Galilee. My welcome back to Burj El Shamali camp where I grew up was overwhelming. It was a little before midnight and my parents couldn't conceive that I was back amongst them, having seen me reporting live just the day before from the Gaza Strip. My mother cried uncontrollably when I told her that I had prayed at the Al Aqsa Mosque in Jerusalem. Her wish to pray there before she dies is still unfulfilled.

As I lay in bed that night, I mentally reviewed the experiences of my trip. I had seen at first hand Palestinians living in the camps of the occupied territories, and I found they were just as determined and ready to endure whatever it takes to get their own identity and live in dignity – just as those who live in my family's refugee camp in Lebanon.

Since that first visit to Palestine, I have returned several times. First to cover the suspicious death of the Palestinian leader Yasser Arafat, then the assassinations of both Sheikh Yassin and Dr Abdul Aziz Al Rantisi. I speculated then, as I do now, how much more blood will be shed in order to influence decision-makers to take the difficult steps to bring peace and justice to the Palestinians and peace and security to the Israelis.

1

Choreographed Victory

A few blocks down from the White House, in the State Department's Harry S Truman building, US Secretary of State Condoleezza Rice had called an out-of-hours Saturday meeting of her staff.[1] On the agenda was Hamas' surprise landslide victory in the Palestinian national elections. 'Why was it that nobody saw it coming?' Rice asked. Answering her own question, she continued, 'It does say something about us not having a good enough finger on the pulse.' One of her staff said it showed how deep the divisions were between the Palestinians and the Israelis, despite the support and encouragement both had received from the international community to solve their bitter enmity. Fatah, the ruling party which had been dominated by Yasser Arafat's leadership since the 1960s, had been in peace negotiations with Israel for over a decade, yet Palestinians had turned their backs on it, instead casting their vote for Hamas, a party which condoned violence and refused to recognize Israel. The vote was a crystal clear expression of how the Palestinians viewed their traditional political masters. 'I don't know anyone who was not caught off-guard by Hamas' strong showing,' Rice reflected.[2]

The following day, Rice flew to London for a two-day conference attended by delegates from seventy countries to discuss the situation

1

in Afghanistan as well as the Middle East conflict and the emerging tension with Iran. In yet another demonstration of America's failure to keep its finger on the pulse, Rice was heard to comment: 'Some say that Hamas itself was caught off-guard by Hamas' strong showing.'[3]

But Hamas had not been caught off-guard. In fact many Palestinian commentators were bewildered by the ignorance displayed by Rice and other US officials of the depth of hostility felt by Palestinians towards their own leadership and Israel. Hamas' success can be credited, in some part, to an artfully choreographed strategy of deception.

On the day of the Palestinian elections, 25 January 2006, which saw 1,073,000 Palestinians going to the polls,[4] I met one of Hamas' top leaders, Dr Mahmoud Al Zahar, a physician who was subsequently appointed Foreign Minister in Ismail Haniyeh's Hamas-led government. Over a cup of tea in his house in the centre of Gaza City, Abu Khalid, as he is known, smiled broadly as he told me how Hamas had been well prepared for this so-called shock. In the six months leading up to the elections, the party faithful had worked tirelessly with their activist base to ensure that everyone – including Fatah and Hamas supporters – remained in the dark about their forthcoming victory. Zahar revealed how Hamas voters had been instructed to react if asked about their voting preference. They were advised to avoid the question if possible but, if pressed, they were told to give a misleading response. In this way, the pollsters were tricked months ahead of the election into predicting that Fatah would once again form the next government.

On the eve of the elections, the Israeli army's Chief of Staff, Lt. General Dan Halutz, confidently told the Committee for Foreign Affairs and Security in the Knesset that he expected the Fatah movement to win, but with a small majority. His prediction was based on 'the wise men of Israeli intelligence',[5] in reference to a special military intelligence department, *Aman*, which, among other things, produces national intelligence estimates and predictions for the Prime Minister and his Cabinet.

The failure to foresee the election's outcome was a huge embarrassment for the intelligence agencies. 'If they don't know what's happening in the Palestinian territories, how are we going to rely on them for what's happening in Iran?' asked an editorial in the Israeli daily *Yedioth Ahronoth*. Looking for a scapegoat, the intelligence outfits targeted Professor Khalil Al Shikaki, a sociologist and specialist in opinion poll surveys, claiming that he had grossly misled them. Not only had the polls carried out by his institute, the Palestinian Center for Policy and Survey Research (PSR),[6] misled Israeli intelligence agencies and their government; the views expressed by Shikaki's centre were taken seriously by decision-makers and institutes worldwide, due to his reputation as a respected Palestinian political analyst. Despite being the brother of Fathi Shikaki, the leader of Islamic Jihad, Shikaki doesn't share his brother's extremist views. With degrees from the American University of Beirut and Columbia University, he has for the last decade coordinated his research with organizations such as the Royal Institute for International Affairs in London and the Harry S Truman Institute for the Advancement of Peace at the Hebrew University of Jerusalem. It eventually emerged that information gleaned from the Internet was the main source for Israeli intelligence agencies' analysis of the elections.

After a day spent interviewing party candidates and the electorate on their way to the polls, I drove to my hotel, passing deserted traffic junctions lit with burning car tyres. In the distance, car horns tooted and blared, sounded by supporters and the military wings of both Hamas and Fatah – each of whom were celebrating long before the victor had been declared.

From my room at the Palestine International Hotel overlooking the harbour of Gaza City, I settled down to watch the post-election analysis on television. Late into the night, Shikaki appeared on Al Jazeera in a live interview from Ramallah. 'How did you get it so wrong?' he was bluntly asked. Shikaki appeared embarrassed and hesitant and found difficulty in justifying how his polls had continually misjudged the intentions of the electorate in the months leading up to the elections. In one survey, published on 11 December 2005, he had talked about the rise of Fatah's fortunes. 'The improvement in the popularity of Fatah in the Gaza Strip in the last three months was as a result of the public reception to the

3

Israeli withdrawal from the Gaza Strip, one month before.' At that time, he had predicted that Fatah would get fifty per cent of the votes, while Hamas would get thirty-two per cent, with nine per cent going to the other candidates and another nine per cent of the voters undecided. In an earlier public opinion poll, issued by his centre on 25 September 2005, he had predicted that forty-seven per cent would vote for Fatah, thirty-two per cent for Hamas, eleven per cent for 'others' and twelve per cent undecided. (He had allowed for a margin of error of three per cent.) Shikaki had expected Fatah to lose about ten per cent of the vote if it failed to choose the right candidates in some of the constituencies but, on the day of the poll, Hamas won more than half the seats while the previous ruling party, Fatah, managed just one third. The final result: 74 of the 132 seats in the Palestine Legislative Council went to Hamas, while 45 went to Fatah.

Nine months earlier, following a three-day round of talks in Cairo attended by delegations from thirteen Palestinian factions, the Hamas delegates had declared their intention to take part in the forthcoming election process. They had previously boycotted the 1996 elections in protest at the Oslo Peace Accords signed by the Palestine Liberation Organization (PLO) with the Israeli government. Mainstream groups like Fatah interpreted Hamas' about-turn as a de facto acceptance of the Oslo agreements and a climbdown from their position concerning Israel's right to exist.

After their return to Gaza from Cairo, Hamas leaders appointed a campaign team drawn from experts in communications, sociology, politics, and economics – covering every sector which affects society and the Palestinian way of life. The Islamic University in Gaza became the nerve centre for their election strategy. One of their first tasks was to divide voters into three categories: supporters, waverers and rivals. The waverers received maximum attention because Hamas strategists believed that the majority of voters fell into this camp. Their ploy was not necessarily to convince them to accept Hamas' policies but to highlight the inadequacies of their opponents. By exploiting Fatah's previous history of bad governance, corruption and failure to achieve any real progress in its negotiations with Israel, they duly persuaded sufficient numbers of waverers to vote for the Hamas candidate. One group Hamas worked hard to lure was the young. Again they used the record of the Fatah government on issues relating to high unemployment, the poor economic situation, corruption and the need for transparency in government to convince them to vote for change. Women waverers were particularly vulnerable to Hamas' tactics at a time when the Gaza Strip was blighted by kidnapping and violence.

In choosing a slogan for the election list, Hamas was careful to avoid anything which hinted at its military agenda, settling instead for an upbeat rallying cry which translated as 'For Change and Reform!' Hamas was now the voice of social concern. They would change people's lives. In order to woo the Palestinian vote, they omitted any reference to their ambitions to destroy Israel, even hinting at a measured rapprochement. 'We won't rule out negotiations with the Jewish State,' said the group's number two candidate, Sheikh Mohammed Abu Teir, in an interview outside Jerusalem's Al Aqsa Mosque. 'Israel and a future Palestinian state could live side by side.' At least for a generation or two, he qualified. I was reminded of something the late Sheikh Ahmed Yassin, the spiritual leader of Hamas, had told me ten years earlier. In the presence of Ismail Haniyeh, he told me that Hamas was prepared to negotiate a truce as a long-term solution to the conflict with Israel but he felt it would be impossible to sustain. He preferred to leave the dilemma to future generations when the current old vanguard of fighters and politicians had died off to be replaced by younger blood. With his impish smile, he said his instinct predicted that the Jewish State would no longer exist in three decades.

Hamas wasted no opportunity convincing the wavering voters to place their X with the Hamas candidate on election day. They targeted mosques, family contacts, neighbours, schools and workplaces. On the media front, a Hamas spokesperson was always made available to answer journalists' requests for interviews, provide background information or accompany them on the campaign tour. These requests were given priority according to the importance of each TV channel or publication and its audience reach. If there was to be a radio or TV debate between Hamas candidates and their rivals, such was their media savvy that Hamas officials would negotiate with the producers to be the first to start the debate and be given the final word.

It is unclear how much Hamas invested financially to achieve its triumph. Their Fatah rivals gave me figures ranging from $22 million to $30 million. The official figure given to me by the Election Commission was $3 million. Their political rallies in Gaza City were attended by tens of thousands. Programmes informing the public of these rallies were distributed well in advance from mosques, libraries, schools and universities. They were aired over local radio stations or posted on the Internet, which became one of Hamas' strongest weapons of communication. Their rallies were peaceful and slick. On election day, there were marshals to organize the traffic and marshals to control the crowds. All their campaign workers were given sandwiches and cold drinks to sustain them through the day.

The count was still in progress in the early hours of the following morning when I telephoned the constituency office of Fatah's rising star, Mohammed Dahlan, to enquire about the results. I was told by a member of his staff that Dahlan was already holding a meeting in his Khan Younis constituency and suggested I go there. By the time I arrived in Gaza's second largest city, convoys of cars, open-topped trucks and buses were converging from nearby Rafiah and the outer fringes of Khan Younis to celebrate Fatah's victor in the movement's stronghold. They must have been relying on exit poll predictions delivered by pollsters including Shikaki, whom TV stations such as Al Jazeera, Al Arabia and western news networks were authoritatively quoting. A casually dressed Mohammed Dahlan was following the news while fielding a plethora of congratulatory calls from all over the Palestinian territories. He calmly tried to curb their enthusiasm, asking people to be patient and wait for the official results. He then decided to take a drive around the streets of Khan Younis to experience for himself the mood of the electorate and asked me to accompany him. Mohammed's distinctive convoy was recognized by passers-by, whom he saluted in response as we drove to Al Amal Hospital, where he had set up an office for his election campaign team.

Dahlan, who was sceptical about the accuracy of opinion polls, was the only politician I encountered throughout the election period who refused to depend on independent polls. He preferred to rely on the research of his campaign team, each working independently of one another to analyse voter preferences. His workers found a conflicting picture developing to that being offered by the opinion polls. Dahlan began to receive worrying news that large numbers of the Palestinian police and security services had voted in favour of Hamas. His advisers predicted that at least forty per cent of these civil servants attached to the Palestinian Authority had voted for Hamas, which dramatically swung the results in favour of his rivals. Dahlan, who had by now realized that his movement's chances of victory were fading, pleaded with his callers to allow a peaceful transfer of power if Hamas won the election. Despite the movement's failure, Dahlan, together with one other Fatah candidate, Sofyan Al Agha, guaranteed his seat and secured the largest number of votes in his constituency with 38,349 votes, just ahead of his closest rival, Younis Al Astal of Hamas, who gained 37,695 votes.[7] Another factor contributing to Fatah's downfall was the defection by large numbers of its candidates who had failed to secure a place on the Fatah election list and had stood as independents. The votes lost by Fatah to these independents were significant.

Hamas' strong showing in cities like Gaza, Ramallah and even the historically Christian town of Bethlehem was considered a protest vote against Fatah rather than mass solidarity for Hamas. Although recognition of Israel by the Palestinian Authority had improved the image of Palestinians in the international arena, the quality of life for families living in the West Bank and Gaza was worse than it had been before 1993, when Israeli soldiers withdrew from the main Palestinian cities and the Palestinian Authority began what was intended to be self-rule.

During Israel's weekly Cabinet meeting on Sunday 29 January 2006, directly following the Palestinian elections, the following Cabinet Communique was issued:

Acting Prime Minister Olmert said: 'As soon as the results of the PA elections became known, I consulted with various elements in order to analyse the new situation that has been created. Following these consultations, we announced that the State of Israel will not negotiate with any Palestinian administration even part of which is composed of an armed terrorist organization that calls for the destruction of the State of Israel. This position has won admiration in both Israel and around the world to the best of our knowledge. It has also met with the widespread agreement and understanding of almost all international elements. At the same time, we announced that Israel would continue to act against terrorism everywhere, at any time; there is no intention to compromise on these matters.'

Ehud Olmert had taken over up reins of government while Ariel Sharon lay in a coma in a Jerusalem hospital, felled by a stroke just two months after leaving the hardline Likud Party to form a party of his own which he called Kadima, a Hebrew word for 'Forward'. Olmert was aiming to win the Israeli elections a month later by garnering support from the full Kadima slate and those Likud and Labour figures who had defected to Sharon's new party. Olmert had to walk a fine line following Hamas' rise to power between Sharon's new centrist approach, while talking tough in refusing to deal with a Hamas government whose commitment was to destroy Israel. The former hardliner Sharon's new popular centrist party was built around the notion that Israel's security would be best assured not through endless and fruitless negotiations with the Palestinians, but by disengaging from them altogether on Israel's own terms.

Hamas' victory had an enormous impact on the campaigning in the Israeli election, with opposition politicians pouring scorn on the government for failing to prevent the Islamic movement's rise to prominence. 'We are talking about an earthquake that has sent us back fifty years and will lead the entire region into chaos,' warned Silvan Shalom,[8] a member of the Knesset from the hawkish Likud Party who resigned as Foreign Minister in anticipation of the 28 March elections.

Benjamin Netanyahu, the former Prime Minister and leader of the Likud Party, argued that 'Israel's unilateral withdrawal from Gaza boosted Hamas' victory' because 'it could claim that terror works.' He called on Israeli leaders to 'stop any further withdrawals and move the barrier eastward and deeper into Palestinian land if Hamas sticks to its radical agenda'. Less than a day after the official announcement of the results, relatives of some of the hundreds of Hamas' bombing victims descended on a café in the centre of Jerusalem which had itself been hit by a suicide bomber in 2002. Eli Cohen, the coffee shop owner, said that 'Palestinians had merely exercised their right to throw out an incompetent, corrupt government. They think that Hamas will do better. Not for the terror. This is my opinion. I don't think they vote for the terror. I think they vote for their jobs and food and the kids.' Erik Ascherman, from Rabbis for Human Rights said: 'We also share responsibility for what happened and still have some hope that maybe Hamas will decide they must now be politicians, diplomats, states-people and not terrorists.'[9]

Some Israeli political analysts called on their government to take advantage of the moral odium surrounding Hamas – at least in western political circles – to bolster the image of the Jewish State, which had become tarnished after decades of criticism over its occupation of the West Bank and Gaza and their ongoing construction of a concrete barrier known as the 'apartheid wall' or 'Berlin Wall' by Palestinians and the 'separation fence' by the Israelis. The fence, expected to extend to 650 kilometres and a height of up to eight metres, places the Palestinians in a stranglehold, annexing farmers from their land, businessmen from their premises, families from one another and cutting off many from access to water.

Following my tour of the polling stations of the Gaza Strip and especially in Gaza City, I had speculated on the scale of support for the Hamas movement. The city has its share of well-off citizens and certain families are known for their taste for the good life, enjoying evenings out at the many restaurants and coffee shops which have flourished in the micro-economic boom of Gaza City, while the rest of the territory crumbles into abject poverty. Palestinians from the Diaspora had had high hopes following the Oslo and Washington peace accords with Israel in 1993 and 1994 and returned to the Palestinian Territories. Most of the returnees were members of the PLO and it didn't seem to matter whether they were high- or low-ranking members, their lifestyles exceeded those of many of their fellow Palestinians back in Gaza and the West Bank. They added another tier to the class system and were described by local Gazans as *Al Aedoun*, which literally means 'the returnee' but has connotations of 'nouveau riche'. The Al A'adeen had grown accustomed to the trappings of wealth and a way of life which bore no comparison to life in the territories. But back in the territories there were no houses and apartments of the standard they were accustomed to, so they began to build grandiose villas or six-storey apartment blocks. The camp refugees, so unaccustomed to the sight of such luxury, referred to these apartments as 'the Towers', whose owners drove around in Mercedes cars or the latest 4x4 jeeps which put them totally at odds with the rest of the Palestinian population. This cultural divide was seized on by Hamas and its followers and used to criticize the PLO and its officials of corruption and the vulgar misappropriation of money intended for its poor citizens. One city resident told me, 'We want to teach them [Fatah] a lesson so that they will not ignore us in the future. We don't believe in Hamas' political views, but we want to show the Fatah leadership that we have alternatives, and if they want to make a comeback they have to consider our views and respect us as voters.'

I had lunch with Ismail Haniyeh at his home in Al Shati camp the day after the election following an invitation from his son. Despite the clear blue sky, sunlight barely penetrated the densely packed houses of the refugee camp. By the time I arrived, hundreds of well-wishers, including a large contingent of Ez Ed Din Al Qassam fighters, were winding their way through the narrow alleyways towards Haniyeh's house. The sounds of victory songs and gunshots punctuated the air, competing with the high-pitched ululating of the camp's elderly women – a tradition in the Middle East during times of joy and sadness. One of the black-clad women, a close neighbour of Haniyeh, told me: 'Abu Al Abed [Haniyeh's familiar name] is a good leader. We feel safe in his hands.'

Forging my way through the joyous crowds, I found Abed waiting for me outside the metal gates leading to their two-storey house. Haniyeh's elder brother, also known as Abu Al Abed, was visiting and I congratulated him on his brother's list victory as he offered me some Arabic sweets in welcome while we waited for Ismail who was giving thanks at the mosque. People of all ages and walks of life lined up outside the house to offer their congratulations and I was surprised to see amongst them high-ranking Palestinian police officers and civil servants. It was proof that Hamas had support even from the Palestinian Authority. By their easy conversation, it appeared they were continuing a dialogue which was established long before election day. It was then that I fully understood to what degree the hopes of the Fatah candidates and their leadership had been dashed. It was taken for granted that the majority of Palestinian Police – which number more than 80,000, together with those working for the different security organizations, not forgetting their families – would automatically vote for Fatah. As it turned out, at least forty per cent of these cast their votes for Hamas.

The buzz travelling through Ismail Haniyeh's house that morning was inevitably about their victory. Haniyeh's eldest brother was keen to engage me in conversation, telling me about the hard work invested by his brother to achieve his success and that he had no concerns about forming an alliance with others to appoint a government. Manoeuvring his way through the throng of TV cameras, Ismail finally returned home looking every inch the statesman with his embroidered brown *abaya*, short-trimmed beard and a white scarf to keep out the January chill despite the sunny weather. In no time a tent was erected and chairs laid out to act as an alternative reception room to his home, which was unable to accommodate the swell of well-wishers. After apologizing for his delay, he reminded me of our first meeting back in 1996, which had taken place at Sheikh Yassin's house. Haniyeh's habitual calm manner made him the natural first choice as the new leader of Hamas. He had no history of confrontation with other Palestinian leaders and he spoke deferentially towards Mahmoud Abbas (also known as Abu Mazen), whom he referred to as 'the President'. He told me, 'We in Hamas only took it [victory] for granted when Abu Mazen himself announced that Hamas had won the election.' The first to call and congratulate him on his movement's victory from Fatah was Hussein Al Sheikh, a senior member of the party in Ramallah in the West Bank.

Despite his hectic day, the new leader of Hamas insisted that my cameraman and I share lunch with him and his son and brother, ordering a takeaway version of a celebratory meal of chicken and rice. Over lunch, Haniyeh outlined his vision for the future of his government and expressed his relief and happiness about the smooth running of the election, which won praise around the world, including from former US President Jimmy Carter, who was in charge of the foreign observer team.

By the early hours of 26 January, it was all over for Fatah. The extent of their loss was devastating. Calls went unanswered. Mobiles were switched off. It wasn't until the early afternoon that they started wakening up to the many questions they had to answer, from their families, friends, followers and sympathizers, regarding their performance as guardians of the national cause.

As evening fell, Fatah's military wing was unable to contain its anger. Fatah militiamen took to the streets of Gaza and Ramallah, directing their ire towards the skies with hundreds of rounds of machine-gun fire and accompanied by chants calling for their leaders to be held accountable for the defeat. Dahlan's phone was ringing incessantly. He was the only Fatah leader left holding things together, at least in the Gaza Strip. After answering calls from Mahmoud Abbas and talking to other senior Fatah leaders, against his advisers' wishes, Dahlan took the decision to face the fury after watching what appeared to be alarming television images showing members of Fatah's militias occupying the offices of the Legislative Council. Some news channels were even suggesting civil war brewing. Dahlan, who is considered enemy number one amongst Hamas followers because of his popularity within his own party and for his tough rhetoric against Hamas, succeeded in defusing the situation after promising the Fatah fighters that whoever was responsible for Fatah's defeat would indeed be held accountable. Magnanimously, he also called on them to respect the democratic and fair elections which had brought his rivals to power.

Of the other political factions, the Popular Front for the Liberation of Palestine (PFLP) founded by George Habash won three seats; the Democratic Front for the Liberation of Palestine (DFLP) led by Nayef Hawatmeh, the Third Way, a newly launched independent movement led by Salam Fayyad, a former World Bank official, and Hanan Ashrawi, an ex-minister and spokeswoman for the Palestinian Authority, and Dr Mustafa Barghouti, a principled advocate of non-violence who stood as an independent candidate of

Independent Palestine, won two seats apiece and the Independents won four. Other Palestinian factions failed to earn a place in the Legislative Council, particularly those who had been active on the political scene since the 1960s, such as the Palestinian National Front (PNF) led by Samir Ghouseh.

I was not surprised by the poor performance of these decades-old factions. Growing up in Burj Al Shamali, a refugee camp close to the city of Tyre in Southern Lebanon, my experience of these factions was that they were on the far left of the Palestinian political movement with sympathies more in line with Marxism. Some refugee camps were represented by several different movements and their individual camp headquarters were decorated with iconic photographs of Che Guevara or pictures of Lenin and Mao Tse-tung. Moscow was the focus for their ideology and we used to have a saying that 'if it was cloudy in Moscow, it would rain over their camp headquarters.' Many Palestinians studied or received military training in Russia, Cuba and China and would bring back literature which took pride of place in their particular factions' HQs. The Little Red Book in Arabic would be propped up against works of Lenin and Marx while the floors would be littered with magazines from Russia containing articles written in Russian and Arabic. Refugees in general were not in favour of their left-leaning politics. They were more concerned about adequate sanitation, improving their cramped housing conditions and eking out the little money they earned from poorly paid seasonal agricultural work. These factions had to work hard to attract followers, managing to a certain degree by providing some social activities in order to draw young kids and women to attend their functions and training courses.

But their time had passed. That was obvious in the early hours of 26 January 2006, as a surging tide of rippling green was the sight greeting anyone out on the streets. Flags and banners bearing the slogan 'Islam Is the Solution', baseball caps and scarves, cardboard Islamic crescents and sweat shirts, weaved and waved in the united colour of victory: green for Hamas. Despite the crowds and the unexpected outcome of the election, no violent incidents were reported that day. Even the burning car tyres outside my hotel, which would normally signify trouble, were shrugged off by the receptionist at the front desk as 'just Hamas celebrating'.

In stark contrast, I visited friends in a known Fatah stronghold in Al Zahraa, a suburb of Gaza. There was absolute silence. The streets were deserted. Dr Zahar had warned me that not only was Hamas planning to win the majority of seats, but they intended to leave Fatah activists with a sense of shame and embarrassment. Only hours before, Fatah supporters had been driving around Gaza City in large convoys, car horns blaring and giant-sized yellow flags waving in euphoric anticipation. They had prepared only for victory. The bubble had burst and the atmosphere plummeted into one of mourning. A sense of foreboding about the future hung in the air.

2

Hamas
Is Born

At ten past two on the afternoon of 6 June 1989, Sheikh Ahmed Ismail Hassan Yassin, a resident of Gaza City, collapsed in Gaza Central Prison at the sound of Israeli jailers beating his son Abdul Hamid. He had been tortured for many days, and this finally drove the disabled Sheikh to make a full confession about his role in launching Hamas. He had previously denied being the 'Father' of the Hamas movement, but compromising statements written by his comrades under duress, together with the torture of his son, forced the Sheikh into a volte-face. Israeli investigator number 54962, Shoki Amzayj, was summoned by one of the torturers and told that Sheikh Yassin was ready to confess. Amzayj, pen and paper in hand, prompted the Sheikh and the confessional began.

Sheikh Ahmed Yassin was born in 1938 in the village of Al Jourah near the coastal town of Al Majdel in what was then southern Palestine under the British Mandate. Al Majdel is now the Israeli city of Ashkelon, but the prison is still referred to by its old Palestinian name. His father Abdullah died when he was just three years old, and he became known in the neighborhood as Ahmed Sa'adeh after his mother Sa'ada Al Habeel. This was to differentiate him from the children of his father's other three wives. Sheikh Yassin had four brothers and two sisters, who, with their mothers, fled their village to Gaza during the 1948 conflict and became refugees in Al Shati Camp beside the sea on the northern side of Gaza City. The tented camp accommodated 23,000 refugees at that time, all crammed into an area of just under one square kilometre.[1]

It was thirty-seven years before Yassin disclosed to his family the true story of the accident which changed his life in 1952. The reality was that he was injured while wrestling with one of his friends, Abdullah Al Khatib. Young Yassin was scared to name the boy for fear that it would cause a rift between the two families, so he concocted a story that his injuries were sustained playing leapfrog during a sports lesson with his school friends on the beach. His neck was kept in plaster for forty-five days and, when the plaster was removed, it was clear that he was going to live the rest of his life as a quadraplegic.

He had damaged his spinal chord, which caused severe paralysis to much of his body leaving him incapable of walking or even holding a pen or a pencil. Although he applied to study at Al Azhar University in Cairo, he was unable to pursue his studies because of his deteriorating health. He was forced to study at home where he read widely, especially on philosophical matters and on religion, politics, sociology and economics. His worldly understanding, his followers believe, made him one of the best speakers in the Gaza Strip, drawing large crowds at Friday prayers when he delivered his weekly sermon.[2]

After years of unemployment, he got a post as an Arabic language teacher at Al Rimal Elementary School in Gaza. Headmaster Mohammed Al Shawwa had reservations concerning the reception the Sheikh would receive from the pupils, since children can be awkward when faced with disability. According to Al Shawwa, however, Yassin handled them well and his popularity grew, particularly amongst the more scholarly students.

His teaching methods provoked mixed reactions among parents, who noticed that their kids were keen to attend the mosques to receive religious education. While the majority were happy, a few made complaints to the headmaster. Al Shawwa recalled one father telling him that he was OK about visits to the mosques for religious study 'but too fast at this early age twice a week ... [as

Sheikh Yassin was advising them to go on Mondays and Thursdays]
is not acceptable.' The headmaster stood by his teacher. Having a
regular job gave Yassin financial stability and he was encouraged
to marry one of his relatives, Halimah Hassan Yassin, in 1960 at
the age of twenty-two. Together they produced eight daughters and
three sons.

Sheikh Yassin's contribution to the growth of the Islamic movement
in Palestine emerged out of his conviction that students must have
an Islamic education and understand the meaning of jihad. But he
also knew the value of giving them a rounded education. I spoke to
many from his generation, including his brother Bader, who told
me in 1992 that the Sheikh encouraged the youth to organize sports
teams and participate in social and cultural functions in addition to
their religious studies.

After the Egyptian revolution and the subsequent mass arrests
of members of the Muslim Brotherhood, Jamal Abdul Nasser
extended his crackdown on the outlawed organization to the
Gaza Strip which at that time was under Egyptian control. Large
numbers of Palestinian activists were arrested in 1966 and anyone
engaged in Islamic politics was under suspicion. Among them was
Sheikh Ahmed Yassin, who, together with a number of other young
Palestinians, was accused of trying to overthrow the regime in
Egypt. Yassin's ill health prevented him from going to an Egyptian
prison with the others and Egyptian intelligence decided that his
disability was serious enough to restrict his potential for causing
trouble. He was detained for two weeks, then released and ordered
to remain under house arrest after signing a paper guaranteeing that
he would not deliver any speeches, especially after Friday prayers.
The first Friday after his release, he went to pray in Al Shati mosque,
where his regular audience begged him to give his weekly sermon.
Without hesitation he broke his agreement. Afterwards, the small
bearded figure, dressed top to toe in white robes like some ethereal
figure from a bygone age, was carried aloft on the shoulders of
delighted worshippers, celebrating his return.

A few months later, in June 1967, Israel launched what has
become known as the Six Day War, referred to by the Palestinians
as Al Nakbah. This war ended with Israel seizing control of the Gaza

Strip from the Eygptian government and the whole of the West
Bank from Jordan and occupying the Syrian Golan Heights.

From Al Shati mosque, Yassin began broadening his appeal by
making appearances at other mosques in the area. His was the most
famous voice in the Gaza Strip. He started collecting donations,
placing small boxes in mosques to help the needy and the poor which
was carried out discreetly to avoid yet another arrest by the Israeli
forces. His announcement that special religious lessons for females
were being offered in the mosques was revolutionary. Until then,
only males attending prayers at mosques were eligible for Qur'anic
instruction. In the late 1970s, an official from the Department of
Education, accompanied by a high-ranking Israeli officer, arrived at
his school with the news that the Sheikh was not qualified to teach.
He was forced into retirement and the Sheikh used the situation to
his advantage by concentrating more on his Islamic teachings and
enlarging his circle of followers.

Yassin had been active in Islamic politics in Gaza since the
1970s. Like many of Hamas' early members, he was influenced by
the revolutionary ideas of Al Ikhwan Al Muslimeen – the Muslim
Brotherhood. The Brotherhood was created as an Islamic revivalist
movement following the collapse of the Ottoman Empire, and what
they saw as the creeping secularism and westernization of Egypt.
Founded in 1928 by a religious scholar named Hassan Al Banna,
the Brotherhood became a political group in Egypt in 1936 when
it took up the cause of Palestinian Arabs against the Zionists and
British rule. Al Banna, known as the 'Supreme Guide', dispatched
his Brothers as missionaries to preach the word and perform social,
charitable, educational and religious work in towns and countryside
alike.[3] Al Banna himself visited Palestine between 1942 and 1945,
establishing several branches of the Brotherhood in some of its
major cities. Groups in Jordan and Syria also embraced the Islamic
movement. These branches played an essential role in the 1948 war.[4]
At that time the Gaza Strip was under Egyptian authority, and the
Brotherhood blamed its government for being passive towards the
'Zionists' and sided with the Palestinians in their war against Israel.
According to Abdul Fattah Dokhan, 'More than one hundred Muslim
Brotherhood martyrs died in that war in the land of Palestine.' The

Brotherhood then began to perform terrorist acts on its own soil in Egypt which led to a temporary ban of the movement. A Muslim Brother assassinated the Prime Minister of Egypt, Mahmoud Fahmi Nokrashi, on 28 December 1948. Al Banna was subsequently killed by government agents in Cairo in February 1949. The Brotherhood was legalized again by the Egyptian government but only as a religious organization. This state of affairs proved temporary as a result of the Egyptian Revolution of 1952.[5]

Nasser was wary of the Brothers and their political and military ambitions, and particularly their desire for Egypt to be governed by sharia law. Thousands of Brotherhood activists were imprisoned or executed and once again the movement found itself outlawed, driving it underground. This crackdown stultified the Islamic movement, leaving the 1950s and 1960s to the Arab Nationalists, communists and others on the left of the political spectrum.

After 1967, however, when Israel captured Gaza from Egypt, the Brotherhood's counterpart in Palestine was becoming more active, spreading their ideology and working towards increasing their independent influence within Palestinian society. They set up charitable organizations and established religious schools and kindergartens which were normally attached to the mosques. These activities became more widespread in 1973 when the Muslim Brotherhood, or other Islamist groups sympathetic to them, set up Islamic societies in Gaza, Hebron, Nablus and Jerusalem.

Following the ideas and teachings of the Brotherhood, Sheikh Yassin had set up an Islamic Society in 1976. By 1978, it was felt that a bigger and better-organized institution was needed to promote Islamic values in Palestinian society, which for the Islamists was intimately bound up with resistance to Israel. That year, he helped set up another organization called the Islamic Compound. As President of the organization between 1973 and 1983 (he was succeeded on his imprisonment by one of his fellow Hamas founders, Dr Ibrahim Ali Yazuri), the first thing Yassin did was to register it with the Israeli authorities. A licence was granted within two hours but, barely an hour later, the Israelis came to Sheikh Yassin and withdrew their consent, claiming there had been a mistake. The mosque and its nursery were closed and they took

Sheikh Yassin and Haj Ahmed Dalloul, another member of the committee, for questioning, accusing them of collecting donations without permission and setting up a foundation.

Israel's back-pedalling over the licence followed criticisms from Sheikh Mohammed Awwad, who was in charge of the Islamic courts. The timing was shortly after the Camp David Agreements were signed between Israel, Egypt and the USA. Sheikh Hashem Al Kazandar, who was in favour of Egypt's peace agreement with Israel, planned to send a delegation to Cairo in support of the Egyptian government. Sheikh Yassin took advantage of this plan and dispatched Sheikh Abd Al Aal, a fellow activist, to see Sheikh Al Kazandar 'to tell him that the Israeli authorities were about to imprison us because of the Compound we had established'. Sheikh Abd Al Aal accompanied Kazandar to the Israeli Civil Administration office in Gaza where Kazandar convinced the Israelis to reinstate the approval. Kazandar was reassured that by the time he returned from Egypt, approval would be granted and, according to Yassin, 'that is exactly what happened.'

The Israeli decision, despite obvious second thoughts, to grant the licence to the Islamic Compound in Tel Aviv was an indicator of what would become unannounced, but official, Israeli policy. The Israeli government perceived its staunch enemy to be the nationalist and secular PLO and, by allowing Islamist rivals to flourish, believed that opposing Palestinian groups would do its work on the ground in a way that did not necessitate active Israeli involvement.

During an interview in his office, Arafat's security adviser Mohammed Dahlan once told me that Yitzhak Rabin, Defense Minister in Yitzhak Shamir's coalition government, was questioned by members of the Knesset about his supposed support of Hamas by funding the Islamic Compound and its activities. Rabin's short answer was that it was a tactic 'to undermine the influence of the PLO'. He was also apparently quizzed by another Knesset member about the possibility of Hamas working against Israel. Rabin's reply was: 'This issue can be discussed later.'

The Islamic Compound's activities as defined by its licence were supposed to focus on sports but, in practice, Yassin admitted, 'We were spreading the message of Islam, memorising the Qur'an, and building mosques, schools, and clinics.' When Israel realized what kind of activities the Compound was involved in they began to impose restrictions – decreeing what was allowed and what was not. Nevertheless, the Islamic Compound soon became the largest foundation in Gaza.

'We didn't really have the infrastructure to carry out military activities,' Yassin explained in an interview at his house in the Jourat Al Shams neighbourhood in January 1999. 'But by the 1980s we had grown in strength, and began amassing weapons. Many of us were imprisoned for this but, on our release in 1985, we had developed a strategy. We prepared ourselves and the Intifada began.'

Back in 1983, Yassin and other leaders of his local organization, the Islamic Compound, were looking for weapons to arm their military wing, the Mujahideen Falastine, which Yassin had established the previous year. This was new territory for them and their lack of experience at weapons procurement made them vulnerable to the attentions of Israel's intelligence service, the Shabak. Israeli intelligence succeeded in infiltrating the Islamic Compound and helpfully provided armaments (in other words, conducted a sting operation). Sheikh Yassin, Dr Ibrahim Al Maqadma, Abdul Rahman Tamraaz, Mohammed Chehab, Mohamed Arab Mahara and others were subsequently arrested for possession of weapons. This experience taught them that they needed to time things carefully if they were to evolve under Israeli occupation, and only proceed with the development of a military wing when the social and political conditions were ripe for it.

The founder of Hamas later described to me in an interview the development of his movement in four, clearly defined stages. The first phase was to build its institutions; charities and social committees which would open their doors to the young and old – anyone who could play a role in resisting the occupier. This was a prelude to their confrontation with the Israeli enemy in the Intifada which, according to Sheikh Yassin, was instigated single-handedly by Hamas, without the involvement of other Palestinian factions. The second phase worked on strengthening the roots of the resistance within every household in the West Bank and Gaza, and to bolster its political credibility. The third stage developed its military capabilities from rudimentary stone-throwing and launching Molotov cocktails, to using guns, hand grenades and other explosives. 'Anything which would give the Israelis sleepless nights,' he said. The final stage was to see Hamas moving beyond the Palestinian dimension and establish a dialogue with its Arab and Islamic neighbours. Because, he said, 'our enemy needs confrontation from a stronger force and to have international backing is important for us.' Yassin announced that the Palestinian cause 'had gone beyond the slogans of the PLO', which reminded Arab and Islamic states that they should support the Palestinian cause, while cautioning them to leave the Palestinians to make their own decisions. While Arafat was adamant that they should remain independent of outside interference, Hamas thought this policy foolhardy, arguing that the Palestinian cause is also an Arab and Islamic cause.

By the start of the Intifada, the various Islamist movements that went on to become Hamas had managed to establish themselves (with a little help from the Israelis) as a potent force in Palestinian politics, and one whose outlook and strategy differed in key ways from Fatah. But they lacked unity, direction or a consistent military strategy, let alone weapons. This was partly a reflection of the dividedness of Palestinian society itself. When the Jabaliya refugee camp exploded suddenly into violence on 8 December 1987, it provided the nascent Hamas with an impetus to focus more on their military direction. 'We used to wait for such opportunities in order to step-up our conflict with the enemy, encouraged by a larger consensual support,' Sheikh Dokhan, Sheikh Yassin's deputy in the early days of the movement, later explained to me.

It was at this juncture that Yassin's life became most interesting to the Israeli interrogators in Gaza Central Prison. I interviewed Yassin's lawyers subsequently and was able to find out the confidential contents of his confession. The story of the founding of Hamas, and Yassin's role in it, is a complicated one, the details of which are still contested by different participants. But the two were inextricably interlinked.

The Israeli investigators listened attentively as the wheelchair-bound Sheikh Yassin, in his distinctive reedy voice, described the birth of the movement:

Two months before the start of the Intifada in December 1987, I met with Sheikh Salah Al Shehada to whom I was first introduced in Al Majdel prison.[6] I had decided to establish a movement in Gaza to work against the Israeli settlement policy, resist the occupation and to encourage Palestinians to take part in the resistance effort against Israel. During our meeting we agreed to set up a military wing and a security wing of this new Islamic movement. The military wing was to fight against the Israeli army and its occupation. Salah Al Shehada built up this wing. The aim was to amass weapons to use in the struggle. The security wing was to monitor and arrest Palestinian informants as well as drug dealers, prostitutes and the sale and consumption of alcohol in the Palestinian Territories.

In early December 1987, I organized a group of people to discuss the movement. There was Sheikh Salah Shehada, forty years old from Beit Hanoun working at the Islamic University in Gaza; Issa Al Nasshaar, a forty-five-year-old engineer from Rafiah; Dr Ibrahim Al Yazuri, a forty-five-year-old GP from Gaza; Dr Abdul Aziz Al Rantisi, a forty-year-old GP from Khan Younis; Abdul Fattah Dokhan, a headmaster from Al Nusairat camp; and Mohammed Shamhaa, a fifty-year-old schoolteacher from Al Shati camp. During this meeting we agreed to call the movement HAMAS, an acronym for the Islamic Resistance Movement. Each one of us would be responsible for the areas in which we lived. I was to be the head of the Hamas organization in the Gaza Strip.

The naming ceremony which brought together the various factions under the umbrella name Hamas, was a drawn-out affair, following a series of alternative identities. The political organizational body began life as the Islamic Resistance Movement, which was abbreviated to the acronym HMS from the original Arabic name Harakat Al Mokawama Al Islamiya. It was finally proposed that HMS should become *Hamas*, an Arabic word meaning 'zeal', which embodies the virtues of the Muslim Brotherhood slogan: 'Rights! Force! Freedom!'

Sheikh Dokhan added another explanation for the chosen name:

The name Hamas was less threatening. We wanted something which wouldn't create the impression we were a militant organization to the Israelis, and would lessen anti-Islamic attitudes against the Muslim Brotherhood living abroad as well as avoiding a negative reaction from other Arab governments. Hamas is a movement of resistance and, as we pointed out in our Charter, it is like a coalition, not solely attached to the Muslim Brotherhood, but can embrace all Palestinian resistance organizations and their supporters and friends.[7]

In Yassin's account, both in his confessions and in subsequent interviews with me, the Jabaliya incident was incidental: he, Yassin, directed the Intifada on behalf of Hamas. Other accounts, such as those of Salah Shehada, suggest that it was a pivotal event which led directly to the formation of Hamas.

Jabaliya is the largest refugee camp in the Strip, just north of Gaza City. At that time it had a population of around 60,000 people, living in a rabbit warren of urban squalor. On 6 December 1987, an Israeli settler was stabbed to death in Gaza's main shopping district. Two days later, an Israeli civilian truck driver swerved and hit an oncoming vehicle packed with Arab labourers, in what became known as the 'Maktura' incident. Four of the Arabs died and others were seriously injured. News of the accident was broadcast over the radio. Rumour spread like wildfire around Jabaliya that the so-called accident was in fact deliberate revenge taken by a relative of the Israeli stabbed two days before. As mourners returned from the funerals of the four Palestinians late that same afternoon, they vented their pent-up emotion against the barbed-wire fence of the Israeli army camp surrounding Jabaliya, with cries of 'Jihad! Jihad!' The Israeli army tried to dispel the crowds with tear gas and fired warning shots into the air. But nothing would suppress the Palestinians' anger and they retaliated with stones and fire bombs. The Border Police joined the army as rioting washed through the camp.[8]

The Israeli settler had been stabbed by a member of Islamic Jihad, and the head of the Israeli army's Southern Command at that time, Major General Yitzhak Mordechai's, interpretation of events was that the stabbing and subsequent uprising was a reaction against the army's decision to deport members of Islamic Jihad three weeks earlier on 17 November 1987 (the truck crash was an accident waiting to happen and poured fuel on the flames of spontaneous rebellion).[9]

On that December day, the General Committee of the Muslim Brotherhood in the Gaza Strip, of which Sheikh Yassin was a member, called an emergency meeting to discuss the events which had taken place in Jabaliya refugee camp.[10] Salah Shehada, the nominated head of the military wing in the Gaza Strip, described in his memoirs the evening Hamas was born: 'The eighth day of December 1987 is one of God's days. It commemorates a new beginning that will shine brightly throughout the history of the Islamic Umma.'

Dr Abdul Aziz Al Rantisi who replaced Sheikh Yassin after his assassination, and was himself later assassinated, confirmed that the first meeting to launch Hamas was held in Sheikh Yassin's house on 9 December 1987.[11] He explained that Hamas was a branch of the global Muslim Brotherhood movement and issued its first statement on 14 December. Until that date, there was no united front directing the Intifada in the West Bank and Gaza. Rantisi was arrested by the Israelis for taking part in the establishment of Hamas and distributing written statements. He described how Hamas set its sights on political power: 'Like many successful movements, it began at the grassroots and was not a military organization at the outset.' The movement was governed by a Shura Council,[12] based on the legislative foundations of the Muslim Brotherhood in Palestine which consisted of twenty-four members in the early days. 'But the number would vary depending on how many members were imprisoned by the Israelis at any given time,' Rantisi said in clarification. There was a core group of decision-makers consisting of seven members. Despite numerous arrests, the Israelis never succeeded in dismantling the organization. A new leadership would emerge, and it would be back to the business of issuing statements and once more engaging the Israelis by attacking their army posts and patrols.

The emergency meeting was to begin at 8 p.m., when the dark winter evening would provide better security. Salah Shehada described the atmosphere of that December night as 'cold, but the throbbing blood in our veins was more than sufficient to warm us'.

With seven members in attendance, they evaluated what had taken place in the camps and streets of the Gaza Strip and were in unison that confrontation in all its manifestations had to be scaled up. Shehada claimed to have come up with a plan 'to stoke up the fire in the whole of the Gaza Strip and attack the Israelis not just through stone-throwing by our youth, but to engage the entire Palestinian population in military-style action'.

Dr Ibrahim Al Yazuri, who was also present at the historic meeting, echoed Shehada's words, saying: 'Strong passions were aroused amongst a number of our brothers who were urging for a revolt and to stir up the public, especially the youth, into intensifying their resistance against the occupation and bring revolution to the streets.' It was agreed, Yazuri recalled, that these resistance activities were to be coordinated by the Jihaz Al Ahdath, the organization's under-eighteens wing, to include regular demonstrations, strikes, and confronting the Israeli army with stones and Molotov cocktail attacks.

According to Shehada, the General Committee wrote their first proclamation that same evening, for immediate printing and circulation to all the Gaza Strip mosques. The statement was signed 'the Islamic Resistance Movement'. 'We had previously distributed several public communications under a variety of names such as "the Islamic Faction", "the Path of Islam" and "the Islamic Defence", but the name "Islamic Resistance" was finally chosen for the movement by Allah,' said Shehada.

Sheikh Yassin recalled that the leaflets were prepared in Khalid Al Hindi's house and were then given to Rouhi Mushtaha and others to print on Akram Sharbit's printing press. He used to meet with the group once a month, either in his house in Gaza or in the homes of Issa Al Nasshaar or Ghazi Abdul Aal, where they would discuss the general situation and their plans for future activities.

The issue of whether Hamas started or reacted to the Intifada is an important one. Everyone involved in Palestinian politics tried to take credit for starting the uprising in the late 1980s. At that time, the PLO and the Jordanian government, were at loggerheads. Both wished to put their own interpretation on the Intifada. The PLO wanted to claim that they had initiated it, and co-opt the grassroots legitimacy that the movement had, the Jordanian government wanted to deny it had anything to do with the PLO, who they portrayed as marginal so that they could continue to claim to be the ultimate representatives of the Palestinian people, or at least of the ones who were living in the West Bank.

Yassin wanted to give the impression that his movement had played a leading role in the early days of the Intifada. He insisted that he himself wrote the statement which started the Intifada on 14 December 1987, a week after the start of the uprising, signing it 'H.M.S.', the Arabic shorthand for the Islamic Movement Resistance. 'It never occurred to me at the time that the letters spelt another word in Arabic,' Yassin recalled, 'but, by our third statement, my brothers in the struggle suggested that we should call ourselves "Hamas" [meaning fervour or zeal]. From then on it became the name of our movement.'

There were conflicting arguments about where they should base their operations. The first option was to find a secure base within an Islamic state, but none of the Arab countries neighbouring Israel had an Islamic regime which could provide Hamas with the necessary launch-pad for its organization. Egypt had just signed its Camp David Peace Agreement with Israel to which Hamas was opposed. Jordan was still recovering from its battle with the PLO forces in September 1970, which had threatened the existence of the whole Kingdom. Syria was sharing a peaceful border with Israel thanks to the UN Peacekeeping Force. Lebanon was licking its wounds following the Israeli invasion of Beirut in June 1982 in an attempt to destroy the PLO. Arafat had made his headquarters in Lebanon after the PLO's expulsion from Jordan in 1970–1971 and was using Southern Lebanon to direct attacks against Israel. In a deal brokered by Philip Habib, the US Envoy to Lebanon, and Ariel Sharon, Israel's Defence Minister, the PLO were given a safe passage out of the country in a flotilla of boats which sailed to Greece from where Yasser Arafat travelled to Tunis, his new HQ in exile.

With the immediate neighbours ruled out, the option favoured by Sheikh Yassin highlighted the advantages of controlling the battle from Palestine and more specifically in the occupied territories 'until we find a country which can provide us a secure base from which to fight the Jewish State'.

During his year-long trial, Sheikh Yassin explained to his Israeli investigator how a Hamas branch came to be established in the West Bank. In January 1988, Jamil Hammami, a member of the Muslim Brotherhood in the West Bank, visited Yassin at his home in Gaza. Hammami used to work and teach at Abu Dis Sharia Institute and was later appointed as chief custodian for Bethlehem city. He enjoyed huge popularity at the grassroots level. Sheikh Yassin asked him: 'Why don't you contribute towards the Intifada in the West Bank?' He agreed to set up a faction there, and Yassin promised to help him by sending him leaflets via Rouhi Mushtaha and Fayez Abdul Aal. Once the movement was established in the West Bank, Jamil began printing large quantities of leaflets and distributing them to Hamas members there. Some of these leaflets were also sent to Jordan. Communications between Yassin and other senior members of the movement were either channelled through Jamil or through contacts in mosques. Yassin explained how the movement in Gaza topped up their funds when they were running low:

> I used to tell Jamil who would contact activists in Jordan, or an activist in London called Mounir Al Aachi, would call Jordan and tell them about our needs. I used to give each of our senior activists a code, which was usually a number rather than referring to them by name so that no one could disclose any details about other members of the group in case of arrest.

Khalid Mishal, who went on to play a key role in Hamas' political leadership, recalled that the first meeting between the leaders of Hamas in the West Bank and Gaza and those living in neighbouring Arab countries took place in 1983 before the arrest of Sheikh Yassin, who was unable to attend because of travel restrictions he was under at that time. Mishal said that a strategy to inaugurate a new Palestinian Islamic movement was drawn up at that meeting. Mishal certainly knew about it, but his role was never mentioned by Sheikh Yassin when he spoke about how the founders launched Hamas. It is doubtful that he played a key role at the time.

An Islamic movement had already been established in 1979 inside Israel which was led by Sheikh Abdullah Nimer Darwish.

Sheikh Raed Salah was his deputy. Its members lived in Israel and all carried Israeli citizenship. These Islamic Israeli Arabs were more in tune with those Palestinians from the Islamic Movement and other secular Palestinian factions such as Fatah in West Bank and Gaza. Sheikh Salah was later appointed head of the Islamic Movement following a split with Darwish. Both Darwish and Salah became active in their individual campaigns to fight against Israel which had begun constructing a tunnel beneath Jerusalem's Al Aqsa Mosque. This breach of international law beneath such a sensitive Islamic religious site was recorded on videotape by Sheikh Raed who passed the tape to Yasser Arafat to alert world leaders about Israel's highly illegal activities.

The relationship between the Islamic movements in the West Bank and Gaza, and inside Israel itself, were unconnected at that time. Islamic activists from the West Bank and Gaza would travel between Haifa, Jaffa and Nazareth to take part in their religious activities, while young Palestinians inside Israel preferred to study in West Bank universities such as Beir Zeit and Al Najah. During sieges and Israeli-imposed curfews, the movement would collect food and other supplies to assist those on the other side of the border. Between 1985 and 1986, Hamas activists in Arab countries began collecting donations to finance their activities, and rallied amongst other Islamic movements as well as dispersed Palestinian communities abroad. By that stage, Hamas was proselytising that the Palestinian cause must be the number one cause for Muslim nations worldwide, reminding them that Palestine is the 'land of the Prophets', including Mohammed, Moses and Jesus. It is also the home of Jerusalem's Al Aqsa Mosque, revered by Muslims the world over for 'Al Isra'a Al Mi'raj', Prophet Mohammed's reputed 'Night Journey' from Mecca to Jerusalem from where he ascended to the Seventh Heaven, as described in the Qur'an:

> Glorified is He who took his servant by night from the sacrosanct Mosque to the furthermost Mosque, the precincts of which we have blessed, that we might show him (some of our signs). Truly He is the Hearer, the Seer.[13]

In the early 1980s, the Muslim world was more preoccupied with the Afghan cause. Interest in the Palestinian cause waned after the PLO's military activities cooled down following the Israeli invasion of Lebanon in 1982, which forced Palestinians out of Lebanon and surrounding Arab countries bordering Israel. Donations to the cause slumped until the months following the first Intifada.

The Intifada which erupted in Gaza in 1987 changed all that. Although Hamas did not direct it as Yassin claimed, it was a powerful force on the ground, fighting the Israelis.

Naming of Parts

The individual wings of Hamas were working independently before the Intifada flared up, but without specific names or agenda. After the inaugural meeting on 8 December 1987, they were enshrined under one organizational structure and given specific functions. These included the political, communications, security, youth, Intifada and prisoners' wings. This last wing was established following a significant and worrying rise in the number of their members being detained in Israeli jails. The most prestigious wing of Hamas is the Intifada wing. It is secretive about disclosing military attacks to protect fighters, restricting claims of responsibility through veiled references to these missions in their internal bulletins. The youth wing, or Al Ahdath, consists of young men, usually under the age of eighteen. It was established at the beginning of the Intifada to ensure maximum participation by the public in strikes and demonstrations.

The Israelis would use all means to enforce shopkeepers to keep their businesses open in defiance of the many Hamas protest strikes. Another Israeli tactic was to falsely claim via their informers to unsuspecting shopkeepers that an announced strike had been cancelled. This would create great problems for shopkeepers, who would then be punished by their local leaders for ignoring the call for a general strike. Anyone found strike-breaking would find burning tyres outside their home as a form of humiliation. The pungent reek of smoking car tyres became the defining smell of the Intifada. Israeli soldiers would also confiscate driving licences belonging to Palestinian taxi drivers obeying strike orders. They wanted to keep the roads moving to create the impression that everything was normal and that they were in total control.

Al Ahdath would inform the public about activities and the progress of the Intifada through graffiti daubed on walls, which became their unofficial newsletter, flouting the restrictions placed by the Israelis on public distribution of political literature. Sometimes these wall papers would summon the community to take to their rooftops at midnight and shout 'Allah Akbar!' ('God is Great!') to remonstrate against the Israeli stranglehold on their lives. When a martyr died, the youth wing was there to offer support and organize financial aid for the family. It arranged the burial and the condolences tent where people paid their respects, and provided food for the mourners. Another of the wing's responsibilities was to make arrangements for students to receive tuition from volunteers in homes and mosques to compensate for the hours lost when the Israelis enforced their regular shutdowns of schools and universities. In general, the youth wing ensured that life went on despite the curfews and blockades ordered by the occupation forces.

The communications wing was established prior to the Intifada but subsequently became more active. Its role was to write slogans, to issue statements on behalf of the leadership covering the news of the Intifada in the West Bank and Gaza in detail, and to pass information to local correspondents and other journalists about what was going on. In charge of this wing during the first Intifada were Imad Al Din Al Alami and Yehia Moussa, and Majdi Abu Shemala – all from the Islamic University on Gaza.

The precursor to the military wing which is known today as Ez Ed Din Al Qassam, was formed in 1983 by Sheikh Ahmed Yassin and headed by Salah Shehada. Called Al Mujahidoun Al Falastinioun (Palestine Mujahideen), the wing comprised a tightly knit group of cells composed of two to three fighters each. The first cell was called Al Maghraga Mujahidoun and was led by Yehiya Al Ghoul. This group was established in 1985. A second group calling itself Group 44 was led by Salah Shehada himself and was established in 1986. A further cell, known as Cell 101, was headed by Mohammed Al Sharatha and formed just a few months before the first Intifada. The Islamic Resistance was the original name encompassing all the military cells in 1986. This moniker had a strong impact on the Intifada's initial appeal. The military wing then became known as Al Jihad Wa Da'wa, which was abbreviated and shortened to its acronym MAJD (which was then adopted by the security wing). Finally it settled with the name of Ez Ed Din Al Qassam after the leader of a rebellion against the British Palestine police during the British Mandate period.

Ez Ed Din Al Qassam's fight against the British occupation proved an inspiration for Hamas' own battle against the forces of the Jewish occupation. Hamas divided its organization into separate command units, each responsible for different functions, just as Al Qassam had done, and, in a final symbolic gesture, they adopted his name for their own military wing. The Hamas leadership came under pressure from the military wing's early recruits who were pushing to begin their battle against Israel. The leadership was hesitant for fear of repeating their earlier unhappy experience when most of the leadership was arrested, almost destroying the movement. Unlike other Palestinian factions, they lacked the experience and capability to carry out military campaigns, as the culture of the Muslim Brotherhood which they had grown up with was in general non-confrontational. This was to their advantage in the initial stages. It created a false impression for the Israelis, who left alone this young movement with its seemingly peaceful cultural activities. It served their own interests to let the organization flourish in the hope that it might weaken the PLO, which was Israel's staunchest enemy at that time. Israel later came to regret this strategy once Hamas and its military wing had unleashed itself as a major player in the theatre of the Intifada.

The military wing chief Salah Shehada learned from bitter experience not to depend on outside influence to secure weapons. His small, self-contained cells were designed to be financially and militarily independent. Relying on weapons dealers was dodgy and costly, while stealing weapons from Israeli soldiers and Palestinian informers, was a cheaper if riskier option. For the courageous and ideological generation of young recruits straining to do battle, it was a welcome challenge. The first Israeli-made Uzi machine gun that the military wing managed to acquire cost them the life of Ghassan

Abu Al Nada, who attempted to ambush a well-armed Palestinian informer travelling to one of Gaza's Israeli settlements. The military wing encouraged the Palestine branch of the Muslim Brotherhood to join them in demonstrations and military attacks. The Brotherhood was happy to comply in order to secure a place on the Palestinian political map from which to espouse their Islamic ideology and also to work alongside the secularist and established PLO.

In his confessions, Sheikh Yassin named Yihya Sinwar, a student at the Islamic University, together with Khalid Al Hindi as responsible for setting up the security wing. Yassin gave them the go-ahead to start recruiting, giving Sinwar responsibility for the territory in the southern half of the Gaza Strip while Al Hindi was put in charge of Gaza City and the northern part of the Strip. 'The security wing began to collect information,' Sheikh Yassin recalled, 'and I told Sinwar: "Any Palestinian informer who confesses to cooperating with the Israeli authorities – kill him straight away".'

MAJD developed into a rudimentary intelligence operation. In 1989, a large number of its members were detained on suspicion of spying for the Israelis. After their interrogation and the subsequent recording of their confessions, the security wing issued death sentences to those found guilty. Ironically, Sinwar got caught in his own trap and found himself telling his Israeli investigators that he was responsible for killing four informers. The security wing would first issue warnings before taking action. Hundreds of informers' cars were burnt and a written caution would be posted on the walls or doors of mosques or in strategic places in the *soukhs* to give them a chance to abandon their Israeli minders. If these warnings went unheeded, they were killed after interrogation and a signed confession. The confessions would subsequently be posted in strategic places to act as a deterrent for others.

The main obstacle facing the fledgling Hamas was its relationship with the Unified Leadership of the Intifada, led by Yasser Arafat's Fatah movement. This became strained after Fatah found Hamas in competition with it, winning over many of its supporters. Conflicts would flare up from one city to another depending on the relative numbers of Fatah and Hamas supporters. According to Salah Shehada, there were several incidents which could have led to the derailment of the Intifada and given Israel the upper hand. 'We were aware that from the beginning of the uprising that the Zionist intelligence were trying to create discord by publishing derogatory statements, purportedly in the name of Hamas and sending them to the Unified Leadership. We uncovered the plot and, while the Intifada did witness strained relationships between the two organizations, we overcame those thanks to the efforts made by our brothers in Hamas and the loyalty of other factions. We were able with God's support to gain more control over conflicts and nip potential conflicts in the bud.'

Father of the Movement

A strong leader around which the nascent movement could unify was essential in the early days of Hamas and the Intifada, and the charismatic Sheikh Yassin, with his learning, his asceticism and his bravery, fitted the bill. The Israelis unwittingly helped by giving him unprecedented publicity. After his arrest on 18 May 1989, his trial, which lasted for about a year, was broadcast live by Israeli TV stations and was presided over by the military court judge in Gaza Central Prison. According to Yassin's defence lawyer, Nazem Oweida, the Israelis were very conscientious and attended every session. 'The witnesses standing against him were Israeli intelligence as well as Israeli police. There were no Arab witnesses.' This bolstered Yassin's standing yet further in Palestinian eyes and made him a public martyr. The accusations directed against Sheikh Yassin were: the establishment of the Palestinian mujahideen organization (MAJD); their possession of weapons; and their ambition to eradicate Israel and replace it with an Islamic nation. Israeli intelligence produced weapons in court as evidence against the Sheikh. According to Nazem, 'It was a limited number of weapons, for manual use.' In reply to Nazem's initial defence statement, the head of the military court, Zakhria Kasbi, pronounced: 'The educated lawyer claims that his client, due to his medical disability, would find it impossible to have any rational ambitions to eradicate Israel at a time when six million Arabs failed to do so. The situation does not only relate to his financial abilities but rather it relies on the ideological and moral beliefs that the accused holds.' Nazem told me that the Israeli judge made a comparison with the Ayatollah Khomeini's ambitions in Iran and the success of the cleric in abolishing the existing secular political system and establishing an Islamic state.

Yassin's lawyer estimated that ninety per cent of the detainees who were convicted asked – as their final wish – for forgiveness and mercy and showed remorse for what they had done. Sheikh Yassin and a few others refused to express any form of apology in front of the court. Though this might have been good for his standing in Gaza, it resulted in a severe verdict: the court's final decision was a lifetime sentence. Later, however, on 1 October 1997, Sheikh Yassin was released. His freedom was mediated by King Hussein of Jordan in exchange for the two agents of the Israeli intelligence agency, Mossad, who had carried out a failed assassination attempt on Hamas leader Khalid Mishal. Yassin believed that Israel ensured his return home was 'late at night so there would be no celebrations or crowds gathering to welcome me back'. He likened his time in prison to 'staying in a five-star hotel', because it gave him the time to memorize the Qur'an and pray to God. 'If it wasn't for the fact that prison distances me from my family and other people I love, I could stay there forever. I am tired of having my home searched by the Israeli army and continually having to report to Israeli intelligence centres.'

Hamas activist and engineer Farid Ziyadeh was one of a group of Palestinian prisoners who cared for Sheikh Yassin in Kfar Yuna prison during 1994 – a prison which was mainly used to house Israeli criminals and Arabs jailed for security reasons. Ziyadeh, from Madma village south of Nablus, recalled the buzz of excitement circling around his fellow Palestinian prisoners in Nablus' central jail, when they learned they were to be transferred to Kfar Yuna. Only one thing was on their minds: how to get close to Hamas' spiritual leader – not just to serve and look after him, but to hear his wisdom. Detailing Sheikh Yassin's daily prison life,[14] Ziyadeh described how he would rise at 3 a.m. to prepare for morning prayers, after which he would read the Qur'an until sunrise. When morning came, Ziyadeh and another prisoner would take him into the prison courtyard and massage the Sheikh's arms to relieve the pain from his long-term illness. Following this short outdoor break, he would be carried back to his cell, where he read from the library of books he had collected. An avid reader, he would learn great tracts by heart. Ziyadeh recalled that Yassin 'never complained and liked to joke with others in the prison to keep their spirits high.'

Samih Alewah from Nablus described the one hundred days he looked after Sheikh Yassin as 'the best hundred days of my life', although they were held in a small cell with no access to sunlight. Alewah said that Palestinian prisoners used to compete to serve the founder of Hamas and would hang on his every word. 'It's true that he didn't often speak,' Alewah said, 'but when he did, it was words of wisdom.'[15] An Israeli prison officer in Kfar Yuna told Israeli television that nothing in his attitude or movements suggested that Sheikh Yassin was aggressive or the type to incite terrorism.[16] The officer, whose name was not revealed, said, 'I used to observe his behaviour and attitude towards the prisoners who looked after him. He was always very kind and considerate and that is why they cared about him. I came to realize that Hamas members would do anything to get revenge if something bad happened to Sheikh Yassin, as he was their spiritual leader.'[17]

Nazem described the Sheikh as:

a very quiet person which was part of his personality and had nothing to do with his illness. Even when he was released and was in charge of public issues, he was still not very talkative. What I can remember of him is that he was an ideological individual who didn't feel regret or express apology. He had a way of smiling as if he was confident that he would be released. He used to stress the need for coexistence between Jews, Christians and Muslims, claiming that he was not against Jews as people of a Jewish religion, but rather he was against those who have abused our lands.

Whatever Sheikh Yassin agreed to with Israel concerning Palestine's future and its coexistence with the Jews in one state, whether it be a ceasefire or maintaining a long cooling-off period, were intended as temporary measures, not a prescription for lasting peace. His long-term ambitions were unwavering: to reclaim the whole of Palestine as it had been before 1948, with Jerusalem as the Palestinian capital, to redraw the borders as they existed prior to 1967, and to dismantle the settlements. His heartfelt belief until the day of his assassination was that it should be for Palestinian generations to come to make decisions about their future; not the current generation who are struggling in an era when the balance of power is not in the Palestinians' favour. To date, the Hamas movement has shown no signs of rewriting the charter which was adopted at the movement's launch almost two decades ago.

3

Ez Ed Din Al Qassam Brigades: The Military Wing of Hamas

The military wing's namesake, Ez Ed Din Al Qassam, was born in 1882 in Jabla, a Phoenician settlement on Syria's Mediterranean coast, south of Latakiya. At that time, there were no established schools in the area so Al Qassam's father, Abdul Latif, who was an expert on Islamic sharia, committed himself to teaching the Qur'an, Arabic language and calligraphy, religious poetry and music, and encouraged Al Qassam and other youngsters in the town to understand the doctrine of jihad. Armed with this grounding in all things spiritual, cultural and religious, Al Qassam travelled to Cairo where he became a student at Al Azhar University, at that time the most famous institution worldwide for sharia law and Islamic study. He became interested in some of the freedom movements in Egypt where there was massive support for resistance against the British occupation. He was particularly drawn to writers like Mohammed Abdu, who was inspired by the Salafi school of Islamic thought.[1]

In 1906, Al Qassam travelled around Turkey's mosques to learn about their teaching methods before returning home to teach in his father's school. When the Italian forces occupied Tripoli in Libya in 1911, Al Qassam led a demonstration on the streets of Jabla, calling on fellow citizens to volunteer to oust the Italian occupation. When the French forces occupied Syria in 1920, Al Qassam led the resistance against the French on the northern coast of Syria, selling his house and everything he owned to buy twenty-four guns. The French tried to convince him to abandon his revolution and return to his home town, offering him a position in their administration. He refused and was sentenced to death by the French authorities in Latakiya. He escaped and fled first to Damascus and from there to Palestine where he set up home in one of the old neighbourhoods of Haifa. Al Qassam was drawn towards helping the uneducated and working classes, holding evening workshops to teach them to read using the Qur'an as text, and the duty of jihad. His pupils were a mixture of railway workers, construction workers, artisans, small shopkeepers and tenant farmers who had been driven from their land by Zionist purchasers of the late 1920s. The Muslim equivalent of the YMCA movement, the Muslim Youth Association, was founded by Al Qassam, impressing on the youth their duty of jihad, the danger facing them as a result of the British occupation and the indirect support the British forces were giving to the Jewish movement.

By the time he was appointed as a judge for Haifa's sharia court in 1930, he had strengthened his ties and popularity with Palestinians from all walks of life. He began holding secret meetings in his house, his followers chosen from amongst the people who attended his classes or his Friday speeches at the mosque. Small jihadist cells were formed, whose membership was exclusive to those prepared to sacrifice everything. The cells formed part of a larger jihadist force, which Al Qassam divided into different units: one to buy arms; one for intelligence to monitor British and Jewish activities; a third for military training; another for communications and publicity and calls for Jihad. A fifth dealt with martyrs, prisoners and their families.

Once these units were established, they began attacking settlements in order to stop Jewish immigration to Palestine. The British government made large sums of money available to encourage Palestinian informers to betray Al Qassam's freedom fighters. On 20 November 1935, the British police in Palestine closed in on Al Qassam and his fighters, on the outskirts of Yabud village in Jenin county. Together with a large contingent of British forces, they fanned out in Yabud woods, where a heavy exchange of fire took place. A large number of Al Qassam fighters were killed, including their leader. The rest were taken prisoner.[2] The Friday following his death became a day of mourning observed in mosques throughout Palestine when Ez Ed Din Al Qassam was held up as an inspiration for national sacrifice and jihad.

Whilst Al Qassam's men used firearms to inflict heavy losses on the British forces, fighters with the newly formed Al Qassam Brigades of Hamas were initially armed with nothing more dangerous than plastic guns and knives. Comrades of Imad Aqel, the military commander of Hamas' fledgling military wing, recall how frustrated he was that their weapons were limited to stones and home-made grenades and bombs.

Imad Ibrahim Aqel was born in Jabaliya refugee camp, east of Gaza City, on 19 June 1971. Before the creation of the State of Israel in 1948, Jewish forces had forced Aqel's parents to flee their village close to the town of Al Majdal (now the Israeli city of Ashkelon). The family village was within the Green Line, drawn up in an armistice between Israel and its opponents in the 1948 Arab-Israeli War – Palestine, Lebanon, Syria, Jordan and Egypt. The so-called Green Line delineated the de facto borders of Israel from those countries and their territories which Israel would later occupy in the Six Day War of 1967.

Imad's father, who was working in the Martyrs Mosque in Jabaliya camp at the time of his son's birth, had early aspirations of him becoming a mujahid. He named him after the twelfth-century Muslim hero and swordsman Imad Ad Din Zengi, who captured the land of Edessa[3] from the Crusaders in 1144. This led to waves of Crusades ordered by European rulers to recover Palestine from the Muslims, which witnessed the rise of another Muslim legend – Salah El Din Al Ayoubi – referred to in the West as Saladin, who secured the city of Jerusalem from the marauding Christian armies in 1187.

Imad studied in the camp's UNRWA (United Nations Relief and Works Agency) school where, by all accounts, he was considered an excellent scholar. From the age of twelve, he became a regular attender at the mosques in his neighbourhood, particularly the Al

Noor Mosque, where he earned the respect of the elders and got his first taste of political activism through the Muslim Brotherhood. By the age of seventeen, he had made up his mind to become a chemist but, before he was able save up the fees for his studies, Imad got involved in anti-Israeli protests, daubing slogans on walls and taking part in general demonstrations as the first uprising in the Gaza Strip broke out in December 1987. He launched a group known then as 'Al Sawaaed Al Ramieh!' ('Archer's Arms'), which later became the special military wing for youth called Al Ahdath. Imad's involvement was to lead and encourage teenagers to participate in Intifada-related activities which earned him several months in an Israeli jail. His ideas of becoming a chemist were abandoned but in turn he was accepted to study Islamic sharia law in Amman, where his brother was an Imam of a mosque. This too was thwarted by Israeli intelligence who intercepted his application, and refused him permission to travel to Jordan because of his known participation in the Intifada.

By early May of 1990, the military wing established by Salah Shehada and Sheikh Yassin had a nucleus of fighters. These were expanded by the recruitment of others operating throughout the Strip. The roll call of the early members of Hamas' military wing, with Aqel, their leader at the top, read as follows:

Imad Aqel, born in Jabaliya in 1971, killed on 24 November 1993

Ghassan Musbah Abu Al Nada, born in 1969 in Jabaliya, killed on 2 May 1991

Mohammed Abdul Karim Abu Al Ataya, born in Al Yarmouk neighbourhood in Gaza in 1968, arrested on 29 July 1992 and given seventeen life sentences

Mohammed Gumaaian Abu Aisheh, born in 1967 in Al Yarmouk, and arrested by the Israeli army along with Abu Al Ataya and given five life sentences

Mohammed Ali Harez, also from Al Yarmouk, born in 1968, and arrested with the other two Mohammed's with a punishment of eight life sentences

Majdi Ahmed Hammad, born in 1965 in Jabaliya, arrested on 26 December 1991 and given six life sentences

Talal Saleh, born in 1969 in Al Zaytoun neighbourhood in Gaza, who left the area via the tunnel network together with
Bashir Audi Hammad, born in 1967 in Jabaliya
Nihro Massoud, also born in Jabaliya in 1971.
Saleh, Hammad and Massoud fled the Gaza Strip for Egypt to avoid arrest after their homes and those they visited were raided and searched.

As operational commander of the new organization, Aqel realized he had to source a supply of weapons to arm this new generation of fighters, and began recruiting young men specifically for this task. One Al Qassam leader who spoke to me under condition of anonymity – I will call him Tariq – told me that when Ez Ed Din Al Qassam Brigades began their attacks in 1991, they had at their disposal no more than twenty machine guns which remained the sum total of their arsenal until the year 2000.

Aqel wished to arm a new group he was assembling in the northern part of the Gaza Strip who called themselves the Martyrs Group. An obvious start was to target Palestinian collaborators who were usually well armed by their Israeli minders, to steal their weapons. The first to be killed was Yahya Al Ahwal, shortly followed by an attempt on the life of Mustapha Al Mashlouh.

The northern cells split into two groups and travelled in separate cars on a mission to kill Al Mashlouh who lived in a well-guarded house surrounded by bodyguards and armed Israeli border guards, who had trained in nearby settlements. On 2 May 1991, the two cars tailed Al Mashlouh's movements that morning in the hope of ambushing him and the impressive arsenal of weapons he was known to carry with him, including M16 rifles and Israeli-made Uzi sub-machine guns. When they intercepted his car, Al Mashlouh was, unsurprisingly, armed with a machine gun and killed Ghassan Abu Al Nada outright. Mohammed Abu Al Ataya who was trying to take control of Mashlouh's car, died on arrival at Al Mamadani Hospital where he worked. Mashlouh escaped into a nearby settlement. It was not an auspicious start.

Each fighter has a legend attached to them which is known to all young Gazans. Majdi Hammad's most dramatic moment came on 14 December 1991. The Al Qassam Brigades commemorate the day in 1987 when the Hamas movement delivered an historic blueprint for its fight against the Israeli occupation of the Palestinian territories. On the first anniversary of their inauguration, Ez Ed Din Al Qassam Brigades decided to mark the occasion with a parade in Jabaliya refugee camp. Majdi Hammad who was the leader of a Brigades cell in the nearby Al Shati camp – or Beach Camp, as it is known – attended the parade carrying an old Swedish-designed 9mm Carl-Gustav M45 sub-machine gun, which he had borrowed from a member in his own cell. The Carl-Gustav was the official gun of the Swedish army after the Second World War and between 1965 and 1970 was manufactured under license in Egypt, where it was called the Port Said.[4] None of the other participants in the parade were brandishing guns, real or otherwise, for fear that Israeli intelligence would round them up for being members of an armed militia. Majdi was an extremely well-built figure and, despite swaddling his head with a chequered Palestinian scarf in an attempt at disguise, he was instantly recognizable and a liability as he fired shots into the air from the weapon in celebratory fashion. The leadership of the Martyrs Group called an urgent meeting and voted to send Majdi abroad as he was vulnerable to arrest and could be forced to reveal the identities of his comrades and more.

It was agreed that Majdi should cross the border into Egypt together with Hassan Al Ayidi who was also wanted by Israeli security for his involvement with the Al Ahdath in central Gaza. The pair attempted to bypass the tightly controlled Rafiah border crossing by swimming out into the Mediterranean Sea under cover of darkness, then cutting across to the safety of a beach on the Egyptian side of the border. Israeli forces patrolling the Gaza shoreline spotted Majdi and Al Ayidi in the water and they were arrested and taken to Al Saraya Prison, Gaza's main detention facility, where they were tortured and, as feared by their organization, forced to make confessions. Majdi had served at least four previous jail sentences and had only been released two months prior to this latest arrest.

Majdi's confessions under torture meant that, as of 26 December 1991, Imad Aqel and his support team – Abu Al Ataya, Abu Aisheh, Harez, Bashir and Talal – became wanted men. One of his comrades described Aqel as always on the alert and in charge. One night, with the six men assembled in their safe house, he was asked to join them for prayers, Aqel told them that they should pray together but he would keep watch. It was noticed that he didn't eat much and he would tease his less frugal brothers that it was 'better to eat light so that I won't become lazy or feel the need for a nap'.

Being light on weapons didn't prevent the group from launching attacks against the Israeli army or Jewish settlers. Their first was on 14 May 1992, when Aqel attempted to shoot a high-ranking Israeli police officer in Gaza using the old Swedish warhorse, the Carl-Gustav. The attack damaged the car of his bodyguards but the target survived. The second attack was carried out three days later by Mohammed Abu Al Ataya, who, with one of his comrades, tailed a car driven by David Cohen, an Israeli sheep trader, in their Peugeot 404, on the road to Beit Lahyia. They forced him to stop, then killed him outright.

Apart from attacks against Israeli targets, Aqel and his group killed at least thirteen Palestinians working as agents for Israeli intelligence as well as drug dealers who were operating in Gaza. The Israeli presence in Gaza at that time was heavy, which left Aqel and his group with no choice but to look for refuge elsewhere. Their lack of machine guns forced them to cross to the West Bank, as they had ruled out leaving the Palestinian territories after Majdi Hammad's failed escape to Egypt. With the sole protection of the Carl-Gustav machine gun, they knew they needed back-up, so they obtained a further Carl-Gustav and a pistol through the leadership of the movement.

Aqel and his fellow members in the Martyrs Group consulted the leadership of the Al Qassam Brigades in both regions and devised a plan to leave Gaza for the West Bank. Cells in the West Bank had been successful in stealing a number of ID cards belonging to Israeli Arabs living inside Israel and their idea was to doctor these, replacing the photographs and personal details with those of their own members. The men were to travel separately into Israel, mainly via the Erez border, crossing at the northern tip of the Gaza Strip, beginning on 22 May 1992.

The first to pass through the twenty-two-metre-long passage that feeds into several narrow lanes of iron-barred checkpoints was Imad Aqel. He took his place amongst the long lines of weary Palestinians who would wait for hours on end to enter Israel for work, under surveillance of the looming watchtowers. His forged Israeli ID card seemed to satisfy the border guards, and he was soon on his way to Jerusalem, an hour's taxi ride from the border. He rented a small flat in Abu Dis, a Palestinian village just outside the eastern municipal boundary of Jerusalem on the Mount of Olives. Abu Dis was awarded to Yasser Arafat's authority under the Oslo Peace Accord in 1993, and the view from the town of Jerusalem's famous landmarks, the golden and silver domes of the mosques of Omar and Al Aqsa, has bestowed upon the small village its controversial nomination as the future Palestinian capital.

The following day, Aqel registered at an educational institute to study media and communications as a cover for his activities. He attended classes regularly while waiting for the rest of his comrades to arrive in the West Bank. A few days later, Mohammed Abu Aisheh and Mohammed Harez joined him in Abu Dis, still armed with one pistol. Talal Saleh, who had crossed Erez in the same way, rented a flat in Ramallah along with five students from Gaza. He enrolled at a private institute, also to study media and communications. At that point, having not yet established contact with the Hamas leadership in the West Bank, the sum of the group's armaments was one pistol, two Carl-Gustav machine guns and a few knives.

A few weeks passed before the arrival of Bashir Hammad, followed by Mohammed Abu Al Ataya, whose parting shot had been an attack in Gaza.[5] Two policemen who were standing in front of the Beach Hotel which the Israeli police were using as an office in Gaza City were distracted by two members of the youth wing as Al Ataya opened fire. Later that day, the police made a statement saying that, despite being used at close range, the Carl-Gustav failed to kill its targets. The gun was renowned in the Gaza Strip for its poor performance. It was capable of spitting out six hundreds rounds a minute but, once the barrel heated up, the bullets tended to 'drop' from the barrel rather than becoming high-velocity projectiles.

Three days later, just over the border in Israel, Al Ataya and his back-up team of youths from Al Ahdath wing stabbed two settlers who were working in a citrus-fruit-bottling factory in Kibbutz Nahal Oz. The factory was close to the Karni or 'Oz Shalom' checkpoint which is a commercial zone where food and agricultural products and humanitarian aid enter and leave the Gaza Strip.

Once the Gaza group of six had finally assembled in Ramallah and Jerusalem, they made contact with Saleh Al Arouri, who was responsible for the military wing of Hamas in the West Bank. By then the group was desperate for weapons and were promised reinforcements. In the meantime, they wasted no time and began planning revenge with knife attacks for the massacre which had taken place at the Al Aqsa Mosque in Jerusalem eighteen months earlier.

They selected two of their number and a driver to go on a reconnaissance. They rose at 3 a.m. on Wednesday 29 July and drove to the Old City in Jerusalem. Their target was to be Israeli soldiers who were known to patrol inside the imposing forty-foot limestone walls that enshrine the Old City and its historic churches, mosques and the Wailing Wall of the Jews. The men arrived at about 3.30 a.m. and made their observations for the following day's attack. The driver dropped them back at their flat in Abu Dis and drove on to Ramallah, having made arrangements for an early morning pick-up the following day. Late in the evening of that same day, Israeli intelligence arrested Mohammed Abu Al Ataya, Mohammed Abu Aisheh and Mohammed Harez after besieging one of the flats the group had rented in Ramallah.

The Shabak,[6] together with special units belonging to the Israeli army and the Israeli Border Guards unit, had coordinated an extensive search to trace the Al Qassam group, whose disappearance from the Gaza Strip had raised the alarm. The assassination of a commander from Al Qassam Brigades, Yaser Al Namrouti, on 17 July 1992 in Khan Younis, following a tip-off by a Palestinian collaborator provided the Israelis with vital information. They obtained a recent photograph of Talal Saleh and were made aware that Mohammed Abu Aisheh's appearance was distinctive because of his unusually dark skin. These key visual references helped the Shabak tighten its net around the group. Only a last-minute change of plan saved Talal, Bashir and Imad from capture. A little before 10.30 p.m., Talal had spontaneously invited Bashir and Imad to spend the night at the nearby flat he was sharing, as his student flatmates had returned to Gaza for the holidays. It was more roomy than the other flat and it saved Imad from travelling back to Abu Dis at a dangerous time of night. They drove off in their Peugeot and, along the route, they spotted an Israeli jeep. Imad, whose antennae was always on the alert, was suspicious, but the three men drove on, unaware that their remaining three colleagues had been ambushed.

Nine days after the arrests, an Israeli army spokesperson confirmed that a rubber boat, a Carl-Gustav machine gun, ammunition, knives, videotapes of recorded attacks and faked Israeli IDs had been recovered from the flat rented by the group.[7]

Sheikh Saleh Al Arouri, the leader of Hamas in the West Bank, had warned the group in his first meeting with them about the dangers of living in Ramallah as there were a large number of suspected Israeli informers in the area. They were advised to move from one safe house to another until they decided to relocate to the larger city of Hebron where Hamas has a sizeable support network. There, Aqel became a regular at the local mosques where he used different names, amongst them Hussein and Ayyoub, in an attempt to throw Israeli intelligence off the scent, and later devised new tactics which included kidnapping Israeli soldiers in exchange for Palestinian prisoners in Israeli jails. He sent a messenger, Abbas Chabanah, a twenty-two-year-old Al Qassam fighter, to see Mohammed Abdul Fattah Dokhan, son of one of the founders, who was responsible for the coordination of Al Qassam activities in the West Bank and Gaza. He needed a car with yellow Israeli number plates, weapons and ammunition. Other assistants in Hebron were asked to find a cave in the surrounding hills which could be used to detain kidnapped Israeli soldiers. More than a thousand Palestinian cave-dwellers live a biblical life with their goats and families in the caves of South Hebron. The cave Aqel had in mind would also double as a training facility for four of their new recruits who had just joined the Al Qassam Brigades a few days before.

The most audacious attack carried out by Imad Aqel and his comrades was in broad daylight on 25 October 1992 against a military camp beside the Mosque of Abraham. They shot two soldiers from thirty metres, then escaped the area without trace, despite the large number of soldiers inside the well-guarded camp. Later that day, an Israeli spokesman confirmed that the bullet-proof vests they had been wearing had failed to save one of the soldiers, while the other was seriously wounded. This was only one of a number of attacks in Hebron which forced Israeli commanders to ratchet up their surveillance and recruit more informers in an effort to track down the perpetrators. The Shabak and military intelligence were already pointing their finger towards the Gaza faction of Al Qassam Brigades.

This heightened Israeli activity convinced Aqel to plan his exit strategy from Hebron despite his increased popularity within the Brigades and the Hamas movement in general. He became something of a cause célèbre during the months he was in the city for his well-orchestrated attacks, his courage and cool behaviour. He stepped up the training regimen of his new recruits, passing on his expertise and responsibilities in the region to Hatem Al Muhtasab and Mohammed Dokhan.

On 23 November 1992, Aqel slipped out of Hebron and headed back towards Gaza via the Erez crossing. He surprised his comrades that morning by assuming the guise of a Jewish settler, travelling to his beach settlement in the Gaza Strip.

Gaza was under strict Israeli curfew. Al Qassam fighters had kidnapped and later killed Alon Karfati, an Israeli soldier, and stolen his uniform and gun. Tight security forced the Al Qassam leadership to advise their members to leave Gaza and head for Egypt. Many heeded the advice, but Imad Aqel decided to take the risk and remain in Gaza. The pressure was on not just Imad but his entire family. His brother Adel was detained nine times and later deported to Southern Lebanon on 17 December 1992. In a surprise visit to Jabaliya refugee camp, Yitzak Rabin, the Israeli Defence Minister, met Imad's brother, Adel, and told him that Israel was willing to allow Imad to seek refuge in Egypt for three years and that the International Red Cross would be responsible for the arrangements. But Imad turned down the offer and continued his jihad in Gaza. Surprise raids were made on a regular basis against those houses thought by Israeli intelligence to be harbouring him. Hundreds of armed soldiers equipped with helicopters, tanks and jeeps were deployed in the hunt and their failure led the Israelis to conclude that locals were helping him melt into the background.

A lot of the time he was protected by the mother of one of the other fighters, Nidal Farhat. Miriam Farhat had always sympathized with fighters on the run from the Israeli forces and when she heard about Aqel, she asked her oldest son Nidal to dig a tunnel beneath their home to provide refuge for Aqel and others like him. Nidal and her late husband both approved this plan and she described the honour they felt as a family 'to harbour such a venerable leader in our home'. She admitted that she used to fear for the lives of her sons if there was an Israeli raid on their house: 'They came to our home many times searching for wanted people but, thank God, they failed.' On several of those occasions, Aqel would be digging away in his tunnel hideout. At other times he would return home with blood on his clothes following attacks with his comrades on the Al Zaytoun neighbourhood. Miriam recounted one occasion when the Israeli army surrounded the house:

> I was in the middle of washing Aqel's trousers, which were stained with blood. I pushed him down the tunnel entrance close to the kitchen door, checking that he hadn't left his weapon or any bullets lying around. Then I faced the soldiers and acted innocently when they asked if I had seen anyone with blood on his trousers.

He survived as a fugitive in Gaza for two years before an informer, Walid Radi Hamdaieh, betrayed him and he was killed. Like many of the early founders of the Martyrs Group, he lived dangerously, audaciously and briefly. But he became a legendary figure in the first Intifada, known for his bravery and for his slogan: 'Killing Israelis is *ibada* (an act of devotion).'

The Organization Grows

In the 1967 Six Day War, Israel fought against Jordanian, Egyptian and Syrian forces for the triple prize of the West Bank and Gaza Strip, the Sinai desert and the Golan Heights. It took Arabs and Palestinians some time to absorb the shock of this defeat and organize their resistance to the Israeli occupation.

The Palestine Liberation Organization (PLO) preceded the Islamic movement, at both the military and grassroots levels. Shortly after the Israeli occupation of the Gaza Strip and West Bank began in 1967, there were several Palestinian armed factions, all sheltering under the PLO umbrella with a bewildering array of acronyms: the PFLP, PDFLP and the PDFLP-GC, the PLF and the PLA, and the Al Saeka and Fatah organizations.

The PLO carried out military operations against Israeli forces and Jewish settlers, as well as kidnapping and arresting spies and informers and sentencing them according to their own legal code of practice. In Gaza, the only trained force apart from the Egyptian forces who remained in the Strip until 1967 were called the Palestine Liberation Front (PLF), the military wing of the PLO. The presence of other active Palestinian groups was limited to those few which belonged to leftist organizations such as the Popular Front for the Liberation of Palestine (PFLP), the Popular Democratic Front for the Liberation of Palestine (PDFLP) and Fatah, whose acronym comes from Harakat Al Tahrir Al Watani Al Filastini, which translates as the Palestinian National Liberation Movement. The fighter who gained most notoriety during the 1970s was Mohammed Al Aswad of the PFLP, whose nickname was 'Guevara Gaza', after the Marxist revolutionary hero, Che Guevara. Armed resistance gathered strength during the 1970s, as Palestinian and Arab volunteers flocked in their thousands to join military training camps which had been set up in Syria and Jordan. Israeli forces led by Minster of Defense Moshe Dayan, began to invest heavily in its efforts to bring peace to the fermenting disquiet in their newly occupied lands along the Sinai desert.

During the first Palestinian uprising between 1987 and 1993, Israel's control over the border with Egypt and its heavy military presence in Gaza effectively restricted the quantities of weapons and ammunition that were available to the Palestinian military organizations. Later on, when the second Intifada began in September 2000, Hamas smuggled weapons through the underground tunnel network which connected Gaza with Egypt and transferred some of it to their organization in the West Bank. This underground route facilitated access to weapons in their thousands. In addition, there were large quantities of ammunition left in the Sinai desert by the Egyptians and Israelis after the 1967 war. Egyptian weapons traders would excavate them and sell them on to the Palestinian organizations. These reclaimed explosives were not used until the later stage of the first Intifada, when military operations carried out by Hamas, Islamic Jihad and the PLO in the Gaza Strip became more intensive. Many types of explosives were also manufactured from household materials found in the soukhs.

None of the Palestinian organizations had problems in recruiting members or volunteers. The university campuses were one source, the mosques were another. Al Qassam fighters were chosen from within the ranks of the Muslim Brotherhood movement in Gaza using the selection criteria that they should have a strong religious commitment and demonstrate fiery determination towards the cause. 'In conflict, everything is possible,' my informant, Tariq, said simply. 'Hamas is not an organization with angels for members.'

Like Fatah, the Popular Front, Islamic Jihad and all the other Palestinian organizations, Hamas has been subject to assassination attempts. They have been penetrated by Israeli spies or by Palestinians coerced into becoming collaborators for the Israelis through torture, blackmail or financial remuneration, or all three. In turn, Hamas has infiltrated Israel's intelligence agencies using Israeli collaborators or persuading Palestinians to join the Shabak who would pass on information about their activities to their Palestinian handlers.

Israeli intelligence appeared to keep one step ahead of every move made by the Palestinian resistance. It was only after Israel's withdrawal in 2005 and the subsequent takeover by the Palestinian Authority that the various military organizations gained easier access to their members outside the Gaza Strip. The development and manufacture of locally made explosives and missiles then became possible. Members with expertise who had been living abroad then returned to make their contributions. Israeli military commentators, in an apparent attempt to undermine the Palestinian Authority's political credibility, would claim that explosives experts were part and parcel of the Palestinian Authority and were the major contributors towards the manufacture of weapons in the West Bank and Gaza on behalf of all the Palestinian organizations.

Political leaders of Hamas, including Sheikh Ahmed Yassin, Mahmoud Zahar, Abdul Aziz Al Rantisi and Abu Shanab, would distance themselves from the military wing and deny any personal responsibility for their attacks. This was emphasized in the wake of each attack or suicide mission carried out by Al Qassam Brigades into the heart of Israel. In a typical statement they would say: 'There is no relationship between the political leadership and the Al Qassam Brigades. The political leadership has no interest in forging a connection with the military wing. They have their own leadership and fighters, who plan and execute their attacks and everything related to this aspect.'

Nevertheless, Sheikh Ahmed Yassin, who was in jail at the time the military wing was established, was highly respected by Al Qassam Brigades, and his religious guidance was considered and implemented. Along with other Hamas political leaders, he was kept informed about its developments and relationships with other Palestinian organizations.

There were many interconnecting links within the Palestinian arena which made it necessary for all the Palestinian organizations – Al Qassam Brigades, Al Jihad Al Islami, Al Aqsa Brigades and others – to cooperate and coordinate with one another. Tariq described the intense pressure placed on all factions by the Israelis which forced the Palestinians to demonstrate a unified front and carry out joint operations, 'but unfortunately,' he said, 'there are members of all factions who attempt to stir up conflict, hatred and envy which creates disunity.'

Joint operations began in 1992, towards the end of the first Intifada, when Hamas and Fatah united in an operation in Khan Younis, where they killed Israeli settlers and military personnel. By the beginning of the second Intifada, cooperation between all the groups had become essential.

Al Qassam fighters who were known to the Israelis led a tough existence, according to Tariq, who was on the Israeli Defense Force's hit list for many years: 'The IDF was everywhere in the Gaza Strip.' While the IDF was the visible enemy, it was hard to defend against the invisible enemy – the Palestinian spies who were a dangerous presence throughout the region's neighbourhoods. The Israeli army would make systematic raids on the homes of suspects or those of their relatives and friends, forcing many Palestinian activists to live their lives on the run or to go into hiding. 'This created a great strain on my comrades who tried their best to adjust to this hunted lifestyle.'

Hamas' election victory in January 2006 and its subsequent formation of a government, caused a fracture within the movement which was at odds with its slogan of 'A Hand to Resist and a Hand to Rebuild', the implication of which was that there should be a balance between resistance and political participation. As Hamas propelled itself onto the political scene, it began to realize that there was a contradiction between building a secure society and creating warfare on the streets.

'The Engineer'

Yehia Ayyash was raised in the village of Rafat, north of Jerusalem, which has become the centre for the international outcry about Israel's illegal Wall. Ayyash was born on 22 March 1966 and grew up in a conservative household with little money. He has been described as a shy, quiet, intelligent boy who began memorising the Qur'an when he was just six years old and his passion for the liberation of Palestine grew with him. He studied in the village elementary school and among his abiding memories is that of standing at the side of the road after school, watching the trucks belonging to the settlers widening the village road to accommodate the flow of traffic to the settlement beside his village. The settlement has now merged into the twenty-seven-settlement bloc of Ariel, the largest Jewish settlement in the West Bank with a population of 37,000.[8]

At high school, his political activism began to emerge, along with his gift for sciences, particularly chemistry, which led him to Birzeit University near Ramallah to study electrical engineering. Birzeit is well known as a hotbed for political activists and, on several occasions during Ayyash's degree course, the university was closed down by the Israeli authorities, forcing it to operate underground.

After his graduation in 1991, Ayyash attempted to get an exit visa to pursue his higher education in Jordan, but the authorities rejected his application. Yacov Perez, the head of Israeli intelligence, regretted this decision saying, 'If we had known that [Ayyash] was going to do what he did, we would have given him permission to travel along with a million dollars.'[9] He married his cousin after graduating and had two children: Bara'a, the eldest, and Yehia, who was born on 20 December 1995, shortly before his father's assassination. At the outbreak of the first Intifada, Ayyash sent a letter to the Martyrs wing of Ez Ed Din Al Qassam Brigades outlining his plans to fight the Jews with suicide bombs.

Ayyash changed his appearance daily, rarely sleeping more than one night in the same house. Even his closest comrades were tricked by his variety of disguises. Sometimes he would be dressed as an Israeli settler, complete with sideburn ringlets, a Jewish skullcap and an Uzi machine gun slung over his shoulder. Other times he would be walking the streets of Tel Aviv in the guise of a foreign diplomat, or driving around with the yellow registration plates of an Israeli car. It was said that he attended the funeral of Kamal Khahil, a senior member of Al Qassam, in the West Bank, disguised as a woman. Rabin once remarked in the Israeli Parliament, 'I am afraid he might be sitting between us here in the Knesset.'

Yehia Ayyash was a highly skilled bomb-maker and explosives expert which earned him his nickname 'the Engineer'. Through his leadership of the Martyrs Group, he enacted what he saw as a programme of revenge for those victims of Jewish and Israeli terrorism which had been taking place since the beginning of the last century.

It was the Hebron massacre that provoked Ayyash to step up his campaign. The West Bank city of Hebron in the Judean mountains, where five hundred Jewish settlers live in fortified homes amongst the estimated 120,000 Arab population, has always been a flashpoint for Palestinian and Israeli tension. These settlers are protected by several thousand Israeli soldiers whose watchtowers survey the city from the rooftops of Palestinian houses. The holy city is venerated by Jews, Christians and Muslims alike, as it is believed to be the burial place of the patriarchs and matriarchs of monotheism – Isaac and Rebecca, Jacob and Leah, and Abraham and Sarah. The few tourists who dare venture to Hebron are charmed by its twisty, narrow, cobble-stoned streets and pay pilgrimage at the impressive Al Ibrahimi Mosque ('Mosque of Abraham'). The mosque's history stretches back to Herod the Great, who built it as a Jewish temple. It became a Byzantine church in the fourth century, and was then converted into a mosque in the seventh century with the advent of Islam. The Crusaders turned it back into a church until it was seized and restored once more as a mosque by Saladin. On 25 February 1994, the Jewish holiday of Purim, a Brooklyn-born doctor, Baruch Goldstein, committed a brutal massacre in the mosque. The orthodox Jew from the nearby settlement of Kiryat Arba threw a hand grenade into the throng of worshippers kneeling for Ramadan prayers and then, brandishing an automatic Galil rifle, killed twenty-nine Palestinian Arabs in the packed mosque. Goldstein was beaten to death at the scene by an angry crowd of onlookers. The bodies of Goldstein's victims were buried that day as required in the Muslim faith, but hundreds of bloodied shoes remained at the entrance of the mosque for days as a reminder of the tragedy.

Ayyash's response occurred on 6 April 1994: Raed Zakarneh became the first Hamas suicide bomber. He drove a bomb (wired up with explosives by Ayyash) to a bus stop at Afula and detonated it, killing eight Israelis and injuring forty-four. Ayyash, who was sad to lose Raed for the cause, promised that this was just the tip of the iceberg for what he had planned.

Ayyash was at boiling point and made a commitment to his comrades that his revenge would cause every Israeli and their government to feel deep remorse. He was already number one on the wanted list after the discovery of a car filled with explosives in Ramat Efal settlement two years before in November 1992. Using the forty-day anniversary of the massacre in Al Haram Al Ibrahimi, in Al Khalil, as his launch pad,[10] he engineered a rapid succession of attacks. Less than a week later, on 13 April, Ammar Ammarneh also exploded one of Ayyash's signature bomb bags on a bus in Hadera inside the Green Zone, taking six Israelis with him and wounding twenty-eight, including eighteen IDF soldiers. On 19 October 1994, at around 8.55 a.m. and during the commuter rush hour, Saleh Nazzal boarded a number five Dan Line bus near Dizengoff Square in Tel Aviv. His bomb killed twenty-two Israelis, injuring forty-eight others. This last attack prompted Yitzhak Rabin to cut short a trip to London and immediately return to hold emergency meetings with his security staff to devise a plan to end Ayyash's reign of horror. At this point, the sum of those killed by the Engineer and his students was estimated to be at least seventy with more than four hundred injured.

The Israelis intensified their search, which led to his mother, Hajja Ayesha, his father and his two brothers, Marae and Younis, being arrested several times. His village too was punished. The electricity supply was cut, and streets were left in disrepair. His father lost his hearing as a result of torture under arrest.

It was Yitzhak Rabin who coined the sobriquet the Engineer during a Cabinet meeting. According to Jadoun Azra, a former head of Shabak, Rabin was astonished by the endurance of Ayyash, who had perplexed and outfoxed the army, the Israeli government, the whole country. He was so elusive that he was likened to a ghost who chased them, and a nightmare which overtook their dreams. Israeli analysts wrote at the time that the phantom Ayyash had completely taken over Rabin's life, involving his entire army, security systems and large amounts of money in pursuit of his arrest.

Some Israeli intellectuals selected the Engineer as their Man of the Year in 1995 because of the influence he had over the Israeli people at that time, swaying their choice of government. Many TV and radio programmes were dedicated to discussions about him. The most talked about was an Israeli TV discussion programme aired on 25 January 1995. A panel of four analysts were assembled to discuss his tactics and strategy and, in particular, why the various Israeli intelligence agencies had failed to capture him. The panel included Shimon Romah, a former Shabak commander, and Ehud Ya'Ari, a respected TV correspondent and expert in Middle East affairs. Shimon Romah commented wryly: 'I'm sorry to tell you that I am forced to show some admiration for this man who has displayed abilities and experience beyond all bounds.'

Things became harder for Ayyash after the deaths of his two friends Ali Asi and Bashar Al Amoudi – both Al Qassam activists who were trusted by Ayyash and worked with him closely. He transferred his theatre of operations from the West Bank to the Gaza Strip which was a blow to Israeli intelligence who had felt they were closing in on him.

'A shy man of few words' is how his wife Asrar described Ayyash in an online interview.[11] From the time that it became apparent that her husband was being pursued by the Israelis, she moved with their son to her father-in-law's house in the West Bank. Every so often, Ayyash would send her a handwritten note asking if she would like to join him in Gaza. One of his comrades would arrive at her father-in-law's village using a password to confirm that he was a safe messenger and he would accompany Asrar, her young son and her mother-in-law to Gaza. The young man was armed with many fake IDs which enabled him to pass through Israeli checkpoints with relative ease. They would change cars after every checkpoint as a precaution but it was relatively easy for women and children to pass through at that time.

'Usually my husband doesn't spend more than a few hours in each place and never says where he is going or when,' Asrar explained, talking of her visits to Gaza. She herself didn't stay in one particular house for more than a week:

I hardly met anyone as I didn't want them to have any suspicions about me. I would sleep with hand grenades next to my head and my machine gun as well. I have done my training and I am very good at using them. Our lives were always in danger so I was mentally prepared for any raids. I knew that the Israelis would use me as a means to blackmail my husband. On one occasion, I stayed in a house for a whole week without leaving it once, because I noticed that the neighbours around where we were staying, appeared suspicious. So I kept out of their sight, not meeting anyone, except the wife of one of Yehiya's comrades who used to come once a day to bring food for me and my son and stay for twenty minutes or so, then leave us.

One day the house was raided by the Israelis and I jumped into the cupboard along with my son, Al Bara'a, who was only four years old but he was aware of the dangers both his father and myself were under. Instead of me calming him down and begging him not to make a noise, he put his hand over my mouth so I wouldn't say anything! Even when he went to play with kids in the neighbourhood, he always introduced himself as 'Ahmad'. He never gave up any information about our background.

One Thursday evening, Ayyash was settling in at one of his safe houses in a neighbourhood between Beit Lahyia and Jabaliya refugee camp in the north of the Strip. The sound of an aircraft overhead made him nervous. Always on the move, he made a snap decision to go south to Rafiah and spend the night at another safe house which he had been going to for about five months. It belonged to a long-established friend, Osama Hammad, who had been one of his classmates at Birzeit University ten years before. They had befriended one another when it was discovered they both lived in Abu Kash village, not far from the University compound in the West Bank.

The conversation between the Engineer and his old friend began with the usual kinds of things discussed between friends of long acquaintance. Then Ayyash talked tactics with Osama, saying they should carry out more attacks in the heart of Israel so that Israeli politicians would get the message that their policies would not bring them security but provoke even more killing. Ayyash then switched topics to express how much he missed his parents and family, which reminded Osama to tell him that his father, Abdul Al Latif, had been trying to reach him on the landline at his previous safe house but there was a fault on the line so he called Osama on the mobile number Ayyash had given him for emergencies.

The next morning, at about eight o'clock, Osama Hammad's cousin Kamal came to the house with a message for Osama that someone from Israel had been trying to get in touch with him on the mobile they shared. The three men chatted together and, after some time, the mobile rang and Kamal immediately handed it over to his cousin. It wasn't the expected call from Israel but Ayyash's anxious father. The two cousins left the room to allow Ayyash to talk to his father in private. Shortly afterwards, there was an explosion and smoke billowed from the room. When Osama rushed in, he found his friend lying on the floor with a gaping hole in the right side of his head. He told me that Ayyash must have died instantly and recalled the throb of a departing Israeli helicopter. The Al Qassam Brigades suspected that the helicopter had sent a signal to a tiny time bomb secreted in the mobile telephone. Israeli intelligence had finally succeeded in tracking its quarry, with the help of an informer: Kamal Hammad.

The Hamas membership wondered who could possibly replace the master bomb-maker. Dr Mahmoud Zahar, Hamas' Foreign Minister in the first elected government of January 2006, spoke to me by telephone immediately after the assassination. He told me that Ayyash's death would create 'a huge vacuum in the movement'. But he added: 'The Engineer has passed on his bomb-making skills to a new generation of Gaza's youth.' Continuing, Zahar said that during the month prior to his death, Ayyash had stopped using mobile phones explaining to his comrades that he feared that Israeli intelligence was closing in on him. He even warned his parents that they should only contact him on his landline. Kamal Hammad had taken advantage of an apparent lapse in the security precautions taken by Hamas and informed Israeli intelligence that his cousin Osama was providing a safe house for the Engineer. They invented a scenario whereby a mobile telephone rigged with a small time bomb could be handed to Ayyash whenever the opportunity arose. In a touch of irony, the Engineer, famous for his sophisticated bombs, was killed as if by his own hand, when a mobile telephone exploded in his ear.

Kamal Hammad was the owner of a building in Al Naser Street in Gaza where Moussa Arafat, the head of one of the intelligence organizations attached to the Palestinian Authority, rented his apartment. Hammad told family members that Palestinian intelligence were trying to arrest Ayyash, in an effort to curb Hamas' militant activities which had become a serious embarrassment to the PA. He was presumably trying to deflect from his own shame as a collaborator.

Osama Hammad, the only witness to the assassination, told me that his cousin Kamal, a businessman involved in property, had been hinting to him for some time that he should get a mobile telephone and offered to share his. On occasion, Kamal would lend Osama the mobile for a day or two to get the feel of it and would then ask for it back.

Despite being in the pay of the Israelis, Kamal Hammad had warned Ayyash, in a moment of guilt, about the danger he was under and advised him to be cautious. But Ayyash answered philosophically that no one dies before their time and that he was aware his days were numbered.

Abdul Al Latif would occasionally call his son on Osama's shared mobile but Ayyash, who had grown nervous in the course of his fugitive lifestyle, had asked his father only to use the landline, discreetly arranging that he should call him on Friday mornings only. On that particular Friday, 5 January 1996, the landlines at the various safe houses Ayyash used, appeared to have been cut off. At 9.00 a.m., Ayyash's father anxiously called the mobile to tell Osama that he couldn't get through to his son. Within a few seconds of answering the phone, the last words Osama heard the Engineer say as he was leaving the room were: 'Father, don't call me on the mobile telephone.'

Dr Zahar confirmed to me that Kamal Hammad was a member of Hamas and it was widely rumoured that he was paid a million dollars by Israeli intelligence as his reward for killing Ayyash. Kamal was moved to a safe house inside Israel for his own protection.

Zahar called on the Palestinian Authority to return the weapons which were seized from Hamas so that it could protect its fighters against the large numbers of informers who were still free and active in the Strip. The Palestinian Authority made frequent raids on homes belonging to Hamas military wing activists as the Authority believed that their aim was to derail the peace agreements the PA had signed with Israel.

Mohammed Dahlan, who was in charge of the Palestinian security services, held Israel responsible for Ayyash's death, saying that Hamas had respected the tacit agreement reached with Israel not to carry out attacks which up until that point had resulted in the deaths of a large number of Israeli civilians. He criticized Israel's attitude saying that 'by their reckoning, every Palestinian is wanted by the Israelis, including myself who coordinates with them.' Dahlan predicted that 'Israel would never succeed in securing its borders,' after threats were made by Hamas to take revenge for Ayyash's death – just as there had been after the Baruch Goldstein attack at the Mosque of Abraham.

Hamas and PA officials described the Gaza Strip as being 'riddled' with Israeli informers following decades of occupation and intimidation. Mohammed Dahlan told me:

[The Israelis] force people to work for them through blackmail, turning their lives into hell. If we had chosen to take responsibility for Ayyash's life, the Israelis would never have got close to him. We have many activists under our protection who remain alive … We detained Hani Al Abed, another Hamas activist, for more than two months, but the moment we released him from our camps, he was assassinated.

Dahlan had always insisted that Hamas leaders and their military wing activists were careless. The exceptions were few but he named Mohammed Al Dayef as one.

Mohammed Ibrahim Diab Al Masri, known as Mohammed Dayef from Khan Younis, was named as the Engineer's replacement because of his talent for orchestrating attacks. He was educated at the Islamic University in Gaza and worked closely with Imad Aqel and Ayyash. Dayef has been a target for Israel for more than a decade, who hold him responsible for the deaths of dozens of people in suicide bombings since 1996. He has survived at least five assassination attempts including two helicopter-borne missile strikes in August 2001 and September 2002. The latter left him injured, destroyed his car and killed two bodyguards. Like Yehia Ayyash, he is said to be a master bomb-maker and was part of the team which designed and produced the Al Qassam short-range rocket. He is invariably described as a 'shadowy' figure and his appearance in silhouette in a videotape on 27 August 2005 did nothing to dispel his mystique. In the tape, which was released by Al Qassam, he made several threatening comments towards Israel in the wake of its withdrawal from Gaza: 'You conquered our land. Today you are leaving Gaza humiliated. Hamas will not disarm and will continue the struggle against Israel until it is erased from the map.'

Yehia Ayyash made his final public appearance at his funeral ceremony, his coffin held aloft above a vast sea of an estimated quarter of a million banner-waving supporters. Al Qassam fighters were out in force, displaying the full might of the military wing of Hamas, a stark contrast with the early days when they had been armed with plastic guns, sticks and knives and one solitary Carl-Gustav machine gun. This time, they were defiantly confident that

Israel's dogged pursuit and assassination of Hamas leaders would never succeed in extinguishing the resolve of the military wing.

The Weapons Collector

No one felt the death of Ayyash more keenly than Adnan Al Ghoul. Adnan was responsible for the manufacture and distribution of weapons and the development of Al Qassam missiles under the supervision of Mohammed Dayef. In the early 1980s, prior to the official launch of the Al Qassam Brigades, Al Ghoul had already made a name for himself within the Hamas movement. Along with many other young men at that time, he was a member of the Muslim Brotherhood in his home town of Al Migraha, south of Gaza City. He was assigned as a weapons collector but he also carried out attacks against the Israeli occupying forces, notably killing Ron Tal, the head of the military police in the Gaza Strip, and one of the leaders of the Shabak, Victor Rijwan, in September 1987. Shortly after these attacks, Israeli forces seized large amounts of weapons which Al Ghoul had stockpiled and so Al Ghoul found himself one of the first Hamas leaders on Israel's wanted list, even before the first Intifada.

He escaped from Gaza by sea on 11 January 1988, slipping along the coast into Egypt with the help of fishermen. He was landed at Al Arish, where he spent the night. The following morning, Al Ghoul contacted one of his relatives who advised him to hand himself over to the Egyptian authorities after discovering that he had neither travel documents nor money. He was questioned politely and 'treated with respect', Al Ghoul recalled,[12] but he was told he would have to remain in custody until they could organize his travel arrangements out of the country. Two months later, on 21 March, he was taken to the airport and put on a plane to Syria. He spent five years in exile, honing his skills in Syria, Lebanon and Iran, where he received extensive training and expertise in manufacturing missiles, explosives, hand grenades and light weapons. Many Palestinian military experts called him the father of the weapons industry. He eventually returned to Gaza via Egypt using the swimmers' route in 1994, with forty kilograms of TNT explosives and other 'souvenirs' from his extended trip abroad which were not available in Gaza.

He was immediately promoted to head of weapons for Al Qassam Brigades.

The membership of Al Qassam Brigades in the West Bank and Gaza in the mid 1990s was in double figures at most – it never reached a hundred. Their strategy was to rely on quality not quantity as they saw it, and to operate in small cells. These cells concentrated on selecting targets, watching those intended targets, reconnaissance missions and carrying out actual attacks.

The turning point in Al Ghoul's career was meeting Yehia Ayyash in 1995. Together they formed a partnership designing military operations and manufacturing bombs, initially from everyday materials, and assisted by others from the Al Qassam Brigades such as Youssef Abu Hain and Saad Al Arabid. Following Ayyash's assassination, Al Ghoul was hell-bent on revenge. He masterminded five serious attacks in 1996, which killed sixty-one Israelis and wounded many more. These deadly reprisals forced the Palestinian Authority to make large-scale arrests of Hamas activists and Al Ghoul was rounded up. After a few months, he managed to escape from prison and went on the run. His wife and members of his family were taken into custody in an attempt to flush him out. It was now Abu Bilal's turn (as Al Ghoul was known) to find himself at the top of Israel's assassination list.

The first attempt on Al Ghoul's life was at the hands of an Israeli informer in the spring of 1998. 'W.S.', who had been living in Syria and was a former member of the PDFLP, came to Al Ghoul through a cousin, asking for help in getting a job with the Palestinian Authority. 'I turned him down politely but he returned some time later asking if I would buy a Kalashnikov and a pistol at a good price because he needed the money to travel.' Al Ghoul recounted that they met in the Haifa restaurant in Gaza and from there drove to W.S.'s flat, where they negotiated a cheap price for the weapons. W.S. went to the kitchen to prepare coffee which he offered to Adnan while he checked over the guns. Adnan then paid for the weapons and left. 'Three hours later, I began to vomit every five to ten minutes,' he recalled. At midnight, he was admitted to hospital where he remained for two weeks. A German doctor at the Al Shifa Hospital in Gaza City saved his life. While recovering from the effects of the poison which had laced his coffee, Al Ghoul informed Palestinian intelligence but, by then, W.S. had fled to Israel.[13] Adnan survived the deadly poison but his health suffered as a result of it.

The second attempt on his life was on 22 August 2001, when, together with Saad Al Arabid, Al Ghoul was experimenting with the launch of the first Al Qassam missile in Al Maghraha area. An Israeli plane fired a rocket at Al Ghoul's car in the mistaken belief he was inside. His eldest son Bilal, aged eighteen, had suggested to his father that they should switch cars, after noticing hovering Apache helicopters that day, and it was Bilal who died in his father's place. A third attempt came two years later when his house was raided by Israeli forces. Once again, Al Ghoul avoided death. His second son Mohammed, Imran, a cousin, and a neighbour called Zachariah defended the house by kidnapping one of the soldiers. There was an exchange of fire, with the other soldiers killing many people, including Mohammed, Imran and Zachariah. The house was then destroyed.

Four months before the Al Aqsa Intifada began in September 2000, Salah Shehada, the leader of Hamas' military wing, met with Mohammed Dayef, Adnan Al Ghoul and other senior officials in Al Qassam to discuss a major regrouping of their military cells. The heavy losses they had suffered through arrest or assassination by either the Palestinian Authority or Israeli intelligence were taking their toll. Al Ghoul decided he should concentrate solely on developing weapons. He put together a strategy for arming Hamas, starting with weapons – from hand grenades, anti-tank weapons and explosives belts for suicide bombers to Al Qassam missiles. He was also responsible for training hundreds of Al Qassam recruits.

Nidal Fathi Rabah Farhat, Miriam Farhat's oldest son, was part of Al Ghoul's weapons team and developed the prototype of the Qassam rocket which has been used since 2001 to target several cities and towns in Israel with a range of up to ten kilometres. According to Salah Shehada, one of the founders of Al Qassam Brigades, the rockets, which have an explosives payload of up to 20 kilograms,[14] 'are made from simple raw materials. [Even] the women can make them at home.'[15] The rockets are frequently launched from Beit Hanoun on the east side of the Gaza Strip, earning the town the nickname

'Qassam City'. The Israeli town of Sederot, close to the northern border of the Gaza Strip, has borne the brunt of these weapons.

On 16 February 2003, Nidal received word that the second component of a small, remote-controlled aerial drone he was assembling had arrived at his home in the Al Zeitun neighbourhood of Gaza City. The component had been dispatched through an Israeli Arab agent which, at the time, rang faint alarm bells for Nidal. Nevertheless, he went to Al Zeitun and, by the time he arrived, two groups of Al Qassam Brigades were ahead of him and had offered to supervise the final assembly of the drone on his behalf. Nidal's contact had specifically advised him via his mobile phone to take personal responsibility for its assembly and, according to those at the scene, he immediately set to work, using a detailed instruction manual.

Nidal and his comrades were excited about this futuristic piece of technology, which had great potential to advance their war against Israel. The drone was intended to fly over Israeli settlements as a surveillance device which could double as a pilotless bomb. As they were examining the new part, they became aware of the sound of an Israeli aircraft buzzing the area. A few seconds later, explosives which had been hidden in a section of the drone were detonated, killing Nidal Farhat, Akram Fahmi and Ayman Muhanna, all senior members of Al Qassam Brigades, together with three other members. Hamas leader Abdul Aziz Rantisi held the Israeli Defense Minister, Shaul Mofaz, responsible for their deaths. The following day, more than 50,000 Palestinians took part in the joint funeral procession. Over one hundred armed fighters from Al Qassam Brigades joined top leaders of Hamas – Sheikh Ahmed Yassin, Abdul Aziz Rantisi, Ismail Haniyeh and others – at the vanguard of the procession which began at Al Shifa Hospital in Gaza, and ended at the Martyrs' Graveyard east of Gaza City, where the men were buried together, according to their will.

One of Nidal's comrades in Adnan Al Ghoul's missiles development team was Abu Hussein, who designed a local Rocket-Propelled Grenade (RPG) known as a 'Yassin' rocket in tribute to Sheikh Ahmed Yassin. Abu Hussein claimed he could make a bomb out of nothing. According to his comrades, he had not put aside his weapon in almost twenty years, as he was constantly being pursued by Israelis or informers. 'The orange groves of Gaza know me well!' he told them laughingly, in reference to his habitual hiding place.

On 22 October 2004, Israel finally cornered the forty-six-year-old weapons expert. An Israeli surveillance aircraft launched two missiles at his car as he drove along Jaffa Street in Gaza City on his return from Friday evening prayers. The car, which was also carrying explosives, completely combusted. Ismail Haniyeh, who was then responsible for the office of Sheikh Ahmed Yassin, was at the forefront of the massive funeral procession and described his death as 'a loss for Hamas and a loss for the Palestinian people'.

Leader after leader was being assassinated, including the founding father of Hamas, Sheikh Yassin, and several of his co-founders, including Dr Rantisi, Salah Shehada, Ibrahim Al Maqadma, Dr Ismail Abu Chanab, and a long list of its members. But this did nothing to stop the movement and its military wing. The clandestine organization that had begun operations on 1 January 1992 with just a handful of young fighters armed with an old machine gun was showing the world fourteen years later that they were capable of producing advanced weaponry, explosives and tactics to confront the best-equipped army in the Middle East.

On the morning of 25 June 2006, nineteen-year-old Corporal Gilad Shalit was abducted by a group of Palestinians from three different militant groups including Ez Ed Din Al Qassam. The Hamas fighters crossed the border from Gaza into Israel via an 800—metre tunnel, emerging at an Israeli army post near Kerem Shalom at the southern edge of the Gaza Strip. They stormed the checkpoint, killing two soldiers and wounding another four, before snatching Corporal Shalit and taking him back along the tunnel to the safety of the Gaza Strip.

Next, Hezbollah fighters managed to slip across the border into Israel from Southern Lebanon in an operation called 'True Promise'. On Wednesday 12 July, they waited for an Israeli patrol to pass by and attacked two military Humvees, kidnapped two soldiers and killed at least seven, while twenty-seven others were injured. Hezbollah fighters shelled the area north of Shtula settlement near Nakoura on the border, which prevented the Israeli soldiers from retrieving the bodies of their fellow soldiers. Israeli troops held back for almost seven hours, worried that 'surprises' might await them if they got closer to the bodies and the injured. One tank had already been destroyed after arriving to help the beleaguered Humvees.

Israeli Prime Minister Ehud Olmert's knee-jerk reaction to the Gaza abduction was to repel any conditions made by Hamas and to order his troops to storm the Gaza Strip to release the soldiers. Despite the tough talk by the Israeli Prime Minister, those who know the Gaza Strip and the developments which took place there following Israel's unilateral decision to withdraw, it was clear that the Israeli army could not reoccupy Gaza. The price would have been too dear to bear for a new Prime Minister who had only been in power for four months and lacked the military credentials of his predecessors.

During the early days of the Intifada, Israeli patrols could confidently travel around the Gaza Strip and the West Bank with just a couple of jeeps, a dozen soldiers and perhaps a Merkava tank or two to keep the areas under control. At the very least they would be confronted with stone missiles and the worst-case scenario was that they might come under fire from home-made petrol bombs. Nowadays, Hamas' military wing is producing sophisticated weapons. Even their basic hand grenades are designed to standards as advanced and effective as any hand grenades made in the USA or China. All products are stamped with 'Made in Gaza by Al Qassam'. Their original missiles, known as Al Qassam 1 and Al Qassam 2, regularly targeted settlements and cities in Israel, especially Sederot, the home town of the Israeli Defense Minister, with limited damage. Now these have been upgraded. I was told by Al Qassam senior leaders when I was in Gaza for the Palestinian elections in January 2006 that it is only a matter of time before Hamas' military wing in the West Bank will be capable of manufacturing weapons which will 'give Israel a taste of its own medicine'.

4

The Informers

The constraint on the development of Hamas and the ability of its military wing to carry out military operations has been the extent of Israeli penetration of the organization, both through moles within the group and through informers in Palestinian society. Israel's strategy has focused on removing the influential and charismatic leaders needed to hold the movement together. Salah Shedah, Sheikh Yassin, the Engineer and Abdul Aziz Rantisi were all assassinated using intelligence gleaned from Palestinian collaborators.

The stories of these collaborators reveal the level of infiltration of Israeli intelligence and the methods and tactics its security organizations have employed to recruit Palestinians during the three decades of Israeli presence in Gaza and its continued occupation of the West Bank. Palestinian security organizations estimate the number of collaborators recruited by Israel during this period to be in excess of 20,000. Many of them were forced to flee to Israel, where they are housed in specially built villages following Israel's evacuation of Gaza, for fear of reprisals.

Akram Al Zotmeh

Salah Shehada, as head of the armed wing of Hamas, was Israel's number one enemy for some time. Israel held him directly responsible for hundreds of deaths through his organization's series of orchestrated suicide bombings. He became a fugitive as a result of Israel's pursuit, prompting Shimon Peres, Israel's then Foreign Minister, to describe Shehada as 'a local Osama Bin Laden'.[1] Israel employed many tricks to destroy the powerbase and military arms of the various Palestinian factions. Detailed testimonies from Palestinians describe how they were recruited by Israel using the successful honey-trap tactic and sexual blackmail.

Shortly before midnight on 23 July 2002, acting on information obtained by Israeli intelligence from a Palestinian informant, an aerial raid was launched on an apartment block in a densely populated neighbourhood of Gaza City. At approximately 11.55 p.m., when most of the city's inhabitants were sleeping, two Israeli F-16 fighter jets were observed circling for a few minutes before one of them fired a one-ton precision smart bomb.[2] The two-storey apartment was reduced to rubble and dust, bringing along with it another home and seriously damaging four others. Salah Shehada was killed instantly, together with sixteen civilians, nine of whom were children, two of them babies: Ra'ed Mater, aged eighteen months, and Diana Rami Mater, two months old. As many as 150 people were injured. Covered in blood and masonry dust, the wounded were barely recognizable as they were rushed to Gaza Shifa Hospital, where Shehada's wife, Leila Safira, his daughter, Iman Salah Shehada, and his bodyguard, Zaher Nassar, were among the dead.[3]

Dust was still settling when I arrived at the small alleyways surrounding the demolished buildings where the Palestinian informer had hidden himself while guiding the Israeli planes. Neighbours who survived the bombardment said they would never forgive Israel for the civilian deaths and vowed to take revenge for the death of the founder of Hamas.

Israel's Prime Minister, Ariel Sharon, retaliated against the international condemnation of this deliberate attack on a crowded residential area, which even Israel's staunchest ally, the USA, called 'heavy handed'.[4] Speaking to Cabinet ministers at a government meeting the morning after the aerial strike, Sharon began apologetically enough: 'We of course have no interest in striking civilians and are always sorry over civilians who were struck. But,' he added, dispelling all attempts at contrition, 'this operation in my view, is one of the great successes.' Sharon's Deputy Director of Communication and Information, Gideon Meir, backed up this statement with a full -blown justification, saying that the air strike was directed towards 'a known terrorist, one who was responsible for hundreds of attacks against Israeli citizens in recent years'.

The attack was planned after Israeli intelligence secured information of Shehada's whereabouts from Akram Al Zotmeh. He acknowledged the consequences of his actions only once it was too late. Speaking from one of the Palestinian Authority prisons in Gaza, during his detention, he expressed his belated remorse. 'I feel pain and sorrow. There were lots of casualties. Everyone who commits a crime has to take his punishment.[5]

Akram was twenty-two years old, single and living in Rafiah, one of seven brothers and four sisters. His father owned a grocery store but Akram had plans for higher things and enrolled as a student at Al Azhar University in Gaza City. His association with Israeli intelligence began in the library of the British Council in Gaza. A third-year student in English Literature, he had gone there to do some research on Shakespeare's *King Lear*. Out of curiosity, spotting a foreigner reading a British newspaper, Akram introduced himself. The man told him that his name was Terry, that he was Canadian and was a lecturer in Sociology at the University of Ottowa, and was in Gaza to study the living conditions of Palestinians. By the end of their conversation, Terry had hired Akram to assist him in his research and act as an interpreter in return for $100 a month. Later, as a further lure, he was promised assistance to travel to Canada, for which Akram provided Terry with passport photographs of himself to obtain an identity card from the Canadian Embassy in Tel Aviv.

Akram and Terry made a trip from Gaza to Tel Aviv to visit the Embassy, ostensibly to process a visa application for Akram to go to Canada. Casually, Terry introduced Akram to another Canadian named David. 'I later discovered they were both Israeli intelligence officers,' Akram recounted. Canadian David confessed to Akram that he was in fact Israeli intelligence agent 'Abu Mohammed'. 'They began harassing and blackmailing me with mocked-up photographs showing me in various sexually compromising situations, which they said they would use against me if I didn't cooperate with them.' Al Azhar University is religiously conservative and therefore it would be of profound embarrassment to Akram if the photographs were made public.

Abu Mohammed assigned Akram to monitor 'confrontations' and 'hot events' in Gaza and to supply the names of Palestinian militants who committed attacks against Jewish settlements and Israeli command posts. A short while after starting work with Abu Mohammed, Akram received a telephone call from another intelligence agent who called himself 'Abu Ihab':

> He asked me to start observing martyr Salah Shehada and his home in addition to the people who visited him and details of the cars they drove ... I explained to Abu Ihab more than once that the building in which the martyr lived was crowded with residents. Abu Ihab justified an assassination attack by saying that if Salah Shehada was not killed in such a way, many other civilians could become his victims.

Twenty minutes after Akram reported Shehada's location to his Israeli minder, the F-16 dropped its deadly bomb.

Israel denied Zotmeh's claims that Israeli agents posed as Canadians in a 'false flag' spying operation which would have contravened an earlier promise. Five years before, Canada recalled its Ambassador to Israel after Mossad agents, with faked Canadian passports, were caught during a botched assassination attempt on top Hamas official Khalid Mishal in the Jordanian capital, Amman. Israel apologized to Canada and gave its word that it would never use Canadian passports again.

Haider Ghanem

Further successful operations notched up by Israeli intelligence were due to the recruitment of another Palestinian collaborator: Haider Ghanem. He too was tricked into working for them in ignorance of the fact that the reports he was preparing for the so-called 'Strategic Studies Center in Singapore' were a foil.

Haider Ghanem was unshaven but appeared sharp and confident when I met him in his prison cell.[6] He expressed remorse at betraying the 'friends' who had trusted him, as he revealed how he was coerced into collaborating with the Shabak:

> I read an advertisement in a newspaper inviting unemployed Palestinians to send in their CVs. I prepared mine and sent it off at the end of 1995, and I received a reply early in the new year of 1996. I was told to get in contact with the Strategic Studies Center, regarding their offer of a high-profile job in journalism based on my qualifications. They placed me in their so-called Media Center in the West Bank, and that's how I began my job in journalism, filing stories for their HQ which they said was in Singapore. I was asked to prepare studies about the situation in the Gaza Strip. I worked for them for about six months and then I was told there would be a change in my assignment. I was asked to work as a correspondent for their centre in Gaza, which I did for about another six months until they invited me to visit them in Tel Aviv. They gave the excuse that they wouldn't be able to meet me at their office because it was very busy but, by our third meeting, I was finally invited. A high-ranking Israeli officer was present at that meeting and that was the first time I knew that my bosses were Israelis. When the officer started to discuss the situation in the Gaza Strip, I began to realize what I had let myself in for. When they recognized I was having second thoughts, they started to blackmail me, saying: 'You've been working for us for nearly a year and we have all these reports you have been sending us.'

By this stage, Haider understood that there was no going back. He began working as an undercover journalist in Gaza, reporting in detail about any issue of interest to his superiors in Israeli intelligence. Instead of writing about a demonstration in a journalistic fashion, he peppered his reports with details which would be of great value to Mossad, such as the number of demonstrators, the people behind its planning and the slogans which were being used. He established contacts with the leaders of all the different Palestinian political organizations. He reeled off the names of some of those he interviewed: 'Of course there was Sheikh Ahmed Yassin, the leader of Hamas, I interviewed him on many occasions. Besides Yassin,

I met Ismail Abu Chanab, and Dr Mahmoud Zahar and, from Islamic Jihad, I interviewed Nafed Azzam and Al Hindi and most of the leaders of the Palestinian Authority.'

Haider told me that his minders asked him to concentrate on certain key figures who were involved with their organizations' armed factions, in particular Sheikh Ahmed Yassin, the leader of the Islamist Resistance Movement, Nafez Azzam, the leader of Islamic Jihad, and the head of the Popular Resistance, Jamal Abu Samhadana. 'Information about what they thought, their military orientations as well their future plans in relation to the recent political change, all these were of immense interest to Israel.'

Before each meeting I had to prepare two or more central questions. The questions were obviously connected to Islamist groups and the relationship between their political side and their military wing and the relationship between the movement itself and the Palestinian Authority. I was also expected to present a detailed description of all other persons present at the meeting, as well as reporting side conversations taking place beforehand or afterwards. The meetings were not like a press conference, they were unstructured allowing a free-flow of conversation.

I was very socially active in Gaza, especially in the Rafiah area which was a particular hot spot during the Intifada, with barriers prohibiting entrance. But, because of my connections, I got access to private and confidential meetings and was privy to details without the need for investigating. Unfortunately for them, they were not discreet during their discussions of sensitive internal political and military issues which were discussed freely and casually in front of me. They didn't give a thought to my presence.

The period from the beginning of the Al Aqsa Intifada in the Gaza Strip generated an information overload from informants about the Palestinian grassroots – their impatience, their inability to defend the factions within the Palestinian public, who were part of the resistance. It was a realistic depiction of the situation There is a high percentage of youth who have no choice other than to resist. I tried to look at where violent conflicts were likely to take place within these factions and I reported a realistic image of the Palestinians' position.

The training that agents received, as well as the systems they utilized, were various and largely depended on the personality of the agent and his mental capabilities:

> All I gained during my course of work with them was Internet skills. They put me on an Internet course in a centre in the Gaza Strip. I kept it up until I was proficient. This was my minders' main concern, how emails could be delivered cryptically without the content being deciphered, even if someone surprised me and saw what I was composing. At the beginning we used a system, a small disk, directly connecting to the Shin Bet [Shabak] HQ without having to navigate through a local server but it had a lot of technical faults so I started compressing files and using passwords to enable access.

The bloody assassinations of collaborators, like those happening in Gaza, didn't deter Haider Ghanem from continuing his association with the Shabak:

> I was in Gaza one day when I saw a gathering of people in one of the squares. I was told that a Palestinian agent, like myself, who was working for the Israelis, was going to be executed because of his role in the assassination of Jamal Abdul Razek in Rafiah. Out of curiosity, I went to watch how he was executed.

The development of Israel's intelligence network in recruiting agents throughout the last few decades conformed with the growth of the Palestinian resistance against the Israeli occupation. What facilitated Israel's recruitment of agents was mainly related to the Palestinians' fear of detention by the IDF. This placed them in a position where they could easily be pressured to join. Moreover, Israel would at times arrest Palestinian individuals under the pretext of committing a nationalist crime to take advantage of their presence amongst the Palestinian political arena after they were set free:

In the early stages of the second Intifada, there weren't any assassinations of political figures. It was more a matter of observation and tracing their activities. A month or so after the outbreak of the Al Aqsa Intifada, I began to shadow one of the Palestinian armed militants. Abut ten days later, on 22 November 2000, he was killed.

The man was Jamal Abdul Razek, one of the most significant icons within the Fatah organization. This was to be the first political assassination operation carried out by Israel in the new wave of violence created by the second Intifada, and Haider's role was key.

Razek, at just thirty years old, had already led a full life as a fighter. He spent his twenties between 1992 and 1999 in an Israeli jail accused of throwing hand grenades and carrying out attacks against the Israeli army and settlers in the southern part of the Gaza Strip. His final hour was spent driving from the southern town of Rafiah to Khan Younis, seven kilometres to the north-east in his Korean-export Hyundai car. The road was also the main artery east to the Orthodox Israeli settlement of Morag. Three of his comrades followed behind him in a Mercedes. Razek had intended making the journey the previous day but, ironically, delayed his journey because he thought that the IDF would be on high alert due to an attack on a Sederot settlement the previous day.

According to Haider, a special Israeli unit was lying in wait for him as a result of intelligence they had received from Haider. As Razek was approaching the Morag settlement, just outside Rafiah, the Mercedes which was following overtook him. The Israelis swerved in between the two cars, their patrol jeep dividing them, and opened fire on both cars, killing Razek and his three comrades.

After the Razek assassination, Haider entered a new phase. He had won the trust of his supervisors in the Shabak, and they promoted him to recruit other informers, using email letters as lures:

> I achieved such a level of confidence within Shin Bet [Shabak] that they began to give me money, which I had to distribute to people I didn't know. Money was also sent via the online PayPal system to new recruits and agents already on the payroll. My own salary was

high. It went up from 1,500 shekels to 2,000 per month until the end of the period when it reached 3,000 shekels.

These email letters were initially prepared by Israeli intelligence, and whoever wrote them had to be credibly informed. The letters included Qur'anic verses alluding to the concept of martyrdom, and statements of patriotic and religious interest which were intended to fire up the youth, not necessarily to join Al Jihad Al Islami [Islamic Jihad] but to influence them to work for Islamist groups. I was then asked to correct linguistic and grammatical errors, basically to edit their messages before they sent them on to would-be Palestinian recruits. The emails included a phone number to call for enrolment. They were offered weapons and money as long as they went about their missions in accordance with the instructions. They had to agree to one condition which was that no one should be informed about these email letters.

One of Haider's assignments was to earmark young men who were regular mosque-goers to size up how willing they would be to join Al Qassam Brigades or Al Jihad Al Islami (Islamic Jihad). He would then recruit them into small cells of just two or three people and supply them with money and weapons. One commonly used double-bluff tactic by Israeli intelligence was to command these 'dummy' Palestinian cells to attack Israeli patrols or checkpoints in the Gaza Strip. When they got close and before they had a chance to open fire, they would be killed instead. Israeli forces would then claim they had been forced to attack. Many Palestinian analysts became aware of this and suggested that both the Israeli government and the IDF were using such tactics in order to raise morale amongst their soldiers. It became apparent that these pseudo-attacks coincided with periods when many towns and cities in the heart of Israel were suffering bombing campaigns by Palestinian groups such as Hamas or Islamic Jihad.

In addition to receiving intelligence about activists and their organizations' movements, Israel was particularly concerned to gather information about what was going on in the Gaza Strip. Haider was puzzled to learn that not all the intelligence he conveyed about the comings and goings in the Strip was acted upon:

For example, if I had knowledge that several people from the West Bank had crossed into the Gaza Strip. I would inform them, but their reaction was often indifferent. I eventually realized that the reason they weren't interested was because it was the Israelis themselves who had sent these people to the Strip as informers.

Abu Khoussa

Tawfiq Abu Khoussa, a Palestinian journalist, related an incident which took place late at night on the first day of *Eid Al Adha*[7] in 1992. He was woken by the sound of gunshots close to his home in Gaza City and rushed to the window to see a large gathering of neighbours in front of his house. The gunshots had killed two young men who had been ordered out of the back of a white Peugeot 504 estate car by masked gunmen. Scrawled graffiti on the wall of Tawfiq's house spelled out a sick message: 'This is an Eid present for Tawfiq Abu Khoussa from Ez Ed Din Al Qassam Brigades.'

Tawfiq was shocked by the scene and the ominous message. Two weeks earlier, he had taken part in a public debate in a nearby neighbourhood which was also attended by Dr Haider Abdul Shafi, the head of the Palestinian delegation for the Madrid and Washington peace talks. Tawfiq's defining message of the debate was to plead for an end to the assassinations which had claimed the lives of more than 450 informers in the four years following the start of the Intifada.

But killing informers was nothing new to the Palestinians in the West Bank and Gaza. What was new was that they began to pose a threat to the binding relationships between tribes and families. Killings were taking place on the pretext that there was a spy or informer in the camp, when in fact the real reason was to settle old scores or to take revenge.

Some killings appeared to be motiveless. Around this time, the body of a twenty-nine-year-old blind man named Hosam Mustapha Shabayek was discovered a day after he was kidnapped from a picture-framing shop in the Al Rimal neighbourhood of Gaza City. His grief-stricken parents made appeals through local newspapers and those in the West Bank for anyone who could give information about how and why an unlikely target like their son had been killed.

Everyone who knew Mustapha Shabayek praised his kind nature and warm spirit.

A similar situation took place in Nour Shams (Sunlight) camp in the Tulkarem area of the West Bank, where Yasser Kashmour and his father Said were found murdered. Yasser was kidnapped from his home in front of his wife, children and parents. Earlier, he had received threats telling him to resign from his job as director of UNRWA in the refugee camp. Prior to his kidnapping, Yasser had made contact with Palestinian leaders both inside and outside the Occupied Territories asking to put an end to the threats he had received from different organizations. One was signed 'Al Shabah Al Aswad [the Black Ghost]', another 'the Unified Leadership of the Intifada'. A third was signed by the PDFLP. When contacted, all three organizations denied issuing such threats.[8] Ten masked men armed with axes attacked his father at the end of March 1992, killing him instantly. Yasser was killed a short time afterwards, close to the family home, also in an axe attack. Their neighbours speculated why an Israeli military post, situated just eighty metres from the house, had been vacated during the time of the killings, while leaving a beam of light directed towards the house. They believed that the attackers must have had connections with the Israeli occupation. Fatah made a statement claiming Yasser as one of its members, and that he was considered a martyr. Ibrahim Goshi, a Hamas spokesperson and leader in Jordan, told me that Hamas only executed informers after first confirming in detail their connections and crimes and the final punishment would only be meted out after serious consideration.

Many accused Israeli intelligence of carrying out these and several other crimes against innocent people as a method to discredit the Intifada and its military factions. The theory was that, by carrying out these attacks, Israel was attempting to create the impression that Palestinian militias were shooting or hacking to death innocent Palestinian citizens as well as Palestinian informers working for Israel.

Hamdaieh

Walid Radi Hamdaieh's indoctrination into the Hamas movement and his double life as an Israeli spy earned him plenty of money, for which he paid the ultimate price. He was executed in Gaza after confessing to the Palestinian General Intelligence, and later to the court in Gaza, that he was a collaborator. He provided intelligence which resulted in Israel's assassination of two Al Qassam Brigades leaders and other senior figures in Hamas on Israel's hit list. He named Hamas' military wing leader Yaser Al Namrouti in 1992, Imad Aqel in 1993 and Marwan Al Zayeg, Yaser Al Hasanat and Mohammed Qandeel, killed together in the Al Sabra neighbourhood of Gaza on 24 May 1992.

Hamdaieh was the former head of the Al Da'awa wing of the Hamas movement. In the early 1980s, after studying at the Islamic University, he became a member of a group called Al Mujamaa – the Islamic Compound led by Sheikh Ahmed Yassin. The Compound was the focus for the Muslim Brotherhood movement in Gaza and the precursor to Hamas. Hamdaieh gave an undertaking to the Sheikh that he would 'remain loyal to the Islamic movement' and was sworn to a secret phrase which was to be used in communications with other Islamist activists: 'How is Al Aqsa?' was the greeting phrase. The response was: 'Al Aqsa is wounded', a reference to the Al Aqsa Mosque in Jerusalem.

By 1986, arguments were brewing between budding Hamas activists and other Palestinian organizations, including Fatah, and Hamdaieh got himself involved in a fight with Fatah activist, Assad Saftawi, in Gaza. As a result, Israeli intelligence raided his home in the early hours of 6 October 1987, when he was arrested and taken to Gaza Central Prison for interrogation. He was given two choices: he would be tortured or he could work for them as an informer. An intelligence officer known as 'Maini' supplied him with his telephone number and, in a little under a week, he was released.[9]

Two weeks passed before Hamdaieh received orders to meet Maini in front of the main gates of Abu Kabir prison in Tel Aviv. When the intelligence officer arrived, he indicated that Hamdaieh should follow him to a nearby building. In a second-floor apartment, another officer, calling himself 'Abu Hodaib', began questioning him about the leaders of the Islamic movement. According to Hamdaieh's confession statement, he offered many names, including Sheikh Ahmed Yassin, Abdul Aziz Al Rantisi and Khalil Al Qoqaa.

He continued to pass information to the Israelis until the official announcement of the launch of Hamas as a movement in December 1987, at the outbreak of the first Intifada. Hamdaieh took part in many Intifada-related activities, for which he was arrested in August 1988 and held for seven months, despite working for the Israelis. He said this was to create the impression within Hamas 'that I was one of them to avoid suspicion'.

Another appointment was arranged for him by intelligence officer Maini in Tel Aviv, this time in a hotel. He was introduced to an officer by the name of Abu Sager, who appeared to be of a higher rank. Hamdaieh and Abu Sager had a long discussion about the situation in Gaza and the Islamic movement in the Strip and, as the meeting concluded, Hamdaieh was given 150,000 Israeli shekels (more than US$30,000) and the name 'Abu Jaafar', which he was to use in his communications with them. At the beginning of May 1989, to his surprise, his house was raided and he was once again arrested. 'Abu Jaafar' was told by intelligence officer Maini that a large group of Hamas leaders had also been arrested and held prisoner in Ansar II detention camp in Gaza. After several days, he was ordered to a questioning session attended by Maini where he was told that the entire military wing of Hamas had been arrested. He remained in Ansar II for four months during which time he continued to supply the intelligence officer with information about the detained members of Hamas and Islamic Jihad.

Shortly after his release, Hamdaieh was summoned to meet Maini on the main road to Al Shujaieh. Maini arrived at the rendezvous point driving a Peugeot 404, the most popular car in Gaza before the Palestinian Authority came on the scene. There were others in the Peugeot whom Hamdaieh believed were intelligence officers 'dressed like Arabs'. The car was decorated with Qur'anic verses, with a small carpet for prayers. Lying on the floor were Uzi machine guns. Hamdaieh sat on the back seat beside Maini, who had disguised himself with a wig and a false moustache. Anyone seeing them, Hamdaieh remarked, 'would assume we were a group of Islamists'. They drove to a settlement nearby, where they joined Abu Sager, who taunted him with the question: 'Why haven't you found a leading role yet? Members who join the PFLP can get a leading role within six months!' Hamdaieh pulled some strings and was promoted to head of the Al Da'awa wing, whose mandate was to publicize the cause. The post had become vacant when the Israelis arrested the previous Al Da'awa head in Al Shujai'a, conveniently allowing Hamdaieh to replace him.

In 1991, Hamdaieh made a seemingly strange request to 'Captain Maini', asking to be arrested once again to provide him with authentic cover for his continued relationship with Israeli intelligence. He was detained for five months, during which time he volunteered the names of all the members of the Al Da'awa wing, particularly those who took part in the military parades which regularly took place on Gaza's streets. Hamdaieh was then asked to update Israeli intelligence about some of those on their wanted list who were using safe houses to avoid arrest or assassination. He managed to provide information about one of them – an Al Qassam activist called Mohammed Qandeel. Israeli intelligence gave him a time bomb and a box of dynamite explosives which were to be passed to Qandeel at the earliest opportunity. As soon as they were alerted that Qandeel had received the equipment, they detonated the bomb, which killed Qandeel along with two Al Qassam military wing leaders – Yaser Al Hasanat and Marwan Al Zayeg.

Walid Hamdaieh's statement went on to describe his involvement in the assassination of Yaser Al Namrouti and the near-capture of Imad Aqel and his group at their house in Ramallah. 'I followed Yaser's movements closely. He used to visit my house often. He gave me US$5,000 to buy some equipment and spend on activities for the organization in my region. I then informed my Israeli handler of Namrouti's request for a gun and time bombs, which they supplied to me. After Yaser left my house, Israeli intelligence followed him to an area far away from where I live and killed him in Khan Younis on 17 July 1992. I was rewarded with large amounts of money from Israeli intelligence in appreciation of my services.'

Four days after killing Namrouti, Israeli intelligence decided to arrest Hamdaieh again, and he was imprisoned for forty days. 'After I was released,' Hamdaieh continued, 'Abu Amjad, the Israeli Captain, told me: "You have wasted an opportunity".' Ez El Din Al Sheikh Khalil, who was later assassinated by Mossad in Damascus, had replaced him in Al Da'awa wing. Israeli intelligence decided to arrest Hamdaieh so that he could reclaim his position. He was subsequently arrested and deported to Marj Zhour village, over the border in Southern Lebanon, along with more than four hundred other Hamas leaders. Handing him a five dinar note, the officer told him that his deportation would only be for a short period. On the reverse was written a telephone number which Hamdaieh was to use to contact him.

When he returned to Gaza from Lebanon, Hamdaieh received instructions to track down a big Hamas fish, Imad Aqel. He was aware that Imad was a regular visitor at Nidal Farhat's house. He was told by his Israeli handler that everyone in Israel – from the lowliest person right up to the Prime Minister – was calling for Imad Aqel's head. In front of other high-ranking intelligence officers, he promised a reward of US$500,000. 'I told him straight away that Aqel was in Al Shujaieh neighbourhood in Farhat's house,' said Hamdaieh. He was told to buy two pairs of trousers in the same colour. One pair they retained and in the other they attached a small listening device. Hamdaieh was told to wear these trousers when he visited Farhat's house so that they could eavesdrop on the conversation. Hamdaieh visited Imad Aqel during Ramadan, and Hamdaieh told how they prayed together:

> Imad had been fasting and we took *Iftar* on the roof.[10] Suddenly, Israeli forces surrounded the house in all directions. When he tried to fire, he was hit by an Israeli grenade. We were besieged for two hours, then the Israeli army asked everyone in the house to get out. As we were leaving, the Israeli soldiers said, 'We want this!' in reference to me. They took me away in a car and asked what had happened inside. I told them that Imad Aqel was dead.

They ordered him to take off his trousers to retrieve their listening device, giving him the second pair he had bought earlier to wear. He was rewarded with US$5,000.

Imad Aqel had survived two years as a fugitive, often seeking refuge in the Gaza home of Miriam Farhat, until his luck ran out. It was a huge coup for the Israelis to eradicate the leader and inspiration of Ez Ed Din Al Qassam Brigades. Aqel's background was indicative of the type of young man who becomes a foot soldier for the military wing of Hamas.

In February 1994, just a few weeks after the Aqel assassination, Hamdaieh attended an important meeting with his Israeli minders during which he was reprimanded: 'You are responsible for the deaths of five seniors in Hamas' military wing, who were assassinated by our agents,' they said. 'Yet it is some time since you have supplied us with any information.' He later visited the Israeli crossing point at Beit Hanoun, where he had an assignation with an Israeli officer who asked him not to use his telephone landline, suspecting it might have been bugged by Palestinian security. He was given weapons to pass on to two wanted Al Qassam seniors – Kamal Khalil and Awad Al Salami. 'The Israelis were desperate for any information about Yehia Ayyash, the Engineer,' Hamdaieh's testimony confirmed, but he failed to get to him even though he had tried to lure Al Salami with the promise of weapons and explosives supplied by Israeli intelligence to gain the confidence of Ayyash. The closing words of Walid Hamdaieh's confession said that he was arrested by Palestinian intelligence in Gaza, 'before I got close to Ayyash'.

Four decades of Israeli occupation provided Israel's security agencies with the ultimate environment in which to recruit Palestinian collaborators, coerced into keeping a Cyclops eye on the armed resistance in the West Bank and Gaza Strip. They preyed on the vulnerable, blackmailing them with promises of work, education or medical treatment outside the territories or tempting them with sums of money. They singled out those like Walid Hamdaieh with the potential to get as close as possible to those on the top of their wanted list. Palestinian security officials have estimated that up to 25,000 collaborators of varying importance have been recruited in this way.

5

The
Martyrs

A Mother's Love
The mother of Mohammed, Rawad and Nidal, all Al Qassam
Brigades fighters who died for their cause, was nominated as a
Hamas candidate and is now a member of the Palestinian Legislative
Council. She has become an icon amongst Hamas followers in the
Gaza Strip. Her popularity and fame were brought to the world's
attention through her public support of her sons' decisions. Umm
Nidal, as she is known, is fifty-six and, together with her late
husband, a policeman, she bore four daughters, now married, and
six sons. Three of her sons died as suicide bombers, one is in prison
and, when I encountered her, two were still participating in armed
resistance in the Gaza Strip. She had no regrets.

I met Miriam Farhat at her home on 24 January 2006, the eve
of the Palestinian elections. She told me how her son Mohammed
had entrusted her with the secret of his intended operation long
before he was assigned. Umm Nidal described as a 'momentous
occasion' the day Mohammed returned home with a gun, which
signalled his initiation into Hamas' military wing and his journey
towards martyrdom. She admitted that, from his early teens, she
had encouraged him to fight with guns rather than stones against

the armoured jeeps which pounded the sandy streets of Al Shujai'a neighbourhood of Gaza City which was their home. The fight against the Israelis is such an intimate part of this family's life, that on the wall hangs a framed piece of barbed wire that her son had cut from the protective barrier around the Jewish settlement, hours before he died.

She recalled with sorrow-tinged pride the evening of Thursday 7 March 2002, when nineteen-year-old Mohammed entered the study hall of an academy which combines religious studies with military training, in the Gush Katif settlement of Azmona. Apart from himself, Mohammed killed five eighteen-year-old students. Twenty-three others were wounded. Mohammed's home became a place of pilgrimage for scores of men and women waiting to join the ever-growing list.

The images of Mohammed during his last few days of life were etched like photographs on his mother's mind and she could replay at will, the conversations they exchanged. Umm Nidal began mourning his loss three days before the operation, when she would go to his room in the early hours, simply to stare at his sleeping face. 'He was very handsome. I used to think he should die a martyr to repay what God has given him. For the sake of Allah I suppressed all my maternal emotions. If I let my fears take control I wouldn't have allowed any of my sons to choose the path of martyrdom.'

She remembers crying as he read out his will. When he looked up, seeing her tears he began to laugh, threatening to pull out of the mission. She told him:

I am your mother! It is not easy for me to ask you to leave, I cry for you day and night. Don't misinterpret my tears. They are the tears of a mother who is about to give her son in marriage to the beautiful *houris* in Paradise. You must obey your orders, and maintain your fight until the moment you meet your God.

When the moment arrived, they exchanged their final goodbyes. 'Aim true,' she said. Then he left. He didn't cry. He left smiling. Her first son to die a suicide bomber appeared tranquil and calm. She described as 'unbearable' the hours which elapsed between him leaving home and learning of his death. 'It was as if I was breathing his very breath.' She worried that he would be arrested before he was 'glorified with martyrdom'. Her relief was absolute when the news came that her son's mission had been successful. I asked her how she could cope with supporting her son in this deadly act. 'I was his partner in jihad,' she replied. 'It is a normal thing. It is not as remarkable as people think.' This will seem incomprehensible to most parents but I think it is important to document it as it shows the extremes of psychology which make this conflict so difficult to understand.

Wissam, one of Mohammed's surviving brothers, was sitting beside his mother, nodding in agreement at her words. He told me that he too was supported by Umm Nidal to take part in a suicide mission but it failed. He was arrested in 1993 on his way to target the Beer Sheva settlement in the Negev Desert, south of Hebron. Wissam had only recently been released after spending more than a decade in an Israeli jail.

I asked this mother of four daughters if she approved of women taking part in suicide missions. 'Jihad is open to everyone,' Miriam Farhat replied. 'No one can hold back a man or a woman destined for jihad. The support for women carrying out operations is unconditional. If any of these operations need a female, then there will be opportunities for women to take part.' She complained that the Israeli siege of the Gaza Strip was an obstacle which prevented more Palestinian women from taking part in acts of martyrdom but she added, 'We should not ignore the influential role women are playing in supporting roles – by giving birth to her kids for instance who are willing to die for the cause.'

The first female suicide bomber was twenty-seven-year-old Wafa Idriss, a member of the Al Aqsa Brigades, the military wing of Fatah. A resident of Al Amari refugee camp near Ramallah, the medical secretary for the Palestinian Red Crescent, exploded her bomb in Jaffa Street, Jerusalem, killing an 81–year-old Israeli and injuring over one hundred others.[1]

Two years later, Reem Rayashi became the first female suicide bomber to be claimed by Hamas.[2] Up until then, Hamas was thought to disapprove of sending women on these missions, despite assurances by the movement that jihad was a duty for every Muslim

– male and female. When her name was revealed, many assumed she had belonged to the Al Aqsa Brigades.

According to Farhat, Reem Rayashi's case was all the more emotive because she decided to leave behind young children – Doha, her three-year-old son, and Obeida, her eighteen-month-old daughter. The twenty-two-year-old university student from a wealthy Gaza family tricked border control soldiers into giving her a personal security check rather than passing through the metal detector, claiming that she had metal plates which would set off the alarm. While waiting for a woman soldier to give her a body search, she detonated her two-kilogram bomb inside the terminal at the Erez border crossing between the Gaza Strip and Israel, taking with her the lives of two soldiers, a border policeman and a civilian security guard. She had recorded a farewell video, dressed in combat uniform with a green Hamas bandana around her head and holding an automatic rifle, in which she announced that since eighth grade she had 'hoped that the shredded limbs of my body would be shrapnel, tearing the Zionists to pieces, knocking on heaven's door with the skulls of Zionists'.[3]

Farhat recalled the reaction of other women towards Reem's selection for the mission: 'Hundreds of females came to me to complain about Reem being chosen ahead of them. They were very jealous about that. Many of the young girls descended on my house and begged to be given priority to follow Reem.'

The acceptance of female suicide bombers for military operations created confusion amongst conservative Palestinian society, which questioned its legality under sharia law. After the Al Aqsa Brigades claimed Wafa Idriss as a female martyr, Sheikh Ahmed Yassin, the founder and spiritual leader of Hamas, gave a statement which appeared to denounce their action by insisting that the role of women was to look after the family and children and bring them up in a *jihadi* way. Yassin said, 'For women to carry out such attacks inside occupied Palestine [referring to the Green Line of 1948] is complicated, because the suicide bomber must sleep away from home for days and weeks prior to carrying out a mission. This would be difficult for girls.' Yassin later claimed to have been misquoted, which had created a misunderstanding about his position regarding female martyrs. Following the suicide attack by Reem Rayashi, he delivered another declaration amounting to approval: 'For the first time, Hamas has used a female Palestinian fighter to carry out an attack against the occupation. This is a new strategy for resisting the enemy.' He added: 'We have said before that women are a tactical advantage.'

While Hamas came late to the scene regarding women suicide bombers, it was ahead of the other Palestinian organizations in using female disguise for its male operatives. Shortly before midnight outside the Dolphin disco on Tel Aviv's beachfront, Said Al Hotari worked his way through the queue of teenagers waiting to enter, dressed as a female singer carrying a guitar packed with explosives. He killed twenty-one and injured almost a hundred that Friday night, 1 June 2001. Similarly, suicide bomber Abdul Basset Odeh entered the dining room of the Park Hotel in the Israeli coastal city of Netanya, wearing full make-up, long smooth black hair tumbling below a hat, high heels peeping out from well-cut trousers and a brown leather coat. His feminine appearance created no suspicion, and the Palestinian from Tulkarem in the West Bank was able to carry out his mission in front of scores of horrified diners enjoying a gala Passover dinner. Thirty died and over a hundred were wounded on the evening of 27 March 2002.

At the time of the attack, Ahlam Aref Ahmed Al Tamimi, a twenty-three-year-old university student from Birzeit University and part-time journalist, was the only female member of Al Qassam Brigades. She was given sixteen life sentences, or 320 years in jail, by the military court[4] for assisting Ez El Din Al Masri in his lunchtime attack on the Sbarro Pizzeria in King George Street, Jerusalem on 9 August 2001. The bomb, concealed in a guitar case, killed fifteen Israelis. The Israeli judge said Ahlam was not an important partner in the attack but she had taken some measures to help and was fully aware of what she was doing. Ahlam had chosen to wear western-style clothes at the time of the attack, rather than her usual Islamic dress, so as not to draw undue attention to her suicide bomber companion. They spoke to one another in English, and Ahlam carried a camera in order to pass inconspicuously as tourists.

Despite the ferocious commitment of Ez El Din Al Qassam's volunteers, the political climate had changed by 2003, and the number of suicide attacks claimed by Hamas was the lowest it had been for a year. This welcome respite led many to believe that the military organization had finally bowed under pressure and was curtailing its bombing activities. Israeli analysts put it down to America having reached a ceasefire agreement with the outlawed organization after a meeting was held between Sheikh Ahmed Yassin and an American legislator, Steve Cohen – a member of the Foreign Relations Committee in Congress. When Reem Rayashi detonated her bomb it was a wake-up call that the military wing of Hamas was indeed still active and deadly. The significance of the Rayashi suicide mission was that it was in retaliation for Israeli attacks against Palestinians and was deliberately aimed towards Israeli soldiers. The Israeli government was put under greater pressure to increase its efforts to coordinate a speedy military withdrawal from the Gaza Strip and evacuate its 5,000 Jewish settlers. Israel's prolonged failure to keep the Gaza Strip under control would force Ariel Sharon to order a disengagement from the territory in August 2005.

Mission Aborted

Israel's penetration of Hamas may have been one of the most determined intelligence operations in the world, but such is the devotion of Ez Ed Din Al Qassam fighters that nothing has prevented the organization from nurturing its most efficient product – the suicide bombers. The fervour of these young people cannot be overestimated. In 1997, a suicide attack took place for which, unusually, none of the obvious suspects claimed responsibility – neither the military wing of Hamas nor the Al Quds Brigade, the military wing of Islamic Jihad. Confusion over this particular martyrdom operation arose because the suicide bomber had switched his allegiance from Islamic Jihad to the military wing of Hamas. His reason for abandoning his former organization was simple. Due to the lengthy waiting list of would-be suicide bombers stretching long before him, he was determined to fast-track his journey to Paradise. By transferring to Hamas, he could be assured of his death-wish well ahead of his former brothers-in-arms. This trend of jumping ship by young fighters impatient to achieve martyrdom was confirmed to me by Fathi Al Shikaki, leader of Islamic Jihad, during a telephone interview from his base in Damascus, a few months before he was assassinated by Mossad agents in Malta in 1995.

This burning desire for martyrdom was described to me by 'Salim', a member of Ez Ed Din Al Qassam, whose own failure to achieve this wish had left him a broken man. 'There's nothing more heart-wrenching than to be held back from Paradise because of a technical fault.[5] Back in 1996, Salim was chosen for a suicide attack within the occupied territories which was derailed due to a security lapse committed by his military cell. They failed to predict the movements of the occupation soldiers, which resulted in the would-be martyr remaining alive and in limbo, praying for a new opportunity.

A stocky man in his twenties, Salim refused to disclose his true identity but agreed to talk about his involvement with the Al Qassam Brigades. 'Martyrdom is like a dream,' he told me at his home in Al Breij camp:

I ask God with every prayer to honour me with the gift of martyrdom and its rewards to the extent that it occupies every moment of my conscious and unconscious thoughts. I made my wishes known in the mosque amongst those I understood to have connections with the military wing of Hamas. I went to the funeral procession for the martyr Yehia Ayyash, who had been assassinated by the Israelis and was known as the Engineer because of his skill at making bombs. A guy, one of the brothers from the mosque, approached me and it was clear he had heard about me. I poured out my desire for martyrdom, assuring him of my passion, but he didn't seem to take me seriously. A week later, I was surprised when a man sitting next to me in the mosque, asked whether I was still insistent on martyrdom. I was a bit suspicious which he must have sensed so he reminded me that he was the same guy I had previously met at the funeral. I didn't recognize him as his head and part of his face were covered in a *kuffiyah*. My reply was instantaneous. It's hard to express how ecstatic I felt at his words. It was indescribable. I couldn't believe that I was to become an Al Qassam soldier, a Qassami bomber who would shred the enemy into pieces.

Salim was put through his paces with two other recruits from Al Qassam Brigades, who had been selected for the same mission. A group of mujahideen drilled them through a rigorous training course intended to increase their psychological strength, religious devotion and powers of discretion, as well as intense physical and practical training, which included teaching them how to control and manage their bomb belts. They were given detailed maps of their target site and transportation from the occupied Palestinian territories to cross the border. A four-metre-high barbed-wire fence separates Israel from the Palestinian occupied territories, angled towards the Israeli side. The fence is electrified and connected to a warning centre. If touched, it can kill.

'Words fail to describe my happiness as the date got closer,' Salim continued:

> I would sneak glances at my siblings and parents, wondering if they could guess the reason behind my excitement. When the day finally approached, I kissed my mother's hand and asked her to be proud of me. I told her I was going away on a mission for a month so that she wouldn't immediately worry. I left quickly in case my determination would falter, although the pleasures of life are no comparison to what motivates the martyr, and can never deter him from accomplishing his wish.

The evening was spent in preparation for the mission ahead with his two fellow mujahideen, praying, running through the plans, and reading the Qur'an. Before sunrise, they made their way to a field close to the border which separates Al Bureij refugee camp in the Gaza Strip and the occupied Palestinian territories of 1948, an area known as Goher Al Deek. Al Bureij was established in 1949, in the centre of the Strip. It was built on 528 *dunums* of land,[6] which had previously been a British military base. The abandoned barracks was used to house a large percentage of the 13,000 Palestinian refugees, while the rest were put up in makeshift tents. The crowded camp was eventually made more permanent in the 1950s, when UNRWA replaced the tents with the simple concrete block houses, which typify all Palestinian refugee camps.[7]

As the time for their martyrdom approached, the men received instructions and from the head of their military cell and asked last-minute questions. Salim was assured that everything was in place for a successful operation. The most important instruction was how to avert potential danger through deception. They were told that if they were apprehended by the enemy, one potential martyr should appear to surrender while his mujahideen brothers fled the area, firing their guns to draw attention towards them. The decoy would then position himself as close to the Israeli soldiers as possible and explode his bomb.

By the evening, the group was inching its way towards the barbed-wire barrier marking the border, having sized up the best place for the three suicide bombers to cross. Days and hours had been spent observing the settlements and their routine. How often did the Israeli patrols pass? Which part of the fence was the most vulnerable in terms of security? What time of day afforded them the greatest window of opportunity? Their organization knew how to isolate the electricity supply to the fence but also provided their fighters with rubber wire-cutters and ladders as a fall-back. Despite the meticulous planning, within seconds of their approach Israeli forces appeared in large numbers to confront them. They managed to abort the mission, with no deaths on either side, but Salim was devastated. He admitted to breaking down in tears. His failure was compounded when he learnt that one of his comrades in the West Bank had been successful and was now honoured with martyrdom. Returning home to his mother she sensed the reason behind his anguish. She held his face and told him to be patient and he would achieve his dream on the next mission.

Two years later in 1998, Salim was chosen to embark on a similar mission. Again due to an unanticipated heavy military presence, he was not able to penetrate the barbed-wire border with Beit Hanoun, north of the Gaza Strip. Having built himself up to die twice, Salim returned home to life, his bag still full of his unexploded promise.

Managing the Fallout

A few young children scampered around the shaded alleyways between the breeze-block buildings. Otherwise the dusty rubble-filled streets of Al Amal in the Gaza Strip were deserted. With giggles, the children directed me towards the home of twenty-two-year-old Ismail Ashur Brais, which was in a three-storey building with the characteristic jumble of concrete and iron rods jutting above the upper floor – the hopeful preparation for further storeys to be added in better times. I cautiously trod the dingy crumbling staircase to the first floor, accompanied by the deafening wails of a mother. As I reached the open door to the living room, two close neighbours were pleading with the grieving woman to try to remain calm until they received certain news about the fate of her son. The morning's television news announced that a suicide bomber from the Khan Younis neighbourhood, had blown himself up in Rafiah Yam. A mother's intuition made her fear the worst. Ismail had been behaving differently these past few days.

It was a strangely quiet morning for the first day of the holy month of Ramadan, 6 November 2002. Late the previous evening, the radio news had reported that three Palestinian children had been wounded by Israeli soldiers in an exchange of fire with Palestinian fighters. The Israelis had been positioned in the many observation towers protecting Morag and Rafiah Yam – two Israeli settlements close to Rafiah Palestinian refugee camp on the south-western edge of the Gaza Strip where it meets the Egyptian border. The following morning I decided to follow up the story, which was being updated on the crackling car radio as my driver, Mohammed, took a sharp left turn and switched off the engine in the shadow of the tall buildings surrounding the settlements. He was concerned that we too might become targets if spotted in the cross-hairs of the Israeli snipers' weapons.

The refugee community remained indoors, nervous to venture out after the previous night's fire-fight. I heard the sound of a person walking along the sandy, uneven pathways above the silence. Cautiously, I got out of the car as a local man approached, wanting to see if he could explain what happened. As he was telling me about some of his neighbours who had been injured in the firing, Mohammed interrupted. A friend had called him on his mobile, alerting him that a suicide-bomb attack had taken place less than two hours earlier in the nearby Jewish settlement of Rafiah Yam. A

Palestinian in his early twenties had detonated his bomb alongside an Israeli checkpoint after infiltrating the settlement in the early hours of the morning.

Mohammed, a native of Khan Younis, called his neighbours and, realizing that he knew the identity of the reported suicide bomber, drove us at speed towards his home town, about seven kilometres north-east of Rafiah. The Mediterranean sun was already warming the route as we sped past row upon row of agricultural greenhouses, which line the main road. The olive harvest was in full swing, despite tens of thousands of dunums of olive trees having been burned or razed by the Israeli military since the start of the Al Aqsa Intifada in September 2000. Farmers and their families were beating the trees with sticks to dislodge the fruit onto nets while donkey-carts stood by to transport the ripened olives to the nearest press.

A mobile watchtower supported by a vast crane dominated the landscape as we arrived in the densely packed town of Khan Younis, keeping a military-trained eye on the town's quarter of a million residents. Foul-smelling wastewater permeated the air – there are no sewage pipelines to service the teeming community. Mohammed made a few enquiries, which directed us to a home in a small neighbourhood just west of the town called Al Amal. Ismail lived here with his wife and young son, together with his parents and twelve brothers and sisters. Their home was across the road from the Ganei Tel settlement, whose barbed-wire fences glinted in the autumn sunshine.

As we reached the top of the stairs, we found Ismail's mother, Zeinab, inconsolable. The room had little except pallets along the walls as seating, and a small table for tea. The focal point was a large framed photograph of a gentle-faced young man with a shy smile. Through her sobs, with Ismail's photograph staring down at her, Zeinab, her white veil soaked in tears, described to me how during the previous few weeks she had experienced instincts which only a mother can have which made her suspicious that Ismail, or Abu Mouad as she called him, was planning to take part in a suicide mission. He had become unusually affectionate while spending more time with his mother, asking her for reassurance that she would care for his young son Mouad if anything should happen to him. Zeinab cried discreetly so that no one would guess her fears, not even his wife Nada, who had left that morning for the local clinic and was not yet aware of her husband's fate.

His older brother, Hatam, told me that Ismail's wish had always been for martyrdom. 'I used to joke with him saying, "Be a man and work. Look after your son and don't have these thoughts." He would just retort, "My son is here [to replace me] so it is my time to go."'

It was still dark that first morning of Ramadan when Ismail told the household that he was leaving to perform early morning prayers in the nearby mosque before heading off to work. At that moment, Zeinab had been convinced that her son was giving her his final embrace. As they parted, she prayed without hope of seeing him again and so she was convinced that her eyes were playing cruel tricks when he returned home just a short while later. But Ismail's bittersweet return was a final reminder to his mother to protect his wife Nada and their eighteen-month-old son Mouad, and to be happy.

I left her to grieve privately and, as I walked down the concrete stairwell, an elderly man in his late sixties was beginning his climb. The painful cries of his wife above appeared to trigger instant realization as he too began to weep. Two well-built young men appeared at his side, grasped him by the shoulders and guided him up the stairs to join his grieving wife. His shock was so profound that he collapsed in their arms and lost consciousness. From the language and rhetoric used by the two young men as they attempted to revive the bereaved father, it was clear they were from the military wing of Hamas. They tried to soothe him, saying it was every father's dream that his son be martyred and that he should be proud. If his son was neither religious nor a good person, he would not have the privilege of dying a martyr. 'The first people to follow a martyr to heaven are his parents,' one of them said. 'Your son prayed and we are in the holy month of Ramadan. Would you rather your son had died in a car accident or from drowning or as a drunk than dying a hero for killing Israeli soldiers?' The father's cries subsided and, in less than fifteen minutes, he was thanking God for giving his youngest son this opportunity, and that he yearned for the day they would meet again in heaven. A few months after Mohammed's suicide, his father died, a broken man.

This poignant scene provided an insight into the personal and organizational side of Hamas. The two men were Ismail's comrades in Al Qassam. They knew in advance that he was embarking on his mission, and kept complete secrecy until the news broke of what they considered was his success. They had come not only to comfort the family, but also to perform a typical Hamas public relations mission. It is imperative for the family of a Hamas fighter to be seen in front of the world's media as proud of their beloved son rather than bitter or tragic and they should extol Hamas' belief in the battle and the glorious afterlife their son is destined to experience.

Driving along the road running adjacent to the settlement, the atmosphere felt tense. Children were pointing skywards towards the Israeli observation towers, from which a protective eye was kept on one of their military bases and helipad. Directly behind Ismail's home, I noticed five masked men painting slogans on the wall. We stopped to take some shots and, on seeing us, they asked us not to film their faces, but to focus on what they were writing. It was a statement by Ez Ed Din Al Qassam, claiming responsibility for the suicide attack on Rafiah Yam. The graffiti of the Gaza version of events read:

The Islamic Resistance Movement [Hamas] and Ez Ed Din Al Qassam Brigades announce to our Palestinian people the martyrdom of the hero Ismail Ashur Brais, who carried out the Rafiah Yam martyrdom mission on 6 November 2002. May God grant him forgiveness and bestow upon you long life.

On the more Orthodox radio programme it was announced that Nisam Avraham, a twenty-six-year-old Israeli Defense Force reservist from Lod, had been killed and five soldiers and a civilian wounded. The suicide bomber was named as Ismail Ashur Hassan Brais, who had been wearing the blue tiger-striped uniform of the military wing of Hamas and armed with a Kalashnikov assault rifle, ten ammunition clips, and home-made grenades.

Later that day, the remains of Ismail's body were returned to his family for burial. Hundreds of young men in their teens and twenties, wearing green bandanas around their heads, attended the ceremony carrying black flags painted with the map of Palestine and the Hamas motto. They chanted slogans calling for revenge and promising further attacks. Some denounced the peace talks with Israel as 'useless and a waste of time', while others stirred up passions amongst the gathering to encourage further suicide-bomb attacks 'because the enemy only understands the language of force'. Ismail's Al Qassam comrades could be identified amongst the crowd by their trademark armbands, decorated with words from the Qur'an: 'It was not ye who slew them; it was God.'[8]

One of Ismail's friends told me that he had worked at the Rafiah Yam settlement as an agricultural labourer. Around thirty non-Orthodox Jewish families lived there, and it was one of the few settlements where the community's children were driven across the Israeli border checkpoint each day, on their way to school in the nearby Ashkelon settlement on the Israeli side of the Gaza Strip. While working amongst them, his knowledge of the community made it easy to get as close as possible to his target that morning.

Ismail's comrades were enraged by my use of the term 'suicide bomber'. They shouted abusive words, telling me that I should call the operation 'an act of martyrdom'. Later that evening, as neighbours gathered, bringing food to the bereaved family, the Israeli army, supported by dozens of tanks, armoured vehicles, bulldozers, jeeps and helicopter gunships rolled into Al Amal. Troops massed around Ismail's house, ordering the family to leave and giving them no time to retrieve their possessions or papers. An exchange of fire began with light weapons between local armed militias belonging to different Palestinian groups who tried to halt the Israeli operation. But proximity to the main Israeli military base made it impossible for them to succeed in halting the inevitable. A Caterpillar D9 bulldozer lumbered towards the evacuated building, reducing the family's home and worldly goods to a pile of concrete rubble and twisted steel, an architectural feature which has come to symbolize tragedy throughout the Occupied Territories. In 2000– 2004, more than 2,500 Palestinian houses were destroyed by the Israeli military in the occupied Gaza Strip, leaving 16,000 people homeless.[9]

Visual evidence of Palestine's helplessness in the face of these onslaughts is everywhere. Just a few blocks away was the home of

Rafea Salmah, a young man in his mid twenties and a member of the military wing of Hamas. He had escaped many Israeli raids on his house in an attempt to arrest him, but the most serious was in the early hours of Monday just a few weeks before Ismail's death. More than forty Israeli tanks backed by Apache helicopter gun-ships, tore through the neighbourhoods of Al Amal and Khan Younis. The tanks scoured the area, randomly firing at civilian homes, with no apparent purpose other than to terrorize the inhabitants and break into Palestinian homes.

When a unit of the Israeli forces approached Rafea's house shortly after midnight, Rahima Hasan Salmah, his fifty-two-year-old mother, who had become accustomed to such raids on her home, rushed to waken her wanted son and ushered him out of the house by the back door. Speaking in broken Arabic, the soldiers ordered Rahima and her kids to leave the house. In defiance, she blocked the entrance with her body, telling the soldiers that her son had fled earlier that evening. At this, the commanding officer pulled the trigger of his M16 automatic machine gun, riddling Rahima with bullets in front of her seven children. She bled to death shortly afterwards.

I fingered the bullet holes pockmarking the concrete walls surrounding the door – a permanent reminder of Rahima's fate. Rafea opened the door to my knock after automatically checking me out through a small side window. An Israeli army base was positioned only two hundred metres from the house. Rafea recognized my companion Mohammed, who happened to have lived in Al Amal a few years earlier, and, as he welcomed us, I wondered how he had the courage to sleep in the very house which had been under suspicion and where his mother had been gunned down just a few weeks before. Rafea offered us a cold drink then proceeded to tell us about the night he avoided arrest but which saw the death of his mother. He described his mother as his teacher and mentor and said that he believed in God and that no one dies before his time. Rafea said he would never forgive the Israeli army for preventing the ambulance service from taking his mother to hospital and for killing his neighbour, Abdul Fattah Al Sallout, who ran to the house together with other neighbours in answer to the cries of his brothers and sisters. 'The troops were just shooting at anything which moved,' Rafea told us, 'and Abdul was killed.'

Hours after Rafea's mother was gunned down, a little after 4:30 that morning, Israeli tanks began their withdrawal from the Al Amal neighbourhood. Hundreds of people congregated to discover the reason for the latest night-time raid, as was the case whenever an Israeli incursion took place. As the crowds gathered, an Apache helicopter followed as more than two hundred youngsters were massing in front of Al Katiba Mosque. The Apache hovered lower and lower over the heads of the youngsters, then fired a missile into the crowd. Pools of blood, incinerated flesh and body parts littered the mosque square like a slaughterhouse. Fifteen young men died, with more than 150 wounded. Relatives of the victims shouted cries for revenge against Ariel Sharon as the hospital which received the victims came under heavy machine-gun fire. The continual flow of ambulances to the scene to pick up the wounded also came under fire from soldiers of the IDF, in a sustained attack lasting three hours. Despite international condemnation, Israeli Prime Minister Ariel Sharon described the Khan Younis attacks as 'a successful operation'. He added: 'This operation was complicated, it was a difficult operation … There will be more operations in Gaza.'

The effect these Hamas suicide bombers have on their families differs in the extreme. There are those, like Miriam Farhat, with conflicting emotions. Farhat actively encouraged her son Mohammed to participate in his mission, impressing on him to follow the orders of his superiors. But at the same time, in the days approaching her son's anticipated death, Miriam would sneak into his bedroom to imprint on her memory the sight of his sleeping face before returning back to her room to weep. In contrast, there is the reaction shown by the father of Ismail Ashur Brais, who had no prior knowledge that his son had been planning to blow himself up in a nearby settlement. Close to collapse, he was finally pacified by two Al Qassam activists, trained to offer the reassuring words to the bereaved that their sons and daughters had not died in vain. They had earned their place in Paradise to prepare the way for their families to follow. The thread drawing them together is the shared conviction and determination they feel for their children's

fight against the common
lost hope of living their liv
peace agreement has failed
quo. Israel's quest to ghetto
the population. The desire
of blood and death have c
recruiting ground for Hama

6

The Politics
of the Sheikh

Hamas' political evolution and its shaping up into a (semi-) coherent group with an ability to impact on Palestinian politics were largely due to its paraplegic leader, Sheikh Yassin. I knew the Sheikh well, having interviewed him many times at his home in Gaza City's Jourat Al Shams neighbourhood. Visiting him once on a cold winter's day in January 1999, I glanced over the concrete floor and cracked windows, which clung forlornly to their rotting frames. Yassin's daughter, Miriam, once said that her father had refused many offers, including one from Yasser Arafat, to build him a better house in his latter years. She said he always believed that 'by working hard on earth I will be rewarded with a nice home in heaven.'

A tall, athletic-looking bodyguard brought the familiar figure of Sheikh Yassin in his wheelchair into the sparse front room to meet me.[1] Within minutes of the Sheikh's arrival, five concerned-looking women had entered the room to ask him for help. I overheard one of them explaining in whispered tones that they had come to collect their money. This apparent intrusion appeared to be a regular occurrence for, after patiently listening to the women's financial needs, he called on Abdul Hamid to take their names and addresses before turning back to our conversation. This was just one example of the attention to people and detail which made Sheikh Yassin so powerful. Since this latest release from an Israeli jail, he had travelled to South Africa and several Arab countries, including Saudi Arabia, where he underwent medical treatment for his compound illnesses. Returning to Gaza, he discovered that his hearing had greatly improved and he was able to follow the news and engage in discussions with his visitors without them raising their voices. In the past, he had relied on Ismail Haniyeh, in charge of running Sheikh Yassin's office, to interpret people's needs and concerns. Intrigued by the earlier scene, I asked about the women and was told they were widows of martyrs who had died carrying out Hamas operations.

Sheikh Yassin had no qualms about sending young men to their deaths if it would result in the killing of Israelis. He was confident that this would accelerate his belief that Israel would disappear off the map within three decades. The conviction for his prophecy, he said, came from a Sura in the Qur'an which describes the period when the sons of Israel fled Egypt and were advised by God to go to Palestine. Fearing to follow his advice, Moses cautioned the Israelites with the words:

'Remember my people, the favour which God has bestowed upon you, He has raised up prophets among you, made you kings and given you that which He has given to no other nation. Enter, my people, the Holy land which God has assigned for you. Do not turn back and lose all.'

'Moses,' they replied, 'a race of giants dwells in this land. We will not set foot in it till they are gone. As soon as they are gone we will enter.'[2]

'Lord,' cried Moses. 'I have none but myself and my brother. Keep us apart from these wicked people.'

He replied: 'They shall be forbidden this land for forty years, during which time they shall wander homeless on the earth. Do not grieve for these wicked people.[3]

The previous generation, mused Yassin, 'was unprepared to fight or lose its way in the desert. It will be replaced by a new generation, willing to seize the challenge and win.' Social and psychological changes in society require forty years he argued:

> In 1948, the Palestinian people were defeated and lost large tracts of their country, forcing them into refugee camps abroad. Almost forty years later, in 1987, a new phase began with the Intifada. I believe that this generation will take the battle to liberation. Twelve years have passed since then and so, from today, Israel has only twenty-eight years left. I may be bad at sums, but I'm good at interpreting the meaning of Qur'anic verses.

Yassin was tentatively prepared to sign a ceasefire for a limit of ten to twenty years, on condition that Israel withdrew from the West Bank, Gaza and East Jerusalem to the borders as defined in 1967. Furthermore, the Palestinian people had to have the freedom to decide their own future. Yassin would say that if he was to sit alongside anyone from the PLO, that someone had to be Arafat. That was until the PLO's signed agreement with Israel, which forced Yassin to backtrack. 'I was saddened and angry and it's impossible to think that I could sit with him at this time and for us to remain a united people. I hope that the future will change things.'[4]

Talab Al Sana'a, a Palestinian member of the Israeli Knesset, visited Sheikh Yassin in Kfar Yuna. There, the Sheikh told him that he was emphatically opposed to the agreements signed with Israel because they ignored the main issues: the future of Jerusalem as the Palestinian capital; dismantling the settlements; the Palestinians' right of return to their original villages; and defining the borders. In addition, Yassin predicted that the economy of the occupied territories would be linked to the Israeli economy and this would be taken advantage of by Israel to access other Arab and Islamic economies. 'I believe in phased solutions but there is nothing in this agreement which would achieve the main goals of the Palestinian people,' Sheikh Yassin told his visitor with his customary wry smile. Al Sana'a mentioned that he was travelling to Tunisia in the coming few days and asked Sheikh Yassin if there was any message he would like to relay to the exiled Chairman Arafat, who had set up his PLO HQ in Tunis. Sheikh Yassin's cryptic reply was that Al Sana'a should tell Arafat the following: 'Be mindful of God, your people and your homeland. An unmarried person is not free to behave as he wishes. The land of Palestine is an Islamic *Waqf*,[5] and no president has the authority to give it up. It belongs to future generations.'

When right-wing Likud leader Benjamin Netanyahu narrowly defeated the relative peacemaker Shimon Peres by a one per cent majority in the May 1996 Israeli elections, Hamas was accused of indirectly aiding Netanyahu's appointment. At the time, they carried out a series of suicide attacks inside Israel, which played into the hands of the hawkish candidate. Dismissing the accusations, a spokesman for Hamas said:

> When we decide to attack, we don't care whether it is Peres or Netanyahu in power. What we care about is how to defend ourselves and achieve the goals of our people. Israel assassinated Yehia Ayyash, the leader of our military wing and should be held accountable for this. We retaliated by carrying out suicide missions. For us, Labour or Likud are the same. They're two faces of the same coin.

On the subject of his adversary, Yasser Arafat, Sheikh Yassin was restrained. 'I have friendly discussions with him. He expresses his views and I express mine. Sometimes he uses the dialogue between us for his own purposes in order to put pressure on Israel and make some gains.' Expanding this point, he said that he always felt that the Palestinian Authority was using their dialogue as a pretext to express their willingness to improve their relationship with Hamas. When he returned from his post-prison tour abroad,[6] at the top of his agenda was to hold a meeting with Abu Ammar (Yasser Arafat) to reach an understanding with him about the situation:

> But the way I was treated gave me the impression that they had turned their backs on me and had no interest in any sort of cooperation. When the Wye Plantation Agreement was signed in Washington,[7] journalists visiting my house in Gaza were arrested. I myself was put under house arrest by the Palestinian Authority, after

it was rumoured that one of my bodyguards was involved in plotting military attacks against Israel.[8] The guard was arrested for no reason and my other bodyguards fled the house. They even searched through my robes, which were on hangers. All the accusations against them were unfounded.

What Yassin didn't own up to was the real reason behind his house arrest in 1998. Palestinian security forces had foiled an attempt by an activist from Hamas' military wing, Al Qassam, to carry out a suicide bomb attack against Arafat while he was presenting his annual speech to the United Nations in New York. After questioning the attacker, he confessed that one of the architects of the failed mission was one of Sheikh Yassin's bodyguards.

After the troubled marriage of the PLO and Israel through the Oslo Peace Accords, there had been much speculation about how Hamas would react, considering its vocal opposition to the agreements. Hamas was part of an alliance of ten Palestinian factions based in Damascus which opposed any peace deals with Israel. Yassin had rallied his followers to resort to violence if the Palestinian Authority tried to take control of its Islamic institutions and mosques. He justified this by saying, 'We have opposed self-rule in a civilized way, so we have the right to be in opposition and be responsible for our own institutions.'

In a letter sent from jail in October 1993, not long after the conclusion of the Oslo Accords,[9] Sheikh Yassin cautioned his followers not to become marginalized and urged them to participate in the scheduled 1996 election for Palestinian self-rule. 'If the proposed Palestinian Legislative Council really does have the power to legislate,' the letter read, 'then we must show solidarity with our Islamist brothers at the grassroots level, and not give our opponents a free rein to negotiate our future as Palestinians.'

Even though Sheikh Yassin was keen for Hamas to be part of a broader alliance, he mistrusted the other factions, even those who, like Hamas, opposed the Oslo Accords: 'These factions have nothing in common with us and will put their own interests above everything. If they manage to secure an agreement with Arafat, they might even turn against Hamas.' He added diplomatically: 'But we must still be tactful in our dealings with them.'[10]

This letter had a real-life postscript, when Ismail Haniyeh, who was to become the Prime Minister of the Palestinian Authority in 2006, decided to participate in the 1996 election as a result of Sheikh Yassin's letter. He was accused by other factions in Hamas of being a traitor.[11]

Yassin's visit to Tehran, one of the stop-offs on his grand tour, introduced him to Ayatollah Ali Khameini, who had succeeded Ayatollah Khomeini as Supreme Leader of the Islamic Republic of Iran. The previous year, the Taliban had killed ten Iranian diplomats and a journalist after storming the Iranian Consulate in Mazar-e Sharif, Afghanistan in September 1998. The Sheikh had sent a letter to the President, offering his condolences. Khameini appealed to the Taliban to stop these assassinations to spare Muslim blood, and prevent Iran from being drawn into a battle which could lead to the downfall of its Islamic regime. At the mention of the Taliban, Sheikh Yassin grew angry, describing their understanding of Islam as 'completely wrong and misleading'. 'How dare they ban women from contributing in our lives by preventing them from working and teaching?' he fumed. 'Their ways can only harm the Islamic religion.' While denying any ties between Hamas and the Taliban regime, Yassin's response to a possible link between Hamas and Al Qaeda, was more ambiguous: 'We support and sympathize with any movement which defends the rights of its people to enjoy self-governance and independence, but we are not prepared to seek an alliance with those movements.' As defined by the Hamas charter, he stressed they had no interest in abandoning their battle with Israel to fight abroad and get tied up with Arab, Islamic or even international conflicts. 'We have no intention of intervening in the affairs of other countries in the world,' Yassin said with finality.

Reflecting on his South African stop, the Sheikh claimed that the Palestinian Authority had prepared the ground in advance to maximize the possibility of failure for Hamas in gaining a foothold there as well as other countries he visited. While clearly piqued, he said in a seemingly pious statement that his organization had 'never sought political recognition because it would undermine the PLO as the official representative worldwide of the Palestinian people'. While some Arab regimes gave the impression that they sympathized with and supported his views, Yassin felt it was a front to benefit their own internal politics. But, despite the setbacks, he succeeded in generating financial and moral support from certain countries. 'Following my visit, we initiated a dialogue and some agreed to let us open bureaux, but in an unofficial capacity to avoid media scrutiny.'

Indeed, for all his religiously inspired beliefs, Yassin was a wily and pragmatic operator. He persistently highlighted the need for loyalty, cohesiveness and sensitivity towards the varying political climates, in order to maintain a healthy relationship between Hamas members based in different countries:

> Our loyalties must be with God, his prophets and their followers. No one else. A member or leader of our organization has to take into account their particular environment and one must use different language and tactics accordingly. If a Hamas representative in Jordan wishes to criticize the policies of the Jordanian government, I would expect the invective to be tempered because he lives in Jordan. But if the same person wants to criticize the Palestinian Authority in Gaza, I do expect the statement to contain stronger language. On the other hand, if that same person was living in PA controlled areas, their words might lead to a civil war. When I was in Syria, someone once told me: 'You made contradictory statements. You say you are against the Oslo Agreement yet you talk about "our brothers in the Palestinian Authority" and "my brother Abu Ammar [Arafat]". These are all traitors and you should say so.'

Yassin answered back with: 'You are shooting from abroad. If you say such a thing in Gaza a war would start tomorrow. Followers of Arafat and Fatah would fight followers of Hamas and I am not prepared to get involved in that.'

When I mentioned Hamas' military wing to him in an interview in Gaza on 18 January 1999, Sheikh Yassin was evasive. He was loath to reply when I asked about a member of the Al Qassam Brigades who had resigned. This particular military wing activist had spoken to me of corruption and dictatorship within the movement and said that assassinations had been carried out in a power struggle. 'Tell me who left!' Yassin shot back. A few months after Yassin was released from Kfar Yuna jail, he was visited by a group of twenty-five activists from Al Qassam Brigades, including Abdul Fattah Al Satari, who wanted to put him in the picture about the discord in the military wing. Al Satari told Yassin that they were no longer receiving help from the political leadership despite many of their members being threatened with assassination, or facing the risk of arrest by the Israelis or containment by the Palestinian Authority. Sheikh Yassin appeared surprised and promised his visitors that he would investigate. A Hamas leader, on condition of anonymity, confirmed to me in September 1998 that the meeting had taken place. He also disclosed that Abdul Fattah Al Satari, Kamal Khalifa, Mohammed Al Sinwar, and Atef Hamdan had left the military wing of Hamas to join the Palestinian Authority's security agencies.

I put the names of those who had left to Sheikh Yassin, knowing very well that it was not news to him, despite his apparent confinement. Sheikh Yassin had an unparalleled intelligence network. In his usual tactful manner, Yassin explained that this particular group from the military wing had been under a lot of pressure and its leadership and senior members were either in various jails or on the run. So in the absence of clear instructions and with a lack of communication between Hamas bureaux abroad and the Hamas leadership inside the Gaza Strip, this group had no financial support and found themselves incapable of fighting or even surviving. Some of them were forced to go abroad where they were put under pressure, because each country has its own individual politics, laws and local sensitivities to take into account. These young men wanted to operate independently as they used to do when they were in Gaza, which led to confrontations with their fellow Hamas activists. 'They wrote me a full report about the situation but there was no mention of any killings,' Yassin told me. His assessment of the situation was that Hamas was under a lot of pressure from various foreign intelligence agencies and perhaps individual seniors in the movement sent messages indicating the need to assassinate or get rid of certain elements. But he said the movement as a whole had no knowledge of that and it would never commit such a thing.

'How can I sign an order to kill a Muslim citizen without a crime being committed?' he ventured. 'It's impossible. No one amongst us would ever consider this unless there was strong evidence of wrong-doing, and it was acceptable according to sharia laws.'

A Schism in the Movement

Factionalism has always plagued Hamas. The issue of when and how far to compromise is always a divisive one for Islamic movements. Ismail Abu Shanab, another founding member of Hamas in Gaza, issued a statement after the Cairo Conference in January 1995 to confirm that an understanding had been reached with the Palestinian Authority and other Palestinian factions based in Damascus on the hot-potato issue of a *hudna* (ceasefire) with Israel. Shanab was part of a Hamas delegation to the conference which was to discuss the US-brokered peace agreement with Israel among other things.

It was a controversial statement to some in Hamas, but Shanab had the credentials to make it. Born in 1948, the year Palestine became Israel in Al Jourah village close to Ashkelon, making Abu Shanab one of the youngest refugees to arrive at Al Nuseirat camp in central Gaza. Despite his unprivileged beginnings, he graduated from the University of Manusra north of Cairo where he became influenced by the revival of the Muslim Brotherhood movement. After gaining a masters in civil engineering at Colorado State University, he returned to Gaza in 1976 and co-founded the Islamic Compound, of which he was made deputy under Sheikh Yassin.

Along with Sheikh Yassin and other Hamas leaders, Ismail Abu Shanab was arrested in May 1989 for his role in the first Intifada, and was kept in solitary confinement for seventeen months of his eight years in prison. Considered a moderate, the soft-spoken father of eleven acted as a go-between when things became tense between Hamas and the Palestinian Authority. A few months before his death, he was reported to have said: 'Let's be frank. We cannot destroy Israel. The practical solution is for us to have a state alongside Israel.' But the détente Shanab helped to approve at the Cairo Conference came to an abrupt end when Israel carried out one of its trademark helicopter assassinations on his vehicle, killing Shanab and two of his aides.[12] While Shanab had always championed a ceasefire with

Israel provided the Jewish State withdrew to its pre-1967 borders, his more tough-talking Hamas comrades like Dr Abdul Aziz Al Rantisi and Mahmoud Zahar preferred the rallying-cry for the destruction of Israel and creating an Islamic state 'from the sea to the river' (from the Mediterranean to the River Jordan).

The ceasefire created uproar amongst Hamas leaders in Jordan and Syria, leading to accusations of a fracture in the movement between those living in the West Bank and Gaza, and those living abroad. Sheikh Yassin's reaction was initially guarded. 'I wasn't willing to discuss this through the broadcast media or on the pages of newspapers,' he said,[13] adding that the movement strives to solve its problems internally and that the issue was settled. 'What happened,' he explained, 'was that some of our brothers abroad reacted impulsively without knowing the truth behind what is happening here [the Gaza Strip].' According to Sheikh Yassin, the Hamas leadership abroad in Jordan and Syria was already in disagreement with Abu Shanab, which prompted his rash statement about the ceasefire. Yassin felt Abu Shanab should have been more restrained and not gone public before considering the circumstances, adding that usually there was good coordination and exchange of views between themselves in Gaza and their brothers abroad. But, he admitted, because of the need to be cautious, communications occasionally got delayed or were never received. 'When those conditions arise,' Yassin remarked, 'how can I approve decisions if I am not aware of them? We are a cohesive movement and it is not permitted for anyone within our organization to set up a separate leadership. This is against Islam and our principles. If anyone considers doing such a thing, I have told them it's better they leave.' This point was exemplified in a letter from Sheikh Yassin addressed to the Shura Council of the movement which he sent from Kfar Yuna prison, dated 3 October 1993:

> Bismillah Al Rahman Al Rahim … Dear Brothers, these ideas I am sending to you should be studied and analysed in the Shura Council of the movement in order that we can make collective decisions which stand up to the challenges faced by our victorious movement. God willing. There must be cohesiveness in both internal

and external decisions because the continuation of our work needs support from the outside in. The inside [Gaza and the West Bank] will be responsible for confrontation and sacrifices, and as such is more in a position to evaluate and to provide knowledge about what is needed to spread the message, and make best use of our efforts. I repeat, it is not permissible for any one person or a group to take a decision which would affect the future and decide the fate of our movement. Any decision taken by the majority, should be obeyed whatever it may be.

Fatah v. Hamas

Cairo had for years provided neutral territory where different Palestinian factions could meet. As early as 1995, Fatah and Hamas met in Cairo to peaceably resolve their differences. Arafat's Fatah movement was keen to avoid confrontation with Hamas, despite its continued attacks against Israel. On the Hamas side, the delegation consisted of four leaders from Gaza, Abdul Fattah Dokhan, Mohammed Hassan Chamaa, Said Abu Musamih and Dr Mahmoud Zahar. The West Bank delegation included Jamal Salim, Sheikh Jamil Hammami, Sheikh Mohammed Al Natcheh and Sheikh Hassan Yousif. The Hamas contingent from outside the Palestinian territories consisted of Khalid Mishal, Imad Al Alami, Mohammed Nazzal and Osama Hamdan. The Fatah delegation was headed by Salim Al Za'anoun, known as Abu Al Adeeb. When both factions repeated their old arguments about who started the 1987 Intifada, some Fatah delegates denied any Hamas participation whatsoever. Dokhan, who was leading Hamas in Gaza at that time, smoothed the waters saying that Hamas and their brothers in Fatah and other Palestinian factions had all played their part in the civil uprising.

However, the Hamas-instigated suicide bombings which led to the election of Netanyahu, and the destruction of the peace process on which Fatah had staked its credibility, soured the relationship. Mohammed Dahlan, Arafat's top security adviser in Gaza, accused Hamas of playing dirty tricks with the future of the Palestinian people. 'Hamas was foiling every positive step that the PA was making in its peace negotiations with Israel,' complained Dahlan:

When the late Israeli Prime Minister Yitzhak Rabin agreed that its government would stop financing and building settlements, the Hamas movement immediately carried out suicide attacks. The documents we have confiscated from Hamas followers confirms this and also reveals that they have made every effort to force Shimon Peres' Labour government to fail.[14]

Dahlan saw Hamas as irresponsibly forcing the Palestinian people to pay the price for its own political commitments to other countries in the region (chiefly Iran and Syria).

Dahlan had been active in the Islamic University and launched Fatah's 'Youth Wing' in Gaza. He first met Sheikh Ahmed Yassin when he was the spiritual father of the Islamic Compound, but they became better acquainted when the Sheikh was released from prison in exchange for the two Mossad agents involved in Khalid Mishal's assassination attempt. 'From then on, I boycotted all relations with Hamas representatives,' he recalled. They would have long meetings together with Dr Rantisi and held separate private meetings with Ismail Haniyeh. Dahlan described his relationship with the Sheikh as 'close', adding that he admired and respected him and considered him to be 'the most rational amongst those who are affiliated to Hamas'.

An issue which Dahlan and Yassin would frequently argue over was the regular arrest of Hamas activists by the Palestinian Authority if they were suspected of involvement in attacks against Israel. As Head of Security for the PA, Dahlan would respect Sheikh Yassin's requests to release somebody, 'provided of course that he could convince me they were not directly involved in an attack or its planning or could in any way jeopardize our relationship with Israel'.

Sheikh Yassin established a school named Ibn Al Arqam, but classes were suspended because, according to Israeli law, private education licences are not granted to political parties. Dahlan outlined the behind-the-scenes efforts he made with President Arafat to grant Yassin a licence. 'We discussed this in the presence of Ismail Haniyeh and Dr Ismail Abu Shanab and the licence was finally issued.'

Dahlan described Yassin's feelings towards Arafat as 'very kindly' and that Arafat in turn had great respect for the Sheikh. 'Their ted the manager of the building. But the authorities weren't rmed, as this was Jordan and nothing untoward happens in the ndly Royal Kingdom. Mishal continued:

ollowing consultations with the leadership, we passed the story o Agence France-Presse and it was broadcast on Radio Monte Carlo at 11.00 a.m. Initially, the Jordanian government denied the event, describing what happened as an argument between Khalid Mishal's bodyguard and two Canadian tourists. After we called the Information Minister to correct his version of events, we learned that the Head of the Mossad station in Jordan had been in touch with the Palace. It appeared that Benjamin Netanyahu, the Israeli PM, had asked the Mossad station manager to cover up for the bungled mission and to ensure the safety of its agents.

Two hours after the attack, I started to lose my balance from the effects of the poison. My driver insisted on taking me to the Islamic hospital, which required some arrangements. Members of Hamas' political bureau and leaders of the Muslim Brotherhood movement in Jordan as well as the head of police in Amman, all arrived at the hospital. But when the news that Mossad had tried to poison me reached the Palace, King Hussein instructed his advisers to transfer me to the King Hussein Medical City military hospital. By then, the oxygen levels in my blood had dropped and the medical team were puzzled by what was happening to me. I later learned that this poison would eventually have starved my brain of oxygen.

srael's initial reaction was denial, while King Hussein described Mishal as 'our son' and hinted to journalists in Jordan about the possibility of executing both Mossad agents. Mossad had chosen this covert form of attack to avoid embarrassment to the Jordanian government, which had signed a peace deal with Israel in 1994.

By the time Mishal arrived at Al Hussein Medical City Hospital, he was feeling drowsy then lost consciousness from Thursday evening until Saturday morning.[17] During these two days, King Hussein took firm control of the situation, calling President Clinton and threatening to close the Israeli Embassy. The King's brother, Crown Prince Hassan, was despatched to Washington on 28 September,

relationship was good,' he said simply. In one of the meetings held at Dahlan's house, they were having intense discussions out of earshot of journalists. They discussed the importance of reining back Hamas' military operations, and not giving Israel any excuse to play games and suspend their withdrawal from the West Bank.[15] Arafat also asked for a ceasefire to allow the withdrawal to take place. The session was informal but serious. Sheikh Yassin told Arafat that terminating military attacks was within Dahlan's authority, to which Arafat replied: 'This is political and I understand his position.' So Sheikh Yassin agreed to stop Hamas' suicide attacks, which Dahlan recalled was in the spring of 1998 when Netanyahu was in government. Yassin then asked what Dahlan would do if a military operation was carried out. Dahlan told him jokingly, 'I might arrest you!' There was no argument and the session was very relaxed.

I got to know Arafat at close quarters from the time I first interviewed him in 1981 at his headquarters in Al Fakhani in West Beirut. I followed his travels and covered his wars. Deep down, I felt the maverick Palestinian leader never wanted to see Hamas participate in elections or even take an active role in politics. Whenever the opportunity arose, he would use Hamas to his own ends.

Arafat once invited Sheikh Yassin to attend a meeting of the Central Council, a body somewhere between the Executive Committee and the Palestinian National Council – the Palestinian parliament in exile. The Hamas leader was accompanied by Ismail Haniyeh. At that time many Hamas activists criticized their leader for participating in these discussions because it was a recognition of the PLO and its institutions.

On 17 December 1992, Israel deported 415 members of Hamas and Islamic Jihad to Lebanon, and a Hamas delegation visited Arafat's HQ in Tunisia to ask for help regarding the situation of the deportees. Amongst the delegation were engineer and Hamas spokesman Ibrahim Goshi, Khairi Al Agha and Mohammed Siam. The delegation asked Arafat to use all his diplomatic and international connections to raise the issue of the deportees. During that meeting, Arafat spoke to one of the high-level Hamas deportees, Dr Rantisi, over the telephone. This was followed up with visits from Fatah representatives in Southern Lebanon where the deportees were staying. This contact with Arafat was the first acknowledgement by Hamas of the PLO leader's paramount position in the Palestinian revolution. Hamas had long tried to position itself as a parallel and equal movement, but this appeal was an acknowledgement of where the real power lay, at least at this point. Hamas had modelled itself on the PLO's structure when some leaders were in exile, while others inside the Occupied Palestinian territories led the resistance against the Israelis on the ground.

The Last Years of Yassin

Sheikh Yassin had paramount spiritual authority in Gaza, but younger, charismatic Hamas figures gained prominence as he aged in confinement. In an ironic twist, Khalid Mishal, the man who would later become the leader of Hamas, was responsible for Sheikh Yassin being released from jail, simply because he survived an attempt by Israeli Mossad. On the morning of 25 September 1997, the head of the Hamas political bureau in Jordan left his house in Al Shmaisani district behind King Abdullah Gardens in Amman to travel the half-kilometre route to his fifth-floor downtown office in Garden Street. Mishal was accompanied by a bodyguard and his three children, who were going to be driven on to the hairdressers. He sensed a car tailing them from the moment they drew away from the house. It had tourist registration plates, but his bodyguard, who was on the alert for anything suspicious, didn't seem overly concerned. Shortly before they arrived at the office building, the car overtook them; Mishal's driver drew up close to the entrance of the Chamieh Building and parked the car alongside a row of boutiques. Recounting his ordeal, Mishal said he noticed 'two western-looking men wearing jeans and sunglasses, about two metres from the car who appeared to be waiting for someone'. He felt uneasy and once again told his bodyguard. This time it was agreed that he should be cautious:

> I took a roundabout route to the office by going behind the car to avoid the two men. As I reached the entrance to the building, something the size of a pistol emitted a spray which hit the left side of my head and my ears. My body began to shake and I realized it was an assassination attack but not with a gun. The guy who attacked

> me was wearing white gloves to protect himself
> the poison which had entered my skin. I tried
> my bodyguard intervened to prevent the attacker
> head and managed to throw one of them to the g
> sunglasses. I never thought Jordan would be a plac
> because of its relationship with Israel, and that's v
> with limited security.[16]

What unfolded was worthy of a film thriller. The
to the aid of his colleague and hit Mishal's body
with a sharp instrument. With blood pouring fr
shouted to onlookers that his attackers were M
had just tried to assassinate Khalid Mishal. The tw
the rental car, which was parked outside the Al T
300 metres away.

Abu Saif, a driver for another Hamas leader, ha
at the Chamieh Building to deliver a letter to
heard the commotion and saw the Mossad agents a
Quick-wittedly, Abu Saif flagged down a Jordania
Garden Street to help catch the attackers. Unquest
agreed and gave chase while Abu Saif followed in h
Israeli agents abandoned their car within a short d
everything they used for the attack inside, and n
towards Al Madina Al Monawarra Street, apparentl
they had been pursued. Abu Saif and the Jordanian d
with the men and a public brawl ensued, drawing in
officer from the Palestine Liberation Army in Jordan
to be driving by. The officer helped to overcome t
intelligence agents and they were taken to the police st
Al Saer where they were arrested.

Five days before the attack, the two men had arrive
on false Canadian passports. They had blended in v
group who were basing themselves in the city to take
of Petra, the ruined capital of the Nabateans, the Wadi
and the Roman ruins of Jerash. The concierge at M
building had spotted the two 'tourists' a few days befo
and, thinking it was a strange place for foreigners to h

along with the head of Jordanian intelligence, Samih Al Battiki, to persuade President Clinton to intervene in the diplomatic crisis. King Hussein also demanded that Netanyahu send an antidote for the poison. In a further humiliation to Netanyahu's government, Jordanian security arrested other Mossad agents and the Israeli Embassy in Amman was put under curfew. Under pressure, Israel agreed to a deal. Sheikh Ahmed Yassin and a number of other Palestinian prisoners would be released in return for the Mossad agents. According to Mishal:

> Confirmation that Sheikh Yassin was to be released came when King Hussein visited me in hospital at about 1.30 after midnight. During the five minutes he spent with me, I thanked him for his help and he congratulated me on my survival. I asked him about the rumours I had heard concerning Sheikh Yassin and King Hussein reassured me that the rumours were true.

At around 2.00 a.m. on Wednesday 1 October, Mishal watched a helicopter land from the window of his hospital room. He couldn't distinguish whether it was Jordanian or Israeli but he made out the distinctive figure of Sheikh Yassin being wheeled from the chopper towards one of the hospital's suites. 'Although I wasn't able to walk,' Mishal recollected:

> I insisted on seeing our leader. At 3.00 a.m., I was taken to his room where I shook hands and kissed him. This was to be my first ever meeting with him. Many of my brothers had met other senior Hamas leaders like Abdul Aziz Rantisi when they were deported to Southern Lebanon but, at that time, Sheikh Yassin was already in an Israeli prison.

King Hussein, Crown Prince Hassan and other princes, together with Jordanian ministers and President Arafat, all paid a visit to Sheikh Yassin's hospital bed, where he remained as a guest of Jordan for a week before being flown to Gaza on board a Jordanian helicopter. In a simultaneous move, an Israeli helicopter took off from Amman with the two pseudo-Canadian tourists on board.

Mishal also met Sheikh Yassin during a stopover in Sudan in 1998. After leaving prison, the Sheikh had embarked on his grand tour of Saudi Arabia, the Arab Emirates, Kuwait, Iran, Yemen, Syria, Sudan, Egypt and South Africa before returning back to Gaza. By the time Mishal caught up with him, Yassin had received successful treatment in Saudi Arabia for a chronic ear infection and had been given the opportunity to perform the Hajj, a duty which all committed Muslims aspire to before they die.[18]

Mishal was eventually deported from Jordan in 1999 and was himself on a trip to Tehran in August of that year when Jordan decided to close down Hamas' offices. He claimed that nothing justified the closure and contacted several Arab governments informing them that Hamas had 'no intention of interfering in the affairs of any Arab country.' One of those he contacted was Sheikh Hamad Bin Jassem, the Qatari Foreign Minister, to brief him and ask him to intervene but with no success. After three weeks, he returned to Jordan where he was immediately arrested and taken to Al Jowaida prison, together with Ibrahim Goshi.

Israel's assassinations of Palestinian activists followed weeks and months of intelligence gathering about their chosen victims – the locations of safe houses, the routes taken when moving from one place to another, the daily routines and so on. Hundreds of activists in the West Bank and Gaza have been eliminated by the use of explosive devices set in mobile telephones, by the side of roads, under cars or triggered from the safety of helicopters or F-16 military aircraft. Both Yassin and Rantisi were assassinated in these kinds of sophisticated attacks. Like Rantisi, Yassin refused to take even the most basic security measures.

As was known to everyone in Gaza, Sheikh Yassin regularly attended *fajr* prayers[19] at a mosque just one hundred metres from his home in the Sabra neighbourhood of Gaza. One Monday morning, 22 March 2004, a helicopter dropped three camera-guided missiles, killing the Sheikh in his wheelchair along with the husband of his daughter Khadija and his bodyguard, Khamis Mushtaha. Yassin's wheelchair lay smashed and blood-soaked as the spiritual leader was rushed to Gaza's Dar Al Shifa Hospital, but he was dead on arrival. According to Israeli security sources, Prime Minister Ariel Sharon personally ordered and monitored the helicopter attack against the paralysed cleric, which was thought to be in revenge for a suicide attack two weeks before.[20] Nabil Massoud and Mahmoud Salem, two teenage school friends from Jabaliya refugee camp in Gaza, had pulled off a double suicide mission on the tightly guarded port of Ashdod in the south of Israel which killed ten Israelis, for which Hamas claimed responsibility. Yassin's daughter, Miriam, recalling her father's words whenever he received the news of a suicide bombing, said: 'This is the only way to free Palestine. Unfortunately without blood we can achieve nothing.'

Around three hours before, Yassin's son, Mohammed, had remarked to his father that a reconnaissance drone had been spotted in the sky. 'We seek martyrdom to Him. We belong to Him and to Him we return,' was the Sheikh's reply to his son.[21] As Sheikh Yassin was leaving the mosque after dawn prayers, another of his sons, Abdul Ghani, warned him: 'Father, there is an assassination plane in the sky.'

His philosophical response was: 'My son, I'm waiting for it.'

The Hamas Firebrand

Even the assassination of Sheikh Ahmed Yassin did not seriously damage the power of Hamas' internal leadership. The spiritual leader was replaced by Dr Abdul Aziz Al Rantisi, who was born on 23 October 1947 in a village called Yebna, between Ashkelon and Jaffa in what is now Israel. After 1948, he and his family were resettled in Khan Younis camp for Palestinian refugees in Gaza. Typical of many young boys in large families, at nine years old he began working outside school hours to help support his large family of eleven brothers and sisters, describing his circumstances as 'very poor and what we got from UNRWA was not enough to feed us'. His father died when Rantisi was fourteen and still in secondary school. At that time, Rantisi didn't have shoes and bought a second-hand pair with money he had saved up from his job. When his older brother, Fawaz, was forced to go to Saudi Arabia to find work, his mother asked Abdul Aziz to donate his shoes to Fawaz in order that his brother would have a pair to wear for his job interview. On completing his schooling in 1965, he won a scholarship from

UNRWA to study in Alexandria in Egypt, where he took a degree in medicine, graduating with top honours, and returned to Gaza in 1972 as a fully qualified doctor. He would walk many kilometres with his medicine bag to treat the poor Bedouin tribes on the border with Gaza, shunning payment which made him very popular amongst these tribes. He returned to Alexandria to do his Ph.D. in Paediatrics and, in 1976, he began work at the Nasser Hospital in Khan Younis. At the same time, he worked alongside Sheikh Yassin in establishing the Islamic Compound and its charity works.

The first of his many confrontations with the Israelis began in 1981 when he was held under house arrest on two charges: one for refusing to pay taxes to the occupying force and the second for organizing a demonstration amongst doctors in Gaza calling for a general strike. In retaliation for his tax avoidance, Israel confiscated everything in his clinic. Despite his attempts at negotiation, they sold off all his medicines and medical equipment. Fortunately for him, Hajj Sadek Al Mozani, the well-off son of a philanthropist, bought the contents of the clinic and returned them to Rantisi. He was eventually barred from working as a doctor in 1986 because of his political activism amongst the medical staff. Rantisi turned to lecturing at the Islamic University. From then on, he became heavily involved in the Islamic movement.

By the time the Maktura incident erupted in 1987,[22] Rantisi was one of the top six leaders in Gaza's Muslim Brotherhood and was instrumental in the decision taken by the movement to organize a civil uprising. Along with Sheikh Yassin, he was a founding father of the Hamas movement and became a favourite spokesman on the world's TV networks and in the international press because of his linguistic skills, his pithy soundbites and his no-nonsense attitude when describing Hamas policies. Famous for his fiery rhetoric and outbursts, the tough-talking man with street cred was the polar-opposite to the smooth-speaking, reflective persona of Sheikh Yassin. Rantisi would be the one rallying the troops following a setback to keep the movement motivated.

I first became acquainted with the former doctor over the telephone from London in 1989, and from then on established a long-distance association with him. Despite his extreme views, once politics was taken out of the equation, I found him straightforward and easy-going. After the many telephone conversations I exchanged with him, there came a point when I didn't need to identify myself as he recognized my voice instantly. As a prime target for Israeli intelligence, Rantisi used a more secure wireless landline, becoming accustomed to secrecy. He was very careful about giving away his identity on the telephone and equally the identities of those he was talking to.

His relationship with the Palestinian Authority was always fractious because of his vocal rejection of peace deals with Israel and the measures taken by the PA against Hamas members. Despite the tense relationship, he appealed to them to spare Palestinian blood and not to enter into confrontation under any circumstances. After succeeding Sheikh Yassin, his first statement as leader was that he was ready to reach out to everyone to work together for the interests of the Palestinian cause.

Rantisi was the first Hamas leader to be arrested by Israel following the start of the Intifada when, on 15 January 1988, he was jailed for twenty-one days for wrestling with Israeli soldiers who had tried to break into his bedroom. Less than two months later, on 4 March, he was re-arrested, this time remaining in jail for two and a half years, accused of launching Hamas and editing the organization's first statement, which was signed by Sheikh Yassin. Rantisi refused to admit to either charge. During this sentence, he was deprived of sleep for six days and forced to stay in a refrigerated room for twenty-four hours. At some point in 1990, he found himself sharing a cell with Sheikh Yassin. He was released on 4 September 1990 but, one hundred days later, he was once again detained by the Israeli authorities for one year before being deported to Marj Al Zahur in Southern Lebanon on 17 December 1992.

During his exile, he was chosen as the spokesperson for the large number of deportees in Lebanon and, according to Rantisi, this enforced gathering of the Hamas elite proved to be strategically useful to the movement, giving its leadership the opportunity to coordinate their tactics. It was the first time that they had met with members outside the Gaza Strip, and through them they were able to forge contacts with other Arab, Islamic and even international organizations and movements. Soon after the deportees' return to Gaza, a military court in Israel ordered Rantisi back to jail until mid 1997. In April 1998, following the assassination of the Engineer, Yehia Ayyash, Rantisi was arrested by the Palestinian Authority for his outspoken denouncements of the Oslo Agreements. The condition for his release was that he abstain from further defamatory statements against the PA and its peace agreements.

I visited Gaza for the first time in 1998. Previously I had not been allowed there by the Israeli authorities, despite being an accredited journalist, because my Palestinian refugee status forbade entry. Rantisi was still doing time in the PA jail then and I was keen to interview the Hamas leader face to face, following our many conversations over the telephone. I approached the Minister of Justice, Freih Abu Meddein to authorize a visit to Rantisi which, up until then, had only been granted to his immediate family. Gazi Al Jebali, head of the Palestinian Police in Gaza, told Freih that permission must also be sought from Arafat. I was due to have an interview with the Palestinian leader in his office along the beach in Gaza, and decided to raise the matter with him myself as our interview drew to a close. Arafat was intrigued to learn how I knew Rantisi, never having been to Gaza before. I explained that we had established a good rapport over the telephone over several years and it would be a missed opportunity to leave Gaza without seeing him. Arafat agreed, and arrangements were made for me to go to the Al Saraya, the headquarters of the Palestinian Police in Gaza.

The building was the former Israeli HQ, which had been handed over to the Palestinian Authority when it came into being following the Oslo Agreements. I was accompanied by the Minister of Justice to meet Jebali, who didn't wait long before asking me why I was so keen to meet Rantisi. He ordered one of his senior officers to accompany me to Rantisi's cell, which was directly above his office. As they unlocked the cell door, a large room opened out in front of me, furnished with a neatly made military-style single bed.

Rantisi was sitting on a chair in front of a small table, reading from the Qur'an. I greeted him: 'As Salaam aleykum.' We shook hands and, in front of the officer who was watching from the door, I asked him, 'Do you recognize this voice?'

He waited a few seconds before his face creased into a smile as he responded, 'Are you Zaki?'

I nodded and told him that I couldn't leave Gaza without meeting him in person, whereupon he embraced me. The officer closed the door and waited outside while I talked to the seasoned prisoner for about fifteen minutes, during which I told him that I hoped that he would be reunited with his wife and children as soon as possible.

A year later, I made a second trip to Gaza and decided to call on Abu Mohammed (Al Rantisi) during one of his infrequent spells outside jail. I was invited to his house one afternoon, where I expected to find stringent security, but none was apparent. He would stay away from home for a week or so and dress in different ways as a disguise, but it wasn't enough for someone of his rank, especially after replacing the assassinated Sheikh Yassin. As he offered me hospitality, I queried why he didn't employ tougher safety measures when he was high on the Shabak's wanted list. 'No one dies before his time,' he replied, which was a well-worn phrase within the movement.

Rantisi's political rival, Mohammed Dahlan grew up in the same Gaza refugee camp. Their families were extremely close, and would often exchange family visits. Less than two weeks before Rantisi's assassination, I met Dahlan who recounted a story about the day Arafat had asked him to arrest the Hamas leader. Mohammed told his boss that he couldn't possibly do that, to which Arafat answered: 'Why, are you scared of Hamas?'

'Definitely not,' Dahlan replied, 'but I am scared of my mother who adores Sheikh Abdul Aziz Rantisi.'

Dahlan had recently been in Paris where he had been tipped off by French intelligence that Israel was about to assassinate Rantisi. On returning to Gaza, his priority was 'to alert the doctor to take precautions'. A meeting was arranged for the next day, and they chose to rendezvous in the house of the late Ismail Abu Shanab on the assumption that it was unlikely that anyone would suspect Rantisi might go there. Mohammed was surprised to see the same old familiar faces of Rantisi's bodyguards driving their recognizable cars. Dahlan cautioned him that if he wanted to survive, he had to make changes to his security team, who were well-known to the locals, the media and, more importantly, Israeli intelligence. Dahlan also warned him to stop making TV appearances and giving regular statements. Rantisi took no heed.

Less than two weeks after hearing Dahlan's story, I was saddened to learn that Rantisi had been assassinated in Al Jalaa Street, north of Gaza on Saturday evening, 17 April 2004. He died of his wounds in Gaza City's Al Shifa Hospital after his car took a direct hit from at least two rockets fired from an Israeli helicopter. Two of his bodyguards were killed on the spot.[23] At the time of Rantisi's killing, Mohammed Dahlan had returned back to London, where he was taking an intensive English course at a language school. He was invited by Al Arabiya TV station to appear on its programme and, as I watched Mohammed from a room adjacent to the studio overlooking the Palace of Westminster, I heard him send his condolences to Rantisi's mother and all his brothers and sisters, naming each of them, one by one.

This poignant sentiment reflected the deep relationship the political opponents enjoyed. The hope for a Palestinian future is that these personal relationships always endure. According to Dahlan, his last meeting with Rantisi, which was also attended by Ismail Haniyeh and Said Siam from Hamas and Samir Mushaharawi, a senior Fatah leader in Gaza, lasted two hours. The first twenty minutes involved a very personal exchange between Dahlan and Rantisi. Rantisi asked about Dahlan's mother, whom he referred to as Um Hassan, and, in response, Dahlan asked about Rantisi's siblings, having grown up with them. The meeting had been called at the request of Arafat, the aim being to reach an understanding between the two rival factions. Amongst the many issues which were discussed was the mechanism for reaching a ceasefire with Israel and how Hamas could participate in the political process. A third topic which was introduced by Rantisi was how to incorporate all the many Palestinian factions into one organization. Dahlan was surprised to hear Dr Rantisi presenting an idea to have a national army which all Palestinian factions would contribute towards, providing that this army would not belong to one specific organization. As he presented this idea, Dahlan called Arafat, who was under siege in Ramallah, and passed the phone to Rantisi.

Mohammed Dahlan recalled the old days when he was Head of Preventive Security, and the many occasions that he alerted Hamas senior figures to plans to assassinate them. Amongst those was Ibrahim Al Maqadma. Dahlan said, 'We provided Al Maqadmeh with documents and even a videotape with confessions by a Palestinian collaborator including dates and places he should avoid but he did not act on the warnings and he became another casualty of the Israeli assassination policy.'

7

International Relations

Like most non-state actors, Hamas' ability to survive and develop has been dependent on the actions of other states, which at various points have seen the Islamist organization as an irritant, an enemy, a burden and an opportunity.

Ironically it was Israel's deportation policy which first caused Hamas to forge a base outside of the occupied territories. By 1990, Israel had woken up to the fact that the Islamic movement that had been allowed to flourish was suddenly a real danger. Without seeking permission from the Lebanese government, Israel deported four Hamas activists from Gaza to Southern Lebanon on 29 December 1999. The group settled just outside Sidon in Mieh wa Mieh, a small refugee camp adjacent to UNRWA's largest, Ain el Hilwa, one of sixteen refugee camps established for Palestinians fleeing to Lebanon following the 1948 war.[1] Residents recall how the four deportees held sway over the way the Islamic movement operated in the camp. In Lebanon's scattered refugee camps, the inhabitants lived in cramped conditions below the poverty line, and the Islamic movement took advantage of this situation, giving lectures and attempting to indoctrinate the refugee population with promises to change their lives. The Hamas four were soon joined by a further 415 activists, also banished by Israel to Southern Lebanon. Two Lebanese

Sunni organizations, Al Jamaa Al Islamiyah ('the Religious Group') and Al Ahbash ('the Society for Islamic Charitable Projects'), were drawn in by Hamas' message. A few years later, two of the deportees were elevated to foreign posts within the movement. Imad Al Alami was appointed Hamas' representative in Tehran, and Mustapha Al Qanouaa became the political bureau chief for Hamas in Beirut. The movement worked hard to garner support from Palestinians in Lebanon at a time when the mass appeal previously enjoyed by other Palestinian factions was dwindling, due to the Lebanese civil war and in-fighting between those factions.

The movement became a magnet for Islamist Palestinians throughout the country's refugee camps, rivalling Fatah. Members of the other factions were generally less fervent, but had been motivated to support them by the salary on offer. Besides the political activities taking place in the camps, Hamas and other Islamic groups competed for popularity by developing social programmes which included caring for orphans and widows, running schools and nurseries, building mosques and giving craftwork lessons to women to teach them skills for home industry. Previously, the PLO had been admired for spending generously on these community projects but, following the first Gulf War when Iraq invaded Kuwait,[2] the Gulf States punished the PLO for supporting Iraq, depriving it of the funding it had received since the 1960s. Islamic charities in the Gulf region began switching their financial generosity and allegiances to Hamas.

Prior to the 1987 Palestinian Intifada, a military agenda was never part of the Muslim Brotherhood's strategy. When Hamas burst onto the scene, the Brotherhood's branch in Jordan, which had overall responsibility for the Palestinian branch in the West Bank, was forced to consider the military ambitions of this newly formed movement and whether this was at odds with the social and educational activities which the Brotherhood was championing.

As Hamas gained support during the years of the first Intifada, it added a foreign affairs department to its political structure. It was then that its leadership felt strong enough to extract itself from the Muslim Brotherhood and become an independent body. When Hamas set up a political bureau in Jordan, their channels of communications with the host government were via its security agencies. While Sheikh Yassin was in jail, the leadership was passed to Dr Moussa Abu Marzouk, who had been banned from returning to Gaza by Israel in 1989 and had established himself in Jordan. On a political level, relations with Jordan were good, particularly after the invasion of Kuwait by Iraqi forces, which forced the Kuwait-based Hamas leaders to move to the Jordanian capital Amman. Many at that time believed that the Jordanian government would use Hamas as a bargaining tool in any conflict which arose with the Palestine Liberation Organization.

The host country began to turn against Hamas when its leadership failed to inform the Jordanian government of its intention to mastermind military operations from Amman to be carried out in the occupied territories. The leadership of the Muslim Brotherhood in Jordan was also kept in the dark about Hamas' intentions. In 1991, the Brotherhood and the Hamas leadership reacted with surprise when informed by a high-ranking security official in Jordan that its government had seized a large cache of weapons including heavy machine guns and cannons, stored at four different addresses in the capital. The value of the hoard was estimated to be worth a million Jordanian dinars, or US$1.5 million. Nine Hamas activists were arrested and imprisoned for nine months, only to be released by King's pardon by the Hashemite monarch in 1992.

This was the beginning of the end of the Jordanian government's tolerance. They toughened their stance against Hamas, and began closely monitoring its activities. Both the political wing of Hamas and the Jordanian government were seeking a mechanism for managing their relationship. In 1993, a meeting was organized in the office of Zaid Bin Chaker, the Jordanian Prime Minister, together with Hamas leaders Dr Abu Marzouk, Ibrahim Goshi, Mohammed Nazzal, Imad Alami and others. This meeting was followed by another held in the headquarters of the general intelligence, in order to define the relationship and to inform the movement of what they were and were not permitted to do. It was made clear to Hamas that they were only permitted to carry out media and political activities in the Kingdom which would not damage Jordanian interests. Military activities were forbidden. Jordan's intelligence agencies viewed Hamas with suspicion, concerned that it might morph into a military organization to threaten Jordan's internal security. To this end, they would arrest its leadership whenever they felt there was cause for concern. Their vigilance was heightened after they seized CDs containing detailed information about the organization inside the West Bank and Gaza in November 1995, leading to further arrests.

Rather as Fatah had in the late 1960s, Hamas began claiming responsibility for attacks in Israel in the early 1990s. The Jordanian government, obligated by its 1994 peace deal with Israel, deported Dr Abu Marzouk and Imad Alami. Marzouk was later arrested in the USA, on unsupported charges of terrorism. Despite Jordan's edgy relationship with Hamas, King Hussein played a role in his release and, in 1997, gave permission to the USA to deport him back to Jordan.

When Mossad agents tried to assassinate Khalid Mishal in Jordan, Israel's initial reaction was denial, while King Hussein described Mishal as 'our son' and hinted to journalists in Jordan about the possibility of executing both Mossad agents. Ironically, Mossad had chosen this covert form of attack to avoid embarrassment to the Jordanian government.

Despite this, tensions continued to grow between Hamas and the Jordanian government, not least because they threatened the equilibrium between the government and the Jordanian Muslim Brotherhood. The Muslim Brotherhood complained to the General Guidance of the movement in Egypt, Mustafa Mashour, about Mishal's behaviour and the decisions he was making in Jordan without consulting them. The arrests of several Hamas members, known as the Al Rasifa group, by Jordanian intelligence in the first half of 1999 disturbed and annoyed the leadership of the Muslim Brotherhood. This was compounded when, in mid 1999, Jordanian intelligence arrested two of Mishal's bodyguards for not carrying weapons licences.

The Jordanian government issued a statement on 29 August 1999, indicating it was to close the Hamas office in Amman, ban their activities and issue a warrant for the arrest of the head of its political bureau, Khalid Mishal, along with his comrades.[3] Three weeks later, the Jordanian branch of the Muslim Brotherhood rallied its members and allies amongst the various political parties and unions to campaign against their government's decision. Three Hamas leaders, including Mishal, who were visiting Tehran, heeded the ban and decided to travel to Damascus to get a sense of perspective on the situation and avoid a confrontation with the Jordanian government.

With this action, the relationship between Hamas and Jordan had plunged to a nadir which would have been unimaginable when King Hussein intervened to save the life of Mishal two years earlier. In those halcyon days, Abu Marzouk was even able to contact the King on his private telephone line. That time of cooperation and mutual understanding between Hamas and Jordan ended forever. The disarray in Hamas' external leadership meant that the organization in Gaza became the powerbase.

Hamas struck up a friendship with Qatar in the early 1990s when Sheikh Hamad Bin Khalifa Al Thani was the Crown Prince, and the relationship strengthened when Sheikh Hamad was appointed Emir in 1995.[4] Mishal claimed that Jordan was looking for an excuse to terminate Hamas' presence in the country and seized on rumours that weapons had been found and other irregularities but claimed that 'none of these were true.' Jordan only agreed to release Mishal and Goshi on condition that they left the country. They were escorted from prison on 1 November 1999 and taken to Marka Airport in Amman, where they boarded a private flight, blindfolded and with their hands tied behind their backs. Mohammed Abdullah Al Mahmoud, from Qatar's Ministry of Foreign Affairs was also on board, and the Hamas activists were flown to the Qatari capital, Doha. 'We remained in Qatar for two years,' recalled Mishal, 'during which time we tried to patch up our problem with Jordan but we failed.'

When Sheikh Hamad Bin Jasem Al Thani, Qatar's Foreign Minister, visited Jordan prior to Mishal's deportation to Doha, he was given an audience with King Hussein in the presence of the Jordanian Prime Minister, Abdul Raouf Al Rawabdeh. When the Qatari Foreign Minister raised the issue of the Hamas leadership detainees in Jordan, he asked the King's permission for them to be deported to Qatar. Jokingly, King Hussein is said to have commented:

'What do you need them for?' Sheikh Hamad Bin Jasem's response was that Hamas would provide the Qatari State with a plausible cover for their intentions to open diplomatic relations with Israel. 'By having Hamas as our guests, it will keep relationships sweet with other Arab governments.'

Qatar was playing a sophisticated triple-game. Here was an Arab government with one of the closest relationships to Washington, hosting the HQ of the American Forces in the Gulf region. On top of this, it had just taken in the leaders of the most radical Palestinian movement. Thirdly, through the state-funded Al Jazeera television network, it was openly giving air-time to Israeli officials and their views for the first time.

Goshi, Mishal and Mohammed Nazzal shuttled between Doha and the Hamas bureau in Damascus and, by 2001, Mishal was spending most of his time in the Syrian capital. With the outbreak of the Al Aqsa Intifada in 2000, Mishal described his relationship with Arafat as 'fine', saying that there was no need for third-party negotiations: 'I met up with brother Arafat at an Islamic conference in Doha and I kept in touch with him over the phone.' Mishal denied any efforts by the Qatari government to mediate between Hamas and Israel. 'Our policy is well-known,' he said, 'and we have no intention at any stage to make contact with the Zionist enemy.'

Despite a very Palestinian attempt to paper-over their very deep differences in public, Arafat knew very well that Hamas had no intention of recognizing the PLO, and what was really going on was that it was trying to blaze its own trail to power.

The Iranian Connection

Hamas' most significant foreign relationships today are with Syria and Iran. The Iranian relationship is all the more interesting for the fact that Iran has traditionally supported Shia groups, and Hamas is Sunni Muslim. Nonetheless, the Iranian connection is real and long-standing. It is one whose deep roots I witnessed at first hand.

Whenever I return to Lebanon, childhood memories are evoked by the scent of orange and lemon blossoms from the swathe of orchards fringing the Mediterranean sea. The sharp tang of citrus would drift through our camp on the sea breeze to mingle with the less pleasant stench of high-density living. Burj El Shamali refugee camp provided emergency accommodation for 2,500 families, including my parents, who were evicted from northern Palestine in 1948. As a teenager growing up in the early 1970s, freedom meant a game of football. We were eight brothers and sisters living in our small UNRWA-provided home and we would let off steam on a stony piece of waste ground at the edge of the camp, a few kilometres from the Roman columns of Tyre, on Lebanon's southern Mediterranean coast. All the camp kids would jostle for space on the coarse, uneven pitch, playing in bare feet to protect our costly and only pair of shoes. Our *ad hoc* football team was regularly swollen by a group of Iranians who had left their country in protest against the monarchy of the pro-western Shah of Iran, becoming guests in Lebanon under the wing of the local Fatah movement. The teenagers were just part of a larger contingent of young Iranian revolutionaries in opposition to imperialist rule who were in Lebanon at that time. I knew them as Mustapha, Rafiq and Bani Sadr. My recollection of them was of quiet types who would sit outside their ground-floor rented apartment after sunset, drinking tea and discussing politics in the cooler evening air.

After the fall of the last Shah of Iran, Mohammed Reza Pahlavi, a triumphant Imam Ruhollah Moussavi Khomeini arrived at Tehran international airport, returning from exile in France to an overwhelming hero's welcome of an estimated six million revolutionaries. He established himself as the Supreme Leader of the new Islamic Republic of Iran.[5] The three amateur footballers also returned to their homeland, and it wasn't long before they too were making news. Under the theocratic leadership of the Grand Ayatollah Khomeini, Abu Al Hassan Bani Sadr was elected President, Mustapha Mohammed Najjar became Minister of Defence and Mohsen Rafiq Doust was appointed head of the Revolutionary Guard. The *Pasadaran*, as it is known in Iran, was established to guard the Revolutionary regime and assist the ruling clerics to enforce Islamic codes and morality.

Five years before,[6] an influential Iranian cleric organized a gathering in my home town of Tyre, the size of which probably hasn't been witnessed since the heady days of the Romans.

Following a similar rally held in Baalbeck,[7] more than 100,000 armed Shia from all over the Bekaa Valley, Southern Lebanon and Beirut's southern suburbs assembled in massed support of a new political movement which was to be called the Lebanese Resistance Detachments, later known as 'Amal'. Imam Sayed Moussa Al Sadr, a popular cleric in the region, said that the movement's launch was necessary because Israeli aggression had reached its highest level and the Lebanese authorities had failed to perform their duty to protect their citizens. He felt compelled to organize the Shia into a military faction to defend the southern Lebanese villages, which were suffering regular bombardments during intense exchanges between Israel and the PLO from their military bases in the south. At that time, Lebanon was on the brink of civil war and other religious factions – the Christians, Druze and Sunnis – were already well-organized politically, with functioning militias. Fiefdoms of wealthy landowners had fled the region as Palestinian guerrillas established a strong foothold following their expulsion from Jordan by King Hussein in 1971. These fighters, or *fedayeen* as they liked to be known, had been engaged in a guerrilla war with King Hussein's army in an attempt to overthrow the Jordanian monarch. King Hussein declared martial law and eventually the Jordanian army seized control and the fedayeen were forced to leave. They made their way via Syria to the southern border region of Lebanon, which provided a launch-pad from which to carry out their attacks against Israeli settlements along Israel's northern border.

When I was growing up in Burj El Shamali camp, the Fatah leader and PLO chairman Yasser Arafat was considered a hero. I remember hearing senior Fatah officials, under instructions from Arafat, rally round their members to donate whatever weapons they could to the fledgling Amal militia. The alliance between the Fatah movement and the Amal Shia revivalist movement proved popular. Al Sadr used his party's launch rally in Tyre to issue a *fatwa*, calling on his people to resist helping the Israelis in any way whatsoever in their war against the Palestinians. 'Dealing with Israel is *haram* – against God's will,' he famously said.

'Amal' translates as 'Hope' and, with this optimistic moniker, the Shia militia went on to participate in many bloody battles against a myriad of combatants – Christians, Druze, Palestinians and even the Shi'ite Hezbollah during Lebanon's fifteen-year civil war.[8] The movement provided a dramatic about-turn for a region which was traditionally governed by well-established, conservative Shia families who were rich, right wing, pro-Shah and with western values. Families like the Al Asaads, Al Khalils, Oseirans and Safie El Dins, who owned large tracts of agricultural land. While the Palestinian movement was predominantly Sunni, sizeable numbers of Shi'ites joined its ranks, and two of its main factions were led by Christians: George Habash led the PFLP and Nayef Hawatmeh the DFLP.

The Iranian presence in Lebanon at that time was not just restricted to anti-Shah revolutionaries. The Iranian Communist Party, Tudeh, and other secular movements such as Mujahideen-e Khalq (MEK) were also represented. They joined the leftist Palestinian factions which became active in Lebanon during the 1970s and these Iranian political figures were to become familiar faces to me when I started out in journalism, writing for various Palestinian and Lebanese publications. Their representatives would regularly visit Beirut's newspaper offices to deliver press releases voicing their opposition to the Shah's regime in Tehran.

Uninvited, Arafat and his entourage of fifty-eight PLO officials turned up in Tehran on 18 February 1979, just days after the victory of the revolution. Arafat would have lunch meetings in Moscow followed by breakfast talks in Washington, courting any government no matter what their complexion if he felt it would positively influence the crisis in the Palestinian territories. At such an early stage of their Islamic revival, the revolutionaries were caught off-guard by this unscheduled visit of a foreign dignitary. Nevertheless, several Iranian officials greeted Arafat at the airport and provided the Palestinians with red-carpet accommodation at the former Government Club on Fereshteh Street, in northern Tehran, the city's smartest address.[9]

There is an Iranian trivia quiz question which asks: 'Can you name the only time Ayatollah Khomeini smiled?' Answer: 'The first and only time Ayatollah Khomeini smiled was when he sat next to Mr Arafat in Tehran in 1979.'[10] In greeting, the two leaders clasped hands and embraced. The tall, white-bearded, black-robed and turbaned Ayatollah was photographed in an unlikely clinch with the diminutive Arafat, wearing his trademark fatigues and carefully arranged Palestinian chequered headscarf. Khomeini's normally taciturn expression was frozen into a Mona Lisa-style smile.[11]

In celebration of this cordial meeting, Khomeini announced that the Islamic Revolution would 'march until the liberation of Jerusalem'.[12] Hours after his arrival, Arafat was invited for a two-hour meeting with Ayatollah Khomeini during which, much to Arafat's surprise, Khomeini was quite critical of the PLO and lectured the Palestinian leader on 'the necessity of dropping his leftist and nationalistic tendencies to get to the Islamic roots of the Palestinian issue'.[13]

Accompanied by Khomeini's son, Ahmed, Arafat toured the major cities of Iran where he too received a hero's welcome. His speeches were attended by hundreds of thousands in Tehran's Revolution Square and likewise in the holy city of Qom, which proved an emotional experience for the Palestinian leader. The Iranian Revolution offered a beacon of hope with which Arafat could inspire his people. It illuminated the strength the disadvantaged masses could generate when they collectively stood up to a powerful regime. Iran was a perfect role model for the PLO, and the admiration was mutual. Jerusalem had been a symbol for the Iranian revolutionaries and Khomeini decreed the last Friday of Ramadan as Al Quds Day (Jerusalem Day), when government workers were encouraged to take part in protests against the 'bloodthirsty Zionist state'.[14] A quarter of a century later, this day is still celebrated with rallies and marches, not only in Iran but in every country with a sizeable Shia Muslim minority, where it has become a ritualized outpouring of vitriol towards Israel.

In a gesture both leaders must have enjoyed, Khomeini handed over the keys of the de facto Israeli Embassy in Tehran, to house the new Palestinian diplomatic mission. Hani Al Hassan, Arafat's chief political adviser and a member of the Fatah Central Committee, was appointed as Palestinian Ambassador to Tehran to validate the strength of their alliance. The new Iranian government lavished financial support on groups opposing Israel and its state television described suicide bombings as 'martyrdom operations'.[15] Billboards shouting 'Justice for Palestine!' peppered the country, and every major Iranian city adopted the name 'Palestine' for its squares, streets or avenues.

Arafat was seen as being so close to the Iranians that when student supporters of the revolution stormed the US Embassy in November 1979, taking its inhabitants hostage, he was indirectly approached through a CIA operative in Beirut to broker the situation with Khomeini. The Iranian government was stunned to learn that a Palestinian delegation led by Saad Sayel, a member of the Fatah Central Committee and Commander of military central operations, had arrived in Tehran to mediate in the crisis. The move backfired, and the relationship between Arafat and Iran never recovered from this point. This, however, was Hamas' gain.

Several years later, in 1994, I became reacquainted with one of the Iranian football chums, Mohsen Rafiq Doust, in his grand office in Tehran. He had moved on from his early responsibilities as head of the Revolutionary Guard to become the head of a powerful multi-billion-dollar foundation called Bonyad-e Mostazafan za Janbazan ('the Foundation of the Oppressed and War Veterans'), in charge of a third of the Iranian budget. Described as 'a state within the State', the foundation is one of the richest organizations in the world, controlling more than six hundred key industrial complexes, and some of the country's biggest and most lucrative businesses, firms and hotels, farms and factories which were abandoned by their owners who 'fled the country before the victory of the Glorious Islamic Revolution and settled down in the Land of Infidels'.[16] Properties seized from the former Shah of Iran provided the new foundation with sizeable opening assets. It now owns airline and shipping companies, deals in oil and arms, export and import and above all, claims the *Iran Free Press*, 'facilitates Iranian funding of some Islamic organizations such as the Lebanese Hezbollah of the Palestinian Islamic Jihad'.[17]

The last time Doust met Arafat in Beirut was in 1982 when, as head of the Revolutionary Guard,[18] he accompanied the head of the Iranian Parliament, Ali Akbar Hashemi Rafsanjani to Lebanon. Despite Doust's earlier admiration for Arafat, he quickly became disenchanted with the PLO leader. Arafat's support for Iraq at the beginning of the Iran-Iraq war in 1980 and the peaceful overtures he was extending towards Israel left Doust feeling disillusioned and he told Arafat so in no uncertain terms. In a speech to a Fatah conference in 1981, which earned Doust a rousing reception, he told the assembled delegates: 'The Iranian Revolution learned a lot from the Palestinian Revolution and because of our belief in God we were capable of defeating the might of the imperialist Shah.' Turning to Arafat he chided: 'Carrying an olive branch is the beginning of your downfall, because Palestine can only be liberated through the barrel of the gun.'

By the time Arafat paid a return visit to Tehran on 28 February 1981, the hovering smile of Ayatollah Khomeini had been replaced by a hostile crowd gathered in front of the Hilton Hotel in protest at the Palestinians' lack of support for Iran in their war with Iraq, which had begun on 22 September 1980. Iran had expected their friends in the PLO to side with them, the underdogs in the conflict. Instead, the PLO played the role of mediators alongside the non-aligned countries and the OIC, the Organization of the Islamic Conference,[19] which made many attempts to broker the conflict between Iran and Iraq peacefully.

Not long afterwards, Arafat confirmed his commitment to the peace process with Israel at an Arab Summit held in November 1981 in Fez, Morocco. To talk peace with your enemy and be a friend of 'the Great Satan', as the Iranian revolutionaries referred to the USA, was anathema to Khomeini's revolutionary principles. What's more, Arafat went on to forge diplomatic relations with the Afghan regime of President Mohammed Najeb which was less than complimentary about Iran.

Salah Zawawi, the PLO representative in Iran, believed that Iran's penultimate humiliation towards the PLO came at the outbreak of the Palestinian Intifada in 1987, when Iranian spokespersons and media outlets downplayed the role of the PLO while exaggerating Hamas' and Islamic Jihad's contribution in fuelling the uprising.[20] At the time, Zawawi denied that Hamas and Islamic Jihad representatives in Tehran were attempting to take over or marginalize the PLO, despite having conducted their business without coordinating with the Palestinian diplomatic mission. They established their own separate contacts and circles within the Iranian regime. As the 1980s played out, following ten years of crumbling enchantment with Arafat and his PLO, the Iranian government had had enough.

The *coup de grâce* was struck one Sunday in late November 1994, when students and demonstrators belonging to the Revolutionary Guard broke into Zawawi's Embassy, chanting slogans against the PLO, describing them as 'agents of Israel and the Americans'. During the six-hour siege in which the Ambassador and his staff were held hostage, the demonstrators destroyed the furniture and tore down the PLO flag. They claimed the building was an 'HQ for informers' and demanded that the PLO staff be replaced by officials from Islamic Jihad and Hamas. Zawawi issued a statement to IRNA, the Islamic Republic News Agency, as well as Iranian newspapers, condemning the assault, which, he said, had been planned by pro-government forces. His statements went ignored and the siege of his Embassy went unreported. Around the same time, the Iranian press had published a news item about a clash between Palestinian police and Hamas followers in Gaza in which they criticized the Palestinian Authority and its police in apparent sympathy for Hamas. The beleaguered Palestinian Ambassador was left with no illusions. His Embassy was trashed and the Iranian government was sending overtures to Hamas. The Iranian leadership had finally decided to terminate its stale relationship with the PLO and start afresh with new Palestinian friends, Hamas and Islamic Jihad.

Hamas' spokesperson in Jordan during the early 1990s, Ibrahim Goshi, told me that their relationship with Iran began shortly after Iraq invaded Kuwait on 2 August 1990.[21] At that time, Hamas was a member of a delegation representing Islamic movements and organizations from many Arab and Islamic countries. In October 1991, Goshi received an invitation to take part in a conference in Tehran in support of the Intifada. 'We held meetings at the highest level,' Goshi said, 'and [Iran] agreed to Hamas opening an office. Imad Al Alami who had been deported by the Israelis was appointed as our representative in the Iranian capital.' Goshi shrugged off his organization's relationship with Tehran as nothing remarkable or untoward. 'It's true Islamic Jihad have offices in Tehran, but it's no different from the presence Hamas and other movements have established in many countries worldwide including the United States and the UK.' He also dismissed claims that Hamas was receiving significant financial assistance from Iran.

During 1992, as he recalled, Goshi received further invitations to Tehran together with Dr Moussa Abu Marzouk, head of the Hamas political bureau based in Damascus.[22] They held meetings with the Iranian leadership to discuss financial methods to support the Palestinian cause and agreed to unite against the peace initiatives being forged between the PLO and Israel. Citing a news story published during his visit, which claimed that he had visited Iranian Revolutionary Guards training camps, he said: 'This never took place. There are so many fabricated news stories about the cooperation which existed between Hamas and Iran.' He blamed Arafat for mounting a 'propaganda campaign' to make a connection between Hamas, Islamic Jihad and Iran and to accuse them for the failure of the Oslo Peace Accords.

Osama Hamdan, the Hamas representative in Iran in 1994, admitted that the flourishing relations between Tehran and Hamas were at the expense of the previous marriage between Tehran and the PLO. But, he said, 'There is an absence of any proof or evidence of Iranian financial support to Hamas, Islamic Jihad and other Palestinian factions who have established contacts with Iran. It is merely rumours and speculation.'[23] According to Hamdan, the budget allocated in 1991 by Iran to support the Palestinian Intifada was used to finance political campaigns to increase awareness amongst the Iranian public of the Palestinian cause. He named the Martyrs Foundation, as the organization responsible for giving help and support to about four hundred Palestinian families of martyrs and prisoners. The Martyrs Foundation had been formed in Iran in 1980, during the Iran-Iraq war, specifically to give financial support to the families of those killed, missing or taken captive. As one of Iran's 'means of exporting the revolution', the foundation has branches worldwide. Hamdan thought it unlikely that any illegal money transfers were being undertaken from the outside to the West Bank and Gaza because of the 'stringent measures employed by the Israelis'.

A top Iranian diplomat to London, Mr Gulam Ansari, whom I consulted at the time, laughed off accusations that Iran was funding 'terrorist organizations' as hyperbole manifested by the West. 'If they have any proof about our support, they should come clean and disclose it.' Despite protestations to the contrary by Ansari and others, it became patently clear that the many shipments of weapons which were either intercepted by the Israeli navy in the Mediterranean Seas, seized on land in Jordan or which successfully reached their intended destination, had one thing in common. They all originated in Iran.

Syria

Syria's symbiotic relationship with Hamas harks back to the early 1990s, when the first Intifada was developing into a full-blown military battle. In concert with Iran, disagreement over Arafat's championing of the Oslo and Madrid peace deals with Israel further cemented their bond. Arafat's many encounters with Syria's President Hafez Al Assad had been lukewarm at best; generally, each regarded the other with suspicion, and Arafat held the belief that Syria wanted the last word on any solution for Palestine. I remember, as a young journalist, attending my first meeting of the Palestinian National Council (PNC) which was held at Damascus University in 1979. It was a rare, if not the only occasion Hafez Al Assad attended a session of the Palestinian parliament in exile. In his speech, Al Assad made a reference to Palestine as 'the southern part of Syria'. Arafat, who was presenting the final speech at the conference, retaliated with a hint of humour by calling Syria 'the northern part of Palestine'.

Following Israel's invasion of Lebanon in 1982, Arafat and the PLO were thrown out and given safe passage out of Lebanon. Rather than choose the obvious and transfer his base to Damascus with its significant Palestinian population, he elected to set up base in Tunis where, according to the Palestinian President, he could maintain his independence; this irked the Syrian President. When Arafat later paid a visit to Damascus from Tunis, he was told he was *persona non grata* and asked to leave. Arafat, unaccustomed to diplomatic put-downs at this stage, was escorted to the airport by a low-ranking

Syrian intelligence officer to ensure his swift departure from the country. A few months earlier, signs of tension between Arafat and Al Assad had begun to emerge, as Syria began to show sympathy towards some of Arafat's rivals in Fatah, particularly Abu Moussa, Abu Saleh, and Kadri – all very senior within the organization.[24] After their forced departure from Lebanon, rather than follow Arafat to Tunis, they established an independent HQ in Damascus. Arafat also set up a secondary base in Tripoli in northern Lebanon, returning by sea from Tunis in complete defiance of Israel. Around this time (December of 1983), I accompanied Arafat on a trip to Damascus from his Tripoli base to write a feature article for my magazine, *Al Hawadess*. Arafat had called an emergency meeting of the Fatah Revolutionary Council in an attempt convince dissenting members of his movement to remain united. The meeting was heated and, as the acrimonious session drew to a close, Arafat's bodyguards signalled to me to jump into their car as the Chairman's departure was imminent.

As Arafat strode towards his car, having failed in his mission, anger was written all over his face. We drove off in a large convoy at top speed, hurtling along the newly built highway, back towards Tripoli via the Syrian cities of Homs and Tartus. At about the halfway point, Arafat's car, which was in second position in the convoy, suddenly drove off the highway taking a slip road, forcing the string of Mercedes and four-wheel drives to follow suit. The still-angry Palestinian President emerged from his elderly, bullet-proof American Chevrolet and sat down in a wheat and corn field where he remained in deep thought for several minutes. As the convoy regrouped, Arafat rose from his reverie, announcing that we should abandon the planned route and take an alternative road with no border controls, which wound through a region of hills and caves called Joroud Al Harmel, before slipping down towards the Tripoli coast. The road resembled a dried-up river bed and, as we bumped and swerved our way along the rough and pitted surface, a rock hit the smoke-screen device on Arafat's car creating dense black smoke, delaying the convoy for many minutes until the fog cleared. President Arafat was fully prepared for an assassination attempt and this sudden route change signified what had been occupying his mind. Following the failed Damascus trip, Arafat's relationship with Syria plunged to new depths and pitched battles between pro-Syrian Palestinian factions and Arafat's fighters became frequent. By the summer of 1983, Arafat was forced out of Tripoli, and with a guard of French navy ships, he travelled by sea via the Suez Canal to Al Hodeida in Yemen.

The political network between Iran, Syria, Hamas and Islamic Jihad strengthened following each suicide bombing or military attack attributed to these groups. Hamas opened an information office in Damascus. Soon members of the movement's political bureau moved to the Syrian capital where they became active in the 'Alliance of the Ten Palestinian Factions',[25] meeting regularly to coordinate their activities and reach a consensus on how to confront the USA, Israel and the Palestinian Authority. As support for Hamas swelled inside the West Bank and Gaza, the relationship between Syria and Hamas strengthened.

Many of the Palestinian factions based in Damascus did not share the support Hamas was enjoying, and Syria realized that here was an organization to be reckoned with, hailing it as a legitimate resistance movement against the Israeli occupation. At their 1996 conference, the ruling Ba'ath Party signalled the importance of forming an alliance between themselves, as nationalists, and the Islamists, meaning Hamas.

Syria's earlier associations with Islamists in the form of the Muslim Brotherhood had ended in bloodshed which began with an attack by the Brotherhood on an artillery school in Aleppo, northern Syria, killing eighty-three Alawite cadets.[26] The Sunni Islamist political movement had emerged as a strong force in Syria in the late 1960s, when Sunnis represented a majority of the population. As its influence spread during the 1970s, it began to threaten the secular Ba'athist regime in Damascus, which tried to suppress it. There was continual warfare between the Syrian army and the Syrian Brothers, who made an assassination attempt on President Hafez Al Assad during an official state reception for the President of Mali in June 1980. A few hours later, the Syrian army retaliated by massacring up to 1,000 members of the Brotherhood, who were imprisoned in Palmyra in the Syrian desert. The following month, the Ba'athist regime passed a law making membership of the Brotherhood punishable by death.

The most bloody period in this sectarian battle came in February 1982, when the Brotherhood led a major insurrection in the city of Hama. The Syrian army responded by bombing the city for several weeks, leaving a fatality count of between 10,000 and 25,000 men, women and children.[27] This final massacre marked the defeat of the Syrian Brotherhood and Islamist groups in general until the new millennium, when President Bashar Al Assad succeeded his father and pardoned and released many imprisoned Brotherhood members.

Sweeping aside the historically complex relationship between the Syrian branch of the Brotherhood and the Syrian government, branches from other countries including Egypt and Jordan were invited to take part in a Damascus-based conference to discuss their vision concerning the Israeli occupation of the West Bank and Gaza. Some of its leaders, like Ishaq Al Farhan, head of the Jordan Muslim Brothers, along with other representatives of Arab and Islamic parties, met the Syrian President during the Arab Nationalist-Islamic Conference which was held in Damascus. Khalid Abdul Majid, leader of one of the Palestinian factions in Damascus, told me that Al Farhan had given a speech praising Syria for its stand against Israel.

Despite the cooperation between Hamas and Hezbollah, Hamas is free to operate its own separate strategy inside the occupied territories. While their political relationship stems from the two factions' combined resistance to the occupation, the relationship between Hamas and Hezbollah has undeniably strengthened through their connections to both Syria and Iran. Israel had hoped to create a schism between Sunnis and Shias but they failed to factor in the strength of unity that exists against the common enemy. In Israel's recent war with Hezbollah in Lebanon, which began in the summer of 2006, many Arab countries, amongst them Egypt, Saudi Arabia and Jordan, criticized Hezbollah for initiating the fighting and giving Israel the excuse to destroy Lebanon's infrastructure. According to Hamas officials, however, there was support for Hezbollah: they claimed they had successfully lobbied Sunni

Islamic movements in the Arab world, which held demonstrations in the streets of Egypt, Jordan, and North Africa. Israel's attempts to marginalize Hezbollah as a Shia movement appear to have failed. Sunni religious leaders in the Arab world issued fatwas, which sanctioned Hezbollah's fight against Israel. Mohammed Mahdi Aqel, leader of the Muslim Brotherhood in Egypt issued a statement which expressed his movement's readiness to send '10,000 mujahid to Lebanon'.[28] If the Egyptian government would open its door to jihad, Aqel continued, 'millions of Brotherhood followers in addition to others from outside the movement, would be prepared to participate in the jihad to support Hezbollah and the Islamic resistance in Lebanon.'

Over the last two decades, Syria has been criticized by the USA and Israel for harbouring what have been termed 'terrorist organizations', and this has been raised with the Syrian government during each visit to Damascus by a senior American official or Secretary of State. Syria has always maintained that the various leaders – Khalid Mishal of Hamas, Ramadan Abdullah Shallah of Islamic Jihad and Ahmed Jibril of the Popular Front for the Liberation of Palestine General Command (PFLP-GC) – were in the capital for media and political purposes, not to carry out military operations. After every suicide bombing against Israeli citizens, Tel Aviv would immediately accuse Syria of either initiating or encouraging the attack, based on Khalid Mishal's presence in the country. Mishal became Hamas' political bureau chief and de facto head of the movement following the assassinations of both Sheikh Ahmed Yassin and his successor Dr Abdul Aziz Al Rantisi.

Hamas' former senior commander in Damascus, Ez El Din Al Sheikh Khalil, had been imprisoned many times between 1987 and 1992 and was one of the 415 Hamas and Islamic Jihad leaders that Israel expelled to Southern Lebanon in 1992. The Gaza-born fighter was described by Israeli radio as the right-hand man of Yehia Ayyash, the Engineer, who had been assassinated by Israel nine years earlier. Nicknamed 'the snake's head',[29] for his dangerous stealth and shadowy existence, Khalil chose not to return to Gaza, basing himself in Damascus from where he travelled restlessly between many Arab and Islamic cities including Khartoum, Aden, Sana'a,

Tehran and occasionally Cairo. The forty-two-year-old leader was assassinated in a predominantly Palestinian neighbourhood of Al Zahera in southern Damascus. At 11.15 a.m. Damascus time on Sunday 26 September 2004, explosives planted in his car were detonated as he answered his mobile telephone. Israel's spy agency, Mossad, was widely blamed for his death. This assassination came almost a year after Israel bombed a Palestinian military base, north-west of Damascus in its first attack on Syrian soil since the 1973 Ramadan War (Yom Kippur). Israeli Prime Minister Ariel Sharon was waging a brand-new war against those he claimed were responsible for suicide attacks by dispatching Mossad to carry out assassination missions in capital cities believed to be harbouring Hamas and Islamic Jihad cells.

Khalil's assassination was an embarrassment to the Syrian intelligence agencies and the Syrian government. President Bashar Al Assad, under pressure from the USA and the international community, claimed to have closed down all Hamas and Islamic Jihad command centres, expelled their leaders and disconnected their telephone systems.

Israel's leaked acknowledgement that it had carried out the assassination was denied by Jadon Ezra, acting Minister for Security in the Israeli government, but he said he was happy about the news. Israeli TV described it as a new tactic in fighting Palestinian factions,[30] while Hamas' military wing, Al Qassam, condemned the assassination of what it described as 'one of the founders of Al Qassam Brigades' and threatened to take their battle abroad.[31] But Hamas' representative in Beirut, Osama Hamdan, denied any change in strategy which confines their military activities solely within the occupied territories and Israel.

Hamas pointed its finger at a 'nameless Arab country' for assisting Israel in the assassination.[32] They referred to a front-page newspaper article, which claimed that an intelligence agency in 'an undisclosed Arab country' had passed a file on Hamas to Israel, three days after an official request was made by the Head of Mossad, Mair Dogan.[33] Conspiracy theorists leapt on this veiled reference. Some believed that the unnamed country was Jordan. According to the article, the file contained detailed information about Hamas activists and leaders and their whereabouts in 'Tehran, Damascus, Beirut, Khartoum and Sana'a and certain Gulf States'. Mossad had requested the assistance of those Arab countries following a double bus bombing in Beer Sheva, which had killed sixteen Israelis.[34] Israel accused the Hamas leadership abroad of ordering the attacks, specifically naming Damascus-based Khalid Mishal, and threatened to assassinate him in the Syrian capital. A few days after the kidnapping of Israeli soldier Gilad Shalit in a joint operation by Palestinian factions, including the military wing of Hamas,[35] four Israeli warplanes buzzed the summer palace of President Bashar Al Assad, in Syria's Mediterranean port city of Latakia. Flying in a low-altitude formation, the jets were part of an overall Israeli operation aimed to pressure the Syrians to expel Khalid Mishal, Hamas' political bureau chief from Damascus.[36] According to Israel, Mishal had been calling the shots from the Syrian capital and had orchestrated the joint kidnapping of the Israeli soldier. Justice Minister Haim Ramon said that Mishal was 'a target for assassination. He is definitely in our sights. He is someone who is overseeing, actually commanding the terror acts.'[37] Interior Minister and former head of the Shabak Avi Dichter said that the only reason Mishal was not in an Israeli jail 'is that Israel, as an enlightened nation, has placed certain restrictions upon itself'.

What Dichter failed to reveal was that, two years earlier, Israel had tried to assassinate Khalid Mishal in Damascus. The *mukhabarat*, Syrian intelligence, foiled the assassination attempt with the arrest of four Arabs, including a woman, all Syrian citizens. Mohammed Nazzal, a Hamas leader, confirmed the arrests, which happened around the same time as Ez El Din Al Sheikh Khalil was assassinated. It was unclear if this foursome was involved in his death but, according to sources in Damascus, the Syrian mukhabarat concluded that the group had been recruited in 'an Arab neighbouring country'. Nazzal appealed to all Arab governments to take measures to prevent Mossad from carrying out assassinations against Hamas in their countries, stating that they could only happen with logistical help from local agents of the respective governments.

Funding

The first official confession that Iran had extended its financial influence into the West Bank and Gaza came when I received a phone call from Damascus in early 1994. The person on the other end of the line was the Syrian-based leader of Islamic Jihad in Palestine, Dr Fathi Al Shikaki. He was keen to give me a detailed account of the kind of support Iran was extending to different Palestinian factions at that time and to correct the rumour that Tehran was handing out funds in excess of $20 million. On condition that he should not be quoted, and that I should source my information as coming from a Palestinian official, he told me that Iran had budgeted $3 million to support the families of Palestinian martyrs, together with more than 10,000 prisoners held in Israeli jails, as well as many social projects and institutions in the occupied Palestinian territories. A few years later, Shikaki was assassinated in Malta on his return from a trip to Libya.

Long before Iran became a player in the politics of the Arab-Israeli conflict, Hamas relied – and still relies – heavily on fundraising by wealthy Arabs, mainly from the Gulf region, who finance the organization via *zakat*, one of the five pillars of Islam, which states that every Muslim has a duty to care for the poor, widows and orphans. Zakat became an obligatory tax paid by Muslims all over the world as a percentage of non-essential income. Historically, the giving of zakat, or alms, has been around since the early days of Islam but, following the Soviet invasion of Afghanistan, charitable zakat organizations became more prominent, springing up in cities like Peshawar along Pakistan's border with Afghanistan to assist Afghan refugees who had fled over the border to escape the fighting. In recent times, these charities have provided disaster relief in the aftermath of the tsunami which swept away thousands of lives in several countries surrounding the Indian Ocean on 26 December 2004 and the earthquake which devastated Pakistan's Kashmir region in October 2005. In the 1990s, the USA began to weigh down heavily on these charities, calling on governments to establish procedures to ensure only the genuinely impoverished receive aid, flagging up the danger that these organizations could end up financing the violent activities of Al Qaeda, Hezbollah, Hamas and Islamic Jihad.

Hamas directly benefited from the hostile attitude of Arab governments towards Arafat and his Fatah movement for its support of Iraq's invasion of Kuwait in August 1980. Wealthy Saudis and Kuwaitis offered money to Hamas and publicly supported it through the media. They made no secret of channelling money to Hamas by many ingenious routes. One of these was to set up charitable social institutions such as nurseries and educational facilities attached to the expanding number of mosques in the Palestinian territories.

In the twenty-year span between the 1967 Six Day War and Hamas' emergence on the international stage, the number of Islamic minarets decorating Gaza's skyline tripled from 200 to 600. In the West Bank during the same period, the number of mosques grew from 400 to 750.[38] Sheikh Ahmed Yassin had built up a strong network of welfare institutions based around the mosques during his years as leader of the Islamic Compound and his association with the Muslim Brotherhood. It is no secret that Israel encouraged the Islamists – first the Muslim Brotherhood, then its younger brother, Hamas – to flourish, in order to destabilize Fatah. The money for their mosques was allowed to flow unhindered into the occupied territories from wealthy Islamists in Saudi Arabia and other Gulf States.

When Hamas was added to the terrorist list by the US State Department on 24 January 1995, Washington used its diplomatic channels to ask the Gulf States to take punitive action against all those in the oil-rich states who had donated money to the discredited organization. President Bill Clinton issued Executive Order, No 12947, making it 'a felony to raise or transfer funds to the signated terrorist groups or their front organizations'.

Two Hamas members were arrested on 19 August 2004 for allegedly participating in a fifteen-year racketeering conspiracy. Muhammad Hamid Khalil Salah of Chicago and Abdul Haleem Hasan Abdul Raziq Ashqar of Washington, DC were accused of illegally financing terrorist activities. In addition, an arrest warrant was issued for a third Hamas member, Moussa Mohammed Abu Marzouk, a former US citizen living in Damascus, who was described as 'a fugitive from justice'. This was the first time Hamas had been identified as a criminal enterprise, citing activities which included:

conspiracy to commit first degree murder, conspiracy to kill, kidnap, maim or injure persons in a foreign country, money laundering, obstruction of justice, providing material support or resources to designated foreign terrorist organizations, hostage taking, forgery or false use of a passport, structuring financial transactions and travel in aid of racketeering.[39]

Ashqar was said to have opened various bank accounts in Mississippi, using them as a clearing house for Hamas funds. Abu Marzouk allegedly maintained and shared numerous bank accounts in the USA, which received substantial deposits from overseas, then transferred the funds among other domestic accounts before the money was ultimately disbursed to accounts and individuals abroad to benefit Hamas activities. Salah was alleged to have travelled throughout the United States and to London, Israel and the West Bank and Gaza Strip on behalf of Hamas, meeting with its leaders and members, recruiting and training new members in the USA. Abu Marzouk and Ashqar, together with a man named Elbarasse and other unnamed co-conspirators, were said to have used various accounts at banks in Cleveland, Milwaukee, New York, Louisiana, Mississippi and Virginia from as early as 1989 until January 1993, transferring amounts ranging from tens to hundreds of thousands of dollars at a time into the USA from various sources abroad, including Saudi Arabia, before transferring funds out of the country to Israel and Switzerland.

Following their arrests, Attorney General John Ashcroft said, 'Our record on terrorist financing is clear: We will hunt down the suppliers of terrorist blood money. We will shut down these sources, and we will ensure that both terrorists and their financiers meet the full justice of the United States of America.'

All too often, however, hunting down 'the suppliers of terrorist blood money' meant hurting ordinary charities with humanitarian aims. When a spate of Hamas suicide attacks in Jerusalem and Tel Aviv between 25 February and 4 March 1996 resulted in fifty-nine deaths, the Israeli Ambassador to London, Moshe Raviv, requested a meeting at the office of the British Foreign Secretary Malcolm Rifkind in King Charles Street, London. The Israeli

Ambassador claimed to have clear evidence that a British-based charity was supporting Hamas and funding its campaign of terror. The accusations, which were similar to those published in the *Daily Express* the following day, claimed that bombing campaigns in Israel were being funded by cells operating in the United Kingdom.

The Israeli Ambassador presented Rifkind with signed documents purportedly sent by the London-based charity Interpal to the head of a charity run by Dr Suleiman Igbarieh, the Mayor of Umm Al Fahem, the largest town in Galilee. Commenting on the document, a British Foreign Office official told me: 'Nothing in the information supplied to us through our diplomatic channels contains enough evidence to pursue or make any arrests of a member of Hamas or its sympathizers.'

Nevertheless, the Council of British Jews called on the government to close down all British organizations which had any connections to Hamas and targeted two London-based publications: *Filisteen Al Muslima* ('Islamic Palestine'), published in Arabic, and the English language *Palestine Times*. But it was 'Interpal', the abbreviated name for the International Palestinian Relief and Development Fund, which came in for the heaviest criticism. The Board of Deputies of British Jews published a report on its website in September 2003, describing Interpal as a 'terrorist organization'. This accusation led the charity to file a libel suit demanding an apology for the slur.[40]

Interpal grew out of consultations between active members of the Muslim community in the UK, including Yusuf Islam, the 1970s international heart-throb and folk-singing star formerly known as Cat Stevens, and Bashir Azam, OBE. Despite describing Interpal as a 'well-run and committed organization', the British Charity Commission felt obliged to freeze the Fund's bank accounts in August 2003, while carrying out a thorough investigation of what the USA had labelled a 'Specially Designated Global Terrorist organization' (SDGT).[41] The head of Interpal, Abdul Rahman Dia, speaking to me at the time of the alleged scandal, remarked that one positive outcome was that, within two weeks, Interpal had become 'the most famous Islamic charity in Britain, and this is reflected in the scale of our donations'.

The British Charity Commission found no credible evidence to link Interpal with terrorism, despite five weeks of investigation; it subsequently gave the charity the all-clear. Following an out-of-court settlement, the Board of Deputies of British Jews issued a statement, saying, 'We would like to make it clear that we should not have described Interpal [as a terrorist organization] in this way and we regret the upset and distress our item caused.'[42] It also formally declared not to republish the allegation at any time in the future. The *Jerusalem Post*, which published an article titled 'UK Bank Sued in US for Serving Hamas',[43] was also forced to apologize to Interpal. That apology came six months later.[44]

The decision by the American administration to freeze the assets of 'the Holy Land Foundation' devastated the family of Ahmed Abu Al Kheir. The charity had been providing a small but for them significant monthly sum of money to help the family of eleven. The amount was between US$55 and US$85 each month. Ahmed, aged forty-nine, had been paralysed in an accident. When he heard about the freeze, he asked his wife to go to the Zakat Committee in Nablus to confirm whether the rumours were true. She was not given a satisfactory response. Abu Kheir's family is one of hundreds of Palestinian families in Nablus who receive regular assistance from the US-based Holy Land Foundation. The Head of the Zakat Committee in Nablus, Dr Abdul Rahim Al Hanbali, said, 'The American foundation looks after many poor families, orphans, disabled Palestinians, and students whose families cannot afford to educate them.' But Hanbali said that this assistance did not serve Hamas directly, rather it served the Islamic principles that Hamas and other Islamic movements were trying to preserve. Commenting on the asset freeze, US President George W. Bush said: 'The Holy Land Foundation funds are used by Hamas to support schools that serve Hamas' ends by encouraging children to become suicide bombers and to recruit suicide bombers by offering support to families.'[45]

Hamas has denied any direct links with the Holy Land Foundation, and its leaders have consistently and strenuously denied that they receive financial support from Arab and Islamic governments, Unlike its predecessor, the Palestinian Authority, Hamas has a reasonable reputation for financial transparency and admits to relying heavily on donations from individuals or institutions in the Gulf States or from Palestinians and Arabs in the global Diaspora. Despite denials from Hamas, the USA and Israel have repeatedly claimed that charitable donations received by Hamas are further channelled to its military wing. Mohammed Anati, the Director of the Holy Land Foundation who was questioned by the Israeli authorities, denied the accusation. Israel has not revealed any documents to support their claim. As for Abu Al Kheir, sitting in his poorly maintained house in Nablus, he declared America to be 'the worst country in the world. It supports Sharon and fights the Palestinians.' His wife told me: 'We are poor. We have nothing to do with Hamas and its politics. This Zakat Committee used to give us a few dinars to save us from starving, but now they have cut off our aid.'

Saudi Arabia and other Gulf States have been widely criticized by Israel and America for their system of zakat, allowing Muslims to donate money to Islamic charities operating in many troubled regions of the world, from Afghanistan through to the West Bank and Gaza. Prince Al Walid Bin Talal of Saudi Arabia issued a press release in April 2002, following discussions with the Palestinian President, Yasser Arafat, admitting that he had donated 100 million Saudi Rials – US$26.5 million, half of it in cash – to help the Palestinians rebuild their infrastructure, which had been destroyed by the Israeli army. The other half of the donation was given in clothes and transportation for Palestinian institutions.[46] The Saudi government has long denied either encouraging Palestinians to carry out military attacks against Israel or sending money to the families of Palestinians who had participated in suicide missions. The Saudi government's statements do use the word 'martyrs' to describe Palestinian victims caught up in the conflict with Israel but deny allegations which link Saudi Arabia to funding the families of suicide bombers, describing them as 'misleading and an attempt to drive attention away from crimes committed by Israel against the Palestinians'.

An American newspaper, quoting a Saudi news agency,[47] published an article in which the Saudi Interior Minister, Prince Nayef Bin Abdul Aziz, was said to have sanctioned US$5,300 per family from the Saudi budget to support more than a hundred Palestinian families who had taken part in the Intifada. The newspaper went on to say that Saudi Arabia had joined Iraqi President Saddam Hussein in giving financial support to the families of Palestinian suicide bombers. The Iraqi government had always encouraged suicide bombing attacks against Israel, giving each family US$ 25,000. The families of Palestinians killed in day-to-day fighting with Israel would receive US$10,000.[48] Iraq distributed the money through the Arab Liberation Front in Gaza and West Bank, a local organization with links to the Iraqi Ba'ath Party, and one of the founding members of the Palestine Liberation Organization.

A report prepared by the Israeli Administration in the Gaza Strip in June 2003 named three main societies in Gaza – Al Islah, Al Jumayeh Islamia and the Islamic Compound, founded by Sheikh Ahmed Yassin – which received tens of millions of dollars annually from abroad. One million dollars it claimed was handed out monthly to needy families and large amounts of money were received from Iran and Israeli Arabs who donated generously.[49] According to Sheikh Ahmad Al Kurd, the head of Al Islah Society in Gaza, his organization donates money according to a scale of one-off payments, which depend on the circumstances of the families: $5,300 is given to families whose bread-winner has been killed or has suffered long-term injuries and is unable to work; $1,300 is given to the wounded and $2,650 to families whose home has been destroyed or damaged. Families of prisoners receive $2,600. To put this into context, according to the United Nations, more than half of the Palestinian population are living below the poverty line, so they survive on less than $2 a day.

Ziad Abu Amr, an independent member of the Palestinian Legislative Council, told Human Rights Watch that, in his capacity as head of the political committee in the Palestinian Legislative Council, he had conducted an audit on the accounts of the largest charity connected to Hamas in Gaza, the Al Islah Society, whose offices Arafat had closed in December 2001. Al Islah has large amounts of money but, Amr stressed, 'We didn't find any wrongdoing.' His complaints to Arafat that 'we couldn't find anything suspicious' were met with the response: 'Hamas' military activities must be funded by foreign countries like Iran.' Arafat was convinced that Hamas was abusing the financial support it received for its social programmes to fund their political agenda and military ambitions.

Hamas leader Ibrahim Al Yazuri said the movement was striving to liberate all of Palestine from Israeli occupation. 'That is our main concern but our social provisions are instrumental to achieving this goal.' Documents removed by the Israeli army from the offices of the Palestinian Authority in April and May 2001 showed that sums of money were received from a Saudi committee headed by Prince Nayef Bin Abdul Aziz and used to support the Al Aqsa Intifada, the money was sent to a zakat charity committee in Tulkarem in the West Bank. According to the documents, the money was distributed to fourteen local charities, many with links to Hamas' social projects giving money or food to the needy. Psychiatrist and human-rights activist Dr Iyad Al Sarraj told me that, while he strongly condemned suicide bombings, he supported families in need. 'I can't let children suffer just because their fathers carry out missions like this. I will do whatever I can in my professional capacity to give these kids some hope and dignity.'

Weakening Hamas became Washington's top priority. When Secretary of State Colin Powell travelled to Damascus to discuss the issue of terrorist sanctuary with President Bashar Al Assad in April 2003, he emerged from the three-hour meeting with a pledge from the Syrian President to close down the offices of Hamas and restrict their communications. Three months later, Powell told a news conference that Hamas provides 'good works' for the Palestinians and could be reformed … but unfortunately, it's good works are contaminated by the fact that it has a terrorist wing that kills innocent people and kills the hopes of the Palestinian people for a state of their own.'[50]

The View from the West Wing

'There is no plan; there is no plot,' a State Department spokesman[51] emphatically announced in an attempt to brush off a US newspaper report, which claimed that America and Israel were planning to isolate, destabilize and ultimately bring down the new Hamas government, by starving the Palestinian Authority of cash.[52] The State Department reiterated the Quartet's position that Hamas must recognize Israel's right to exist, renounce terror and accept past agreements which the Palestinians have reached with Israel. 'We are not having conversations with the Israelis that we are not having with others, including the Quartet,' it confirmed with finality.

Plot or no plot, at 4 p.m. GMT on 29 March 2006, the USA severed diplomatic and financial ties with the newly sworn-in Hamas government. While communications would still be permitted with non-Hamas members of the Palestinian Parliament and with the office of President Mahmoud Abbas, an email was sent to every American diplomat and contractor ordering them to cease any cooperation with Hamas-appointed government ministers. America's labelled rebels had already been on the State Department's list of 'Foreign Terrorist Organizations' for several years and therefore subject to American law, which bars the US government from providing direct assistance to the named organizations. The October 2005 list included Al Qaeda, Shining Path, the Tamil Tigers, Hezbollah and several Palestinian factions, including, of course, Hamas. Such a decision by the USA was received in the Arab and Islamic world as yet another example of Washington siding with Israel. The American government would rather look the other way than condemn Israel for its atrocities against the Arab world, and had similarly failed to force Tel Aviv to abide by UN resolutions calling for Israeli withdrawal from the Arab-occupied territories as defined by the 1967 war.

Fortunately for the first elected Hamas government, it is well-equipped with US-trained economists, engineers and planners to handle the financial straitjacket being zipped up around it. In a Cabinet of twenty-four, seven Hamas MP's obtained their university degrees and Ph.D.s in the USA, including Finance Minister Omar Abdul Razzak, who gained a BA with majors in Mathematics, Economics and Computer Science at Coe College, Iowa, followed by a Ph.D. in Economics at Iowa State University. Reminiscing about his university years, where his first-year roommate was Jewish, he sighed: 'They were the best four years in my life, actually.'[53]

Razzak went on to become an economics professor at Nablus University. Of the others, Abdul Rahman Zeidan, Minister of Transportation, gained a BA in Civil Engineering at the University of Alabama; Sameer Abu Eishah, the Minister of Planning, also studied Civil Engineering at Pennsylvania State University; Aziz Duwaik, Speaker of the Palestinian Parliament, gained an MA in Geography at the State University of New York at Binghamton and a Ph.D. in Regional Science at the University of Pennsylvania; Wasfi Kabaha, Minister of Prisoners and Released Prisoners' Affairs, has a BS in Civil Engineering from the University of Detroit; Nasser Al Shaer, Deputy Prime Minister and Minister of Education, was an Institute Fellow at the Multinational Institute of American Studies, New York University, where he studied American History; Moussa Abu Marzouk, Deputy Chief of the Hamas political bureau based in Damascus, obtained an MA in Industrial Science at Colorado State University and also studied Engineering at Louisiana Tech University. Born in 1951 in Rafiah refugee camp in Gaza, Abu Marzouk completed an Engineering foundation course in Egypt before travelling to the USA in 1974 to continue his studies. Between 1981 and 1982, he lived in Falls Church, Virginia, during which time he was elected head of the political bureau of Hamas.

Almost three years before Hamas swept to power, a suicide bomber detonated his five-kilogram device, packed with ball bearings, on a No 2 Egged bus as it passed through Jerusalem's Shmuel Hanavi neighbourhood, killing twenty-three people and wounding more than 130. Many of the passengers had been returning from prayers at the Western Wall. Three days later, on 22 August 2003, President George Bush announced that the US Treasury was labelling six senior Hamas leaders and five Hamas-related charities as SDGTs – Specially Designated Global Terrorists. The six individual SDGTs were named as Sheikh Ahmed Yassin, the leader of Hamas in Gaza; Imad Khalil Al Alami, a member of the Hamas political bureau in Damascus; Osama Hamdan, a senior Hamas leader in Lebanon; Khalid Mishal, head of Hamas' political bureau in Damascus; Abdul Aziz Rantisi, a Hamas leader in Gaza reporting to Sheikh Yassin and Moussa Abu Marzouk, Deputy Chief of the political bureau in Damascus.

Abu Marzouk was arrested in New York on 25 July 1995 and held on an unspecified charge for twenty-two months without trial. The unofficial accusation against him was that he was a 'terrorist'. Within ten days of his arrest, the Labour government of Shimon Peres made a request to the USA to extradite Abu Marzouk to Israel. The extended period of his vague confinement was to give Israel sufficient time to present legal documents to support their extradition charge. They failed to produce anything which carried enough weight and, when elected as Israeli President in May 1996, Benjamin Netanyahu did not pursue his predecessor's request. On occasion, Abu Marzouk's jailors would allow him to speak to the media but they became concerned by his inflammatory statements against Israel and his fighting rhetoric. 'They asked me to acknowledge my involvement with Hamas as a condition to free me,' recalled Abu Marzouk.[54] During the entire period of his incarceration, he claimed he was never questioned by any investigator. A letter addressed to Janet Reno, the Attorney General, from Secretary of State Madeleine Albright expressed concerns that Mr Marzouk's prolonged presence in the United States would 'seriously undermine compelling foreign policy objectives in the Middle East and in the fight against terrorism'. American officials retrospectively realized that the 'terrorist' charge would create a problem for them if, through insufficient evidence, they were forced to release him. Eventually, on 25 April 1997, Abu Marzouk signed an agreement with the American administration which stated the conditions of his release: that he left American soil forever, refrained from initiating any legal action against the US government while seeking compensation for his confinement and desisted from making any press statements. First, though, America had to find a mutually acceptable country which would take him. Their obvious choice was either Jordan or Egypt. According to Abu Marzouk, a delegation from the FBI visited both countries prior to his discharge and requested that they prevent him from carrying out political activities and insist that he renounce violence towards Israel. Both governments turned down the American request.[55] King Hussein of Jordan personally agreed to receive the SDGT and, on 5 May 1997, he was freed.

Hamas didn't register on America's political radar until the series of suicide bomb attacks in Israel which brought Netanyahu, Israel's youngest Prime Minister, to power in 1996. Until then, none of the American officials or secretaries of state or even US President Bill

Clinton had intimated that the Hamas issue was of major concern to them.

While President Clinton was trying to broker an elusive peace between the Israelis and the Palestinians, the FBI was secretly funnelling money to suspected Hamas members in a sting operation to see whether the money would be used to fund terror attacks. The FBI's 1998– 1999 counter-terrorism operation was run from its Phoenix, Arizona bureau in coordination with Israeli intelligence and, according to FBI officials, was approved by the Attorney General, Janet Reno.[56] Several thousands of US dollars were sent to suspected Hamas supporters during the operation as the FBI tried to 'track the flow of cash'. It was a rare acknowledgement of an undercover sting that resulted in no prosecutions.

Officially, America has no contact with SDGT organizations, and rumours that the CIA were covertly in touch with Hamas were brushed off by a former senior US policy adviser I spoke to with the comment. 'The CIA barely [even] talks to Fatah! Israel has the power of veto over whom the CIA in the West Bank and Gaza meets,' he said. 'That's the working relationship between the US and Israel.' He made a distinction between Hamas having contact with 'the Americans' and Hamas having contact with 'the American government'. He named Martin Burton, a former CIA officer, Graham E. Fuller, former Vice-Chairman of the National Intelligence Council at the CIA, and Fred Hof, Former Staff Director of the Mitchell Commission, as Americans who had had discussions with Hamas. They were not flouting the law because they were former government officials. The intention of these 'within the law' meetings was essentially an intelligence-gathering operation. Two such meetings were held on 21– 22 March and 23– 24 July 2005 in Beirut, organized by Alastair Crooke, a former MI6 senior officer. By listening to what Hamas had to say and establishing a relationship with them, they could inform policy-makers in Washington what Hamas was thinking and, more importantly, planning. 'Our discussions were quite detailed,' the US policy adviser continued. 'We talked about how Hamas viewed the resistance; how they defend suicide bombings; what their political position is and under what circumstances they would deal and negotiate with Israel; how they viewed Fatah; and what they intended to do if they were to take office.

The Hamas victory came as a tremendous jolt which rocked the foundations of George W. Bush's administration at a time when it was championing the US war against terror and promoting democracy in the Middle East. In a keynote speech delivered in 2002 from the Rose Garden of the White House, Bush announced a set of conditions which Palestinian Arabs had to fulfil in order to merit US support for the creation of a Palestinian state. Among the major obligations was that Palestinians must 'elect new leaders, leaders not compromised by terror'.[57] Four years later, these words fell on stony ground. The Palestinians made their uncompromising choice, forcing the administration to adopt a balancing act: accepting that they had exercised their democratic choice, while describing it as a protest vote against their previous leadership, which had been tainted by corruption and bad governance. When George Bush was asked if these ambitions were now dead during a White House press conference, he tried his best to sound optimistic: 'Peace is never dead because people want peace. The best hope for peace in the Middle East is two democracies living side by side.' Bush added, 'I don't see how you can be a partner in peace if you advocate the destruction of a country as part of your platform. And I know you can't be a partner in peace if your party has got an armed wing.'[58]

The USA claims to have spent more than US$1.7 billion in the West Bank and Gaza since 1993 to combat poverty, improve infrastructure and promote good governance. Dennis Ross, former Special Envoy to the Middle East under President Clinton, said that Washington was unlikely to change its position on Hamas. 'The only way you will see the administration make an effort to stay involved, is if there is a common front with the international community to insist on a set of standards that Hamas would have to meet if they are to have relations, or be royally receiving material assistance from the outside.' Ross added: 'Hamas did not expect to win the election. They hoped to take over the Palestinian Authority in time. Now they have to deal with the consequences of their success.'[59]

Just as Sharm Al Sheikh provides neutral territory on which to thrash out the Palestinian-Israeli conflict, Doha in the Gulf state of

Qatar plays host to the annual US-Islamic World Forum. 'The stability and prosperity of the Islamic world should be of great importance to the international community, as it represents twenty-seven per cent of the global population,' announced Sheikh Hamad Bin Khalifa Al Thani on 10 April 2005 at the opening of the 2005 gathering, whose guest list from Algeria to Uzbekistan reads like an A– Z of key figures in the world of business, politics, media, academia and civil society. The aim of the Forum is to generate dialogue and prevent discourse between the West and the Islamic world.

Former US Ambassador to Israel, Martin Indyk, Senior Fellow in Foreign Policy Studies at the Brookings Institution and an expert in the Arab-Israeli conflict, gave two different examples of moderate Islam as highlighted at the Forum. One came from Kazi Hussein Ahmad, the Emir of Jama'at-e Islami, the Pakistani branch of the Muslim Brotherhood. Ahmad, considered to be one of the moderate Sunni leaders in Pakistan, told the conference: 'Dialogue is possible for people of all faiths, including Christians and Jews.' But the balance was redressed by Sheikh Youssef Al Karadawi, who has been described as the most influential contemporary Sunni scholar, well-known for his fatwas on many issues relating to politics, women and social concerns. He is progressive and condemned the 9/11 attacks, and many believe that he represents a credible alternative to radical Islam. However, he appeared to toe the more extreme line with the words: 'We can talk to the Christians but we can't talk to the Jews. They are occupying Palestine and until they are no longer in occupation of Palestine, we can't have any dialogue with them.' Al Karadawi called on the USA to make a choice between 'Extreme Islam' and 'Liberal Islam'. Putting himself firmly in the camp of 'Liberal Islam', he said: 'We represent it along with the Muslim Brotherhood worldwide.'

Many Arab intellectuals who have had relationships with consecutive US administrations, believe Washington would prefer to deal with Hamas rather than Fatah or other nationalist factions, provided that Hamas agrees to become part of the political process. The US administration is keen to foster an Islamic Sunni movement which would side with them and with which it could be on good terms – as is the case with the mainstream Sunni movements, namely the Muslim Brotherhood in Jordan, Iraq and Egypt, in order to confront the extreme Islamic elements of both Sunni and Shia sects such as Hezbollah, Al Qaeda and their affiliates.

Martin Indyk, was the US Ambassador to Israel from 1995 to 1997 and then again from 2000 to 2001. Prior to that, he was President Clinton's Middle East adviser at the National Security Council and was responsible for handling the 1993 Oslo signing ceremony. Recalling the moment when Hamas first came to his attention, he said it was early on in the Clinton administration, around 1993, when a diplomat attached to the American Embassy in Tel Aviv who was responsible for the Gaza Strip, had gone to Gaza to meet with a Hamas official. 'I received a call from the Deputy National Security Advisor, Sandy Berger, saying, "What the hell's going on? How come we've got somebody meeting with a Hamas official?" I was in the White House in those days and I said, "Gee, I don't know anything about it." But as a consequence of that meeting, a decision was made at the beginning of the Clinton administration, that there would be no political contact with Hamas.'[60]

The Spy Who Went into the Heat

The West had only three options in dealing with Islamist organizations, according to Alastair Crooke, former Middle East adviser to European Union High Representative Javier Solana. 'We can bomb them, we can ignore them, or we can talk to them. By now the evidence should be clear: the first option has not [worked] and cannot work, while the second is simply a defence of intellectual laziness.'[61]

Crooke favoured the third option. For more than five years, he acted as mediator between Palestinian groups like Hamas, providing Britain, which is officially forbidden to talk to those on the 'terrorist list', with its only link with the organization. The former senior spy for MI6, who spent three decades as one of Britain's intermediaries where he became acquainted with militias in Pakistan, Afghanistan, Namibia, and Northern Ireland, found himself sipping mint tea with members of Hamas on behalf of the EU.

Crooke compared the USA to a juggernaut: 'It is possible to move it but, because of its unwieldy size, it will take time. This can be equated with foreign policy where we don't expect a change overnight.' He has been described as 'brave to the point of madness' for shunning the safety of armoured CIA vehicles, in favour of travelling unarmed by local taxis to shuttle between the West Bank and the Gaza Strip. Crooke was also a key figure in putting together a ceasefire agreed by Hamas in 2002 which he hoped would put an end to the rash of suicide bombings. The deal was scuppered when Israel assassinated Salah Shehada, the Hamas military commander, in an aerial attack on his home.

Despite the delicate links forged by Crooke between the Israeli military and the intelligence service of Hamas, many Israelis and Palestinians were suspicious of the Graham Greene-style Brit. One who particularly distrusted him was Mohammed Dahlan, the Palestinian Authority's security minister who felt Crooke showered too much attention on Hamas. According to Hamas insiders, Sheikh Yassin made the assumption that anything he told Crooke would be immediately passed to the Israeli government, and consequently would deliberately feed disinformation to the Middle East negotiator. Yassin would caution his senior advisers, particularly if they had any connection to the military wing, to be wary of talking to Alastair Crooke, and he transmitted similar warnings to Hamas leaders in the West Bank.

The Hamas meeting was attended by Sheikh Yassin, Dr Abdul Aziz Rantisi and Dr Mahmoud Zahar, and the minutes were taken by Mohammed Al Najjar. Parallel meetings were held abroad. Crooke was heavily involved in the arrangements for the ceasefire, which was negotiated by Hamas and the PA and announced in Egypt on 29 June 2003. He stressed the importance of understanding the views of Hamas, saying, 'the EU was in favour of following a policy which would ease the tension and diffuse the violence.'

Crooke was cautious that the meetings should be kept secret to prevent Israel and the US from 'taking advantage of such information'. However, he assumed Israel was aware of such meetings, 'because they were watching everyone who was communicating with Sheikh Yassin or visiting his house, and these meetings took place there'. The 'secret' eventually became public after documents seized by the Israeli army from the Palestinian Authority Preventive Security

Compound in Gaza in November 2002 were found to contain transcripts of the clandestine meetings, written in Arabic on Palestinian Authority headed notepaper.[2] The transcripts revealed that Crooke congratulated the Hamas organization for its welfare programmes and for being an important political factor, saying 'The main problem is the Israeli occupation.' He added that it was necessary to initiate trust-building measures and a mutual lowering of the level of violence, and Crooke assured Sheikh Yassin and the Hamas seniors that the Europeans were unequivocally opposed to Israel's settlement activities. On his side, Sheikh Yassin agreed that the root of the problem was the Israeli occupation, which, as he defined it, extends over the territories of 1948, not just 1967 (meaning the liberation of the entire territory of Palestine and not just the post-1967 'occupied territories'). Sheikh Yassin told Crooke that he was unhappy with the EU's decision to include Hamas on its list of terrorist organizations and asked that the Europeans support him and resist the American policy. Crook's response was: 'We do not consider Hamas' political wing to be a terrorist organization.'

In September the following year, the British Foreign Secretary, Jack Straw, ordered the MI6 agent to leave Jerusalem, claiming fears for his safety. Closer to the truth was that Straw was under pressure from Israel, who felt that the British negotiator was getting uncomfortably close to Hamas. Undaunted, the man with a mission for dialogue in peace building went on to coordinate an unusual pair of meetings held in Beirut's chic Hotel Albergo and an undisclosed location in the city in March and July 2005. Coordinated by Crooke and Dr Beverley Milton-Edwards, a specialist in Middle Eastern and Islamic politics at Queen's University, Belfast, the two-day meetings were attended by an august group of specialists in global conflicts together with members of Hamas, Hezbollah, Lebanon's Muslim Brotherhood and Pakistan's Jama'at-e Islami. Apart from representatives from political Islam, the eclectic gathering included a former UK Ambassador to Syria, a former station chief in Kabul, Afghanistan during the Afghan War, a key negotiator of the 1998 Good Friday Agreement, a former National Intelligence Chairman at the White House, an independent delegate from the Kingdom of Saudi Arabia, Chairman of the Board of the Vietnam Veterans of America Foundation and a former Executive Producer of the American investigative news programme *60 Minutes*, who joined other delegates from the Conflicts Forum.

Hamas has a shared ideology with its sister branches in the Muslim Brotherhood movement and Washington and London has enjoyed a warm relationship with the Brotherhood branches in Egypt, Jordan, Iraq and even Syria. Some see it as only being a matter of time before Hamas comes on board, as all the signs are hinting at a sea-change in the movement's attitude towards Israel. At the end of June 2006, Prime Minister Ismail Haniyeh announced Hamas' willingness in principle, to sign a document drawn up by Palestinians from all factions, that they accept the existence of Israel.

This recognition of the Jewish State by Hamas is exactly what the international community demanded following the movement's success in the Palestinian elections, but their olive branch appears to have gone unheeded or misunderstood. This was illuminated by Prime Minister Tony Blair, just one month after Haniyeh's announcement. Speaking to a gathering of the press at his monthly conference in Downing Street in August 2006, he described the Hamas situation as a 'conundrum' to be resolved. 'We recognize the mandate of a democratically elected people' but, he said, 'the negotiation cannot be taken forward unless it is on the basis that people accept Israel also has a right to exist.'

Made in Tehran

Getting arms to an organization whose military operations are based in Israeli-occupied Gaza and the West Bank is tricky, and has to be done through cooperation with non-Hamas actors outside the Palestinian territories. How countries like Iran get weapons through to Hamas is illustrated by the 'Santorini' incident.

The Mediterranean was particularly choppy on the morning of 6 May 2001, causing the *Santorini* to dip and rear in the swell of the turbulent waves. The twenty-five-metre fishing boat was being tracked by Cypriot, Syrian and Lebanese coastguards, because of reports that a vessel was in trouble in international waters. In reality, the *Santorini* was being refuelled after delays left it short of petrol. In addition to the extra fuel, it was being loaded with weapons from Zodiac inflatable craft, which were escorting the boat until it reached high seas. Radio communications between the ship's captain and the Mediterranean coastguards were intercepted by the Israelis who sent a navy plane to investigate. They reported back that the boat was behaving suspiciously for a fishing trawler. 'It was a fishing boat that was not fishing,' the commander of Israel's navy, Admiral Yedidia Ya'ari, said at his office in Camp Rabin, the headquarters of the Israel Defense Forces, in Tel Aviv.[63] The vessel was about 150 kilometres west of Tyre. They waited for the boat to head towards the Israeli coast before sending two Israeli missile boats, shortly joined by two attack boats from Flotilla Thirteen, the naval commando unit, then boarded the boat in international waters, meeting no resistance from the crew. They found thirty-nine barrel-loads of weapons which were to be dropped into the water off the Gaza coast at a pre-selected location.[64] The explosive cargo included fifty 107mm Katyusha missiles with a range of 8.5 kilometres, four SA-7 'Strella' anti-aircraft missiles with a four-kilometre range, twenty rocket-propelled grenade launchers (RPG), 120 anti-tank grenades, two 60mm mortars with ninety-eight mortar shells, seventy mines, thirty Kalashnikov assault rifles and some 13,000 rounds of 7.62 ammunition.[65]

Under interrogation, one of the *Santorini* crew, a Lebanese called Deeb Mohammed Rashid Oweida, told the Israelis that the smuggling operation involved twenty-five members of Hezbollah. Some of them secured the shore, while others participated in loading the weapons. Oweida had been involved in sourcing a suitable boat for the operation and had found a fishing boat called *Abed Al Hadi* in Arwad port in Syria. The deal to buy the boat was struck in the Shahin restaurant in Tartus, northern Syria, and a Syrian crew transferred it from Tartus to Tripoli port in Lebanon. The boat was then registered as Lebanese and the *Abed Al Hadi* was re-floated as the *Santorini*.[66]

Israeli intelligence were quick to suspect Lebanese-based Jihad Jibril, the son of Ahmed Jibril, leader of the PFLP-GC, whose headquarters were in Damascus. According to Fadel Chororo, a member of the PFLP-GC political bureau and its head of communications, previous shipments had successfully made their

way to Gaza and the Egyptian Sinai coast. He was uncertain of
the exact dates but said that from November 2000 three cargo-
loads of weapons had arrived at intervals of between fifteen days
and one month. The shipments had been delivered by the *Santorini*
and another boat named *Calypso 2*. Chororo blamed bad weather
and choppy conditions for this failed mission, creating difficulties
in loading the *Santorini* which subsequently aroused suspicion.
At a press conference in Damascus a few days later, Ahmed Jibril
proudly announced that the weapons belonged to his organization
and boasted of three previous successful deliveries of arms to the
Gaza coast. 'This was not the first shipment, nor will it be the last,'
he said defiantly. 'What we are doing is in fact legal and the PFLP-
GC had the right to arm the Palestinian people who are dying at
the hands of Israeli aggression.'[67] Other commanders within the
PFLP-GC freely admitted that they lacked a significant presence
in the West Bank and Gaza and had established links with Hamas
in order to support the armed struggle in the region. According
to Chororo, the first high-level meeting between leaders of Hamas
and the PFLP-GC took place in Lebanon straight after Israel had
expelled hundreds of Hamas activists and leaders to Marj Al Zahur
in Southern Lebanon in December 1992.

Chororo told me that meetings took place between leaders of
Hamas, who were amongst those who had been deported to Lebanon,
and Ahmed Jibril, in which they agreed to set up a committee to
coordinate activities in the West Bank and Gaza. Talal Naji, the
number two in the PFLP-GC, and Fadel Chororo both attended
the meeting. Dr Abdul Aziz Al Rantisi, subsequently assassinated
by the Israelis, and other senior Hamas leaders were also present.
Chororo himself was appointed to head the PFLP-GC side of the
committee, whilst Hamas would be represented by 'engineer' Imad
Al Alami. Al Alami is described by Israeli intelligence as the man
responsible for coordinating the activities of Hamas' military wing.

As a child, Jihad Jibril spent much of his time in military camps
in Lebanon and Syria. His father, Ahmed, gained notoriety for his
creative schemes to reach enemy targets. The PFLP-GC's prime
period of guerrilla activity had been during the 1970s and 1980s,
and it was the first organization to carry out kamikaze-style attacks.

In one such operation, a member of PFLP-GC flew a hang-glider into an Israeli base near Kiryat Shemona, killing six officers and soldiers on 28 November 1987. Jibril junior would follow his father from military camps in Lebanon to military camps in Syria and back again. Jihad survived numerous assassination attempts, until he was finally killed by a powerful car bomb in the Mar Elias district of Beirut on 20 May 2002.

Israeli generals, who had become concerned at the scale of Palestinian efforts to arm themselves, kept a watchful eye on those involved in the arms trade. At the top of their list was Jihad Jibril who, along with other Fatah commanders, was scouring the world's weapons markets, shopping for armaments which could be delivered to the closest point to the Palestinian territories. The obvious country was Iran, and Fatah and others cultivated a hotline to Hezbollah. Although Fatah had decided to go along with the peace process, failure in achieving any progress forced Arafat and his commanders to prepare for the worst, especially after Israel destroyed his military infrastructure which was supposed to have been protected under the peace treaty.

At noon on Monday 21 May 2002, Mar Elias, West Beirut's busy commercial centre, was rocked by a huge explosion. A white Peugeot parked in Al Umm Street (Mother Street) had disintegrated. Lebanese police said the bomb consisting of high-explosive plastic, equal to two kilograms of TNT, had been planted under the driver's seat and detonated by remote control. Once the billowing smoke from the explosion had cleared, the dead man was revealed as Jihad Jibril.

PFLP-GC leaders blamed Israel for the killing of Jihad, a charge which the Israeli Defense Minister Binyamin Ben Eliezer strongly denied. Ahmed Jibril, speaking to reporters at his headquarters in Damascus shortly after the assassination, said: 'This time Mossad managed to assassinate my son, having tried in vain four times before.' He told Qatar-based Al Jazeera television that his son had been supervising the training and arming of the Islamic Palestinian group Hamas, which would have been almost unthinkable some years ago for a radical movement such as PFLP-GC.

Jibril senior believed his son's killer was Hussein Khattab, a forty-year-old Palestinian from Lebanon's Ain Al Hilwa camp, who had been working undercover for the Israeli intelligence services. According to Fadel Chororo, Ahmed Jibril said that Khattab had been arrested by the Israelis in the early 1980s and was recruited by Mossad during his time in jail. He was released on 25 April 1985 during the prisoner exchange agreement with Israel that had freed Sheikh Ahmed Yassin, when the PFLP-GC traded three captured Israeli soldiers for 1,150 Palestinian and Lebanese prisoners held in Israeli jails. The International Red Cross had mediated the exchange.

The most infamous arms smuggling bust occurred on 3 January 2002, less than nine months after the Santorini episode. The Israeli navy seized a ship called *Karine-A* close to the Island of Kish, south of Iran, which turned out to contain fifty tonnes of weapons and was apparently bound for the Palestinian territories. According to the results of the investigation subsequently intiated by Israel, the weapons were part of an arms deal between Iran and Yasser Arafat's Palestinian Authority.

Illicit weapons finding their way into the Palestinian territories by land, sea and air from Jordan, Egypt and Lebanon as well as Iran do so in violation of the 1994 Gaza-Jericho Agreement.[68] Israel traced arms that had been brought into the territories in vehicles registered to Palestinian officials with VIP-1 status, granting them immunity from security checks. Smuggling weapons via land routes was highlighted by the arrest of a Jordanian truck driver, Abdul Basat Suleiman Dallasheh. He was caught at the Sheikh Hussein Bridge crossing near Beit She'an on 1 March 2001 while attempting to smuggle weapons from Jordan. Israeli customs officials found four Kalashnikov assault rifles, two M16 assault rifles, a Beretta 9-millimetre sub-machine gun and twenty handguns hidden in the fire extinguisher and air pump of Dallasheh's truck.

In another incident, on 25 June 2002, Israeli security forces intercepted a load of contraband weapons hidden in a truck with Israeli licence plates, at the Karni crossing-point between Israel and the Gaza Strip. The driver, an Arab resident of East Jerusalem, had unsuccessfully attempted to conceal an M16 assault rifle, a pistol and various types of ammunition. In October of the same year, Israeli police stopped a truck, which was on its way to Gaza and contained thousands of bullets hidden behind a double wall. Ali Abu Al Ragheb, the Jordanian Prime Minister, commenting on a haul of twenty-five mortars seized from a Lebanese man who had smuggled them into Jordan from Syria, apparently en route for the West Bank, said:

> In Jordan, we have seen many cases where there has been some smuggling of arms or ammunition ... to various factions through Jordan or to Jordan and it's not new ... We deal with these issues maybe on a monthly basis and it depends on the size and maybe the last one was a big one compared to others.[69]

8

Fiction Precedes Fact: The Al Qaeda Connection

Shortly after sunset on 24 April 2006, three virtually simultaneous explosions ripped apart the Al Capone restaurant, the Ghazala supermarket and a wooden footbridge popular with early evening strollers in the Sinai beach resort of Dahab. Masonry, furniture and lethal shards of glass rained down on horrified tourists as they settled down to dinner or idled amongst the souvenir shops of Dahab's bazaars. A tranquil day spent diving amongst the coral reefs of the Gulf of Aqaba exploded into a violent evening of terror and panic.

Dahab, meaning 'gold' in Arabic, had morphed from a quiet Bedouin fishing village into an idyll for scuba divers and young travellers. The nineteen people who died that night were predominantly Egyptians, enjoying the twin holidays of the ancient festival of Shem Al Nassim, which celebrates the first day of spring, and Coptic Easter.[1] An estimated ninety tourists of many nationalities were wounded.[2]

Tourism is Egypt's largest-foreign currency earner and it would inevitably become a prime target for any organization intent on economic and human destruction. The use of simultaneous explosions and targeting tourists has become the deadly trademark of the multinational Islamic fundamentalist network, Al Qaeda. Tourist havens in Bali, Kenya and Turkey have witnessed the devastating effects of the organization's handiwork and the Dahab attacks also bore the hallmarks of Al Qaeda. Similarities between the Dahab bombings and those in nearby Sinai resorts – Taba in October 2004, which killed thirty-four people, and Sharm El Sheikh in July 2005, with eighty-eight deaths – forced the Egyptian security services to accept that local Bedouin terrorist groups were to blame, while stopping short of admitting an Al Qaeda connection with a nervous tourism industry to protect.

The Sinai Bedouin, traditionally cattle and goat herders, have seen their pastoral way of life eroded by the Egyptian government which, since the mid 1980s, has aggressively exploited Egypt's palm-fringed coastal areas by building lucrative resorts on former Bedouin land, with little recompense to this largely marginalized community. Hotels prefer to bring in their own employees and have no use for the Bedouin's traditional skills. Seashore hotels consume a large amount of water, tapping into the local supply and supplementing it with desalination plants. The Bedouin are left with little to drink or irrigate their land, forcing them away from the coast to settle in the mountainous regions of southern Sinai.[3] Some eke out a living as camel drivers, offering tourists a taste of their cultural way of life. But the mountain landscape provides cover for a more lucrative trade. Many have been tempted into drugs trafficking and arms smuggling via the nearby Rafiah border, supplying the black marketeers of the lawless Gaza Strip.

Al Tawhid Wa Al Jihad (Unity and Jihad), an affiliate of Al Qaeda, became the prime suspects for the blasts. The organization was formed by Khalid Moussaed in the year 2000, with members of the Suwarka Bedouin tribe, which had a long history of resistance against the Israeli occupation of Sinai between 1967 and 1973. The Egyptian Ministry of the Interior stated that security forces first concentrated their search around Jebel Maghara, meaning Mountain of Caves, in Northern Sinai. This area is known to the security forces as a haven for outcast Bedouins like Salim El-Shannoub, nicknamed 'the mountain devil', whose curriculum vitae includes arms dealing, drug smuggling and people trafficking.[4] After a gun battle lasting a few hours, in which six terrorist suspects and a police officer were killed, Egyptian anti-terrorist squads finally cornered several Bedouins holding out in the desert caves of Mount Halal.[5] Mohammed Shahta was subsequently arrested on 29 April 2006, when he confessed to driving the three suicide bombers to Dahab, concealed in his fruit van. Ibrahim Al Sowarki was another taken in for questioning. His brother Atallah was named as one of the bombers. Al Sowarki tipped off the security forces, suggesting they should also concentrate their search 100 kilometres west of Dahab, amongst the caves of the craggy mountains of southern Sinai, where the Jabaliya Bedouin tribe have made their home.[6]

Further clues linking Al Tawhid Wa Al Jihad to Al Qaeda were uncovered during that mountain raid in the form of CD recordings of speeches and declarations made by Al Qaeda's notorious trinity – Osama Bin Laden, his deputy, Ayman Al Zawahiri, and the head of the organization in Iraq, Abu Musab Al Zarqawi.[7] These global electronic communications are periodically aired on various Arab satellite channels and Internet sites, with their familiar call to all Muslims to support Al Qaeda and 'resist a war against Islam'. Bin Laden reiterated these words in a videotape recording transmitted by Al Jazeera television on Sunday 23 April 2006, one day before the deadly Dahab bombings.

The dust was still settling in Dahab when follow-up suicide missions targeted members of the Multinational Force and Observers (MFO) based in the Sinai desert. Their role is to monitor Egyptian Border Guards along the twelve-kilometre border Egypt shares with Gaza.[8] The first would-be assassin ran in front of a passing military vehicle leaving Al Gorah Airport. Thirty-five minutes later, the second detonated his bomb while riding his bicycle towards an Egyptian police vehicle, close to the town of Al Arish. Only the bombers were killed in the botched attempt. This attack fitted the now familiar pattern set by the Taba and Sharm bombings, when the MFO became targets in the aftershocks. One of the failed assassins was named as Eid Salameh Al Taraweh, who was positively identified by his wife, Salwa, despite denials from his brothers.

Egyptian police reported that Al Taraweh, from the coastal city of Al Arish in north-east Sinai, was a commander for Al Tawhid

Wa Al Jihad and the engineer behind the earlier Taba and Sharm El Sheikh explosions.[9] He was on the police wanted list for more than eighteen months after they linked him to the stolen vehicle which had exploded at the Taba Hilton Hotel. Al Taraweh's role was to select the suicide bombers and prepare the explosives for the bombing missions. Explosives like TNT are either smuggled or extracted from old mines and army weapons abandoned in the desert after the Six Day War of 1967 and the Egyptian campaigns of the two world wars. Under cover of the chaos created by the bombings, Al Taraweh fled with other members of the terrorist group, into the desert around the Bedouin town of Rafiah, a frontier town bordering the Gaza Strip.[10] They remained there for some time before returning to Al Arish to regroup with their emir, Khalid Moussaed. Al Taraweh was again appointed chief coordinator for what was to be their next target, the resort town of Sharm El Sheikh.

Nasser Khamis Al Mallahi, the suspected ringleader of the triple Dahab attacks and leader of the group Al Tawhid Wa Al Jihad, was killed three weeks later in a shoot-out with Egyptian police in an olive grove south of Al Arish following a tip-off. Automatic rifles and hand grenades were recovered and an accomplice, Mohammed Abdullah Abu Grair, was arrested.[11]

Despite the Egyptian security forces' reluctance to confirm any direct relationship between the bombers and Al Qaeda, a statement issued by the Ministry of the Interior accepted that Al Qaeda had exported its methods and ideologies which in turn have been taken up by individual terrorist franchises scattered throughout the world including countries in the Horn of Africa,[12] Yemen, Mali, and Indonesia. He added that the local extremist group responsible for the Egyptian Sinai attacks had most probably implemented Al Qaeda's *modus operandi* through videotaped declarations made by Bin Laden and Al Zawahiri, thus strengthening its ties with the terrorist network.

Egypt's diplomatic unease with the Hamas movement was due to the safe passage and protection that Hamas accorded to some of those involved in the two-year wave of suicide bomb attacks against resorts in the Sinai between 2004 and 2006. Egypt's displeasure was articulated by the Egyptian intelligence chief General Suleiman, to Said Siam, Hamas' Interior Minister, on his debut trip to Cairo a few weeks later. The meeting took place on 27 May 2006, in Suleiman's private office within a vast complex of buildings on the scale of a small city. Egypt's State Security Intelligence Headquarters has occupied this site in the Al Qubbah district of east Cairo since the 1950s, when an underground tunnel network was built to connect the complex to Al Qubbah's Presidential Palace. Suleiman presented Siam with documents detailing the plot behind the Sinai attacks. Amongst the evidence were confessions made by three Hamas members who were arrested by the Egyptian security forces. Suleiman told Siam: 'On the one hand, you ask us to help you while, on the other hand, you are meddling in our internal affairs.'

Suleiman was ready with a conclusive portfolio detailing the exact involvement of Hamas members, including their names and movements. Siam was left red-faced. Egypt confirmed that, following the triple bombings in Dahab, three Hamas members had been arrested, who had admitted they had links with the Islamic radical organization Al Tawhid Wa Al Jihad. Suleiman named Yusri Muhareb as one of those behind the attacks. Yusri had entered the Gaza Strip via the underground tunnel network assisted by Hamas members, including Magid Al Deery, where he trained in explosives and weapons technology. Egyptian security forces stated that Yusri and his brothers Munir and Ayman Muhareb were all directly linked to Islamic radical Palestinians. Munir was killed by Egyptian security forces on 1 May 2006. A statement issued by the Egyptian Ministry of the Interior said, 'The group leader, Nasser Khamis Al Mallahi, sent some of his assistants to Palestine for explosives training, including Ahmed Mohammed Al Kereimy, Mohammed Abdulaziz Nafia and Attalla Al Ghiram – the three suicide bombers who carried out the Dahab resort operations.'

Tamir Al Nusayrat, a highly experienced Hamas explosives expert, was smuggled into Egypt by Al Mallahi, the head of Al Tawhid Wa Al Jihad. Nusayrat had connections to Yusri Muhareb, one of the three brothers involved in the planning of the attack to carry out further offensives inside Egypt. Palestinian Abu Suleiman, a frequent visitor to the country, provided Yusri with $1,000 plus a mobile phone with a SIM card connected to an Israeli network. The same SIM card had been used by his brother Munir, to whom Abu Suleiman had also given funds amounting to $500.

The Sinai Bedouin play an influential role in the underground smuggling trade with Palestinians in the Gaza Strip. A network of tunnels running from the Rafiah region of Gaza across the border into Egypt began to emerge in 1982, shortly after Israel's withdrawal from Sinai in compliance with the Camp David Accords.[13] The majority of the Palestinian tunnellers, shunting goods from one side to the other, were young men under twenty years old. For some, it was simply a job with pay, while for others it was a passport to join the resistance. The Palestinian smugglers operated in coordination with their Egyptian counterparts in this illegal cross-border enterprise. Palestinian fighters became experts in the field of explosives manufacture, producing their own from urea ammonium nitrate fertilizer.

Initially, the tunnels were used to smuggle gold, drugs, fertilizers and cigarettes between the two borders, out of sight of the ever-watchful eyes of the Israeli Defense Force. Less conventional goods are also known to have been ferried along the narrow, underground passages like the ostrich and python which stocked the tiny Rafiah Zoo, one of the few recreational places for children.[14] But the zoo no longer exists, having been destroyed by Israeli bulldozers in 2004. Many animals were crushed in their cages, while the lucky ones escaped. The co-owner of the private zoo, Mohammed Ahmed Juma, accused the Israelis of stealing his valuable African Parrots.[15] An IDF spokesman denied destroying the zoo saying: 'It was a very small petting zoo close to a school and the animals just escaped somehow. We didn't hurt them.'[16] I was told by a member of the Al Aburish family in Rafiah that some animals which survived the Israeli bulldozers were rounded up and smuggled back along the claustrophobic tunnels to Egypt. Perhaps there was a happy ending after all for the monkeys, crocodiles, jaguars and snakes reported missing by Mr Juma.[17]

As violence escalated during the second Palestinian Intifada and the sea routes of the Mediterranean and Red Sea used by smugglers were under stricter surveillance, the majority of goods crisscrossing the ever-expanding subterranean network were weapons. The driving force for smugglers was not politics or patriotism but economics. Israel's counter-attack on the black-market arms trade pushed prices ever higher. Kalashnikovs and bullets reaped great rewards for the Sinai Bedouins, which they procured from their sources in Egypt, Jordan, Yemen and, more recently, Darfur, where markings on ammunition boxes identified them as products of Sudan. A Kalashnikov AK-47 assault rifle could earn ten times its purchase price during the short, underground trip, where a nought was added to the $200 price tag on arrival in the black market in Gaza.[18] Bullets too were lucrative, with as much as $7 profit being made on a single one. Violence was good for business and for dealers it was a money-spinner. The tunnels themselves had become more valuable than real estate with wealthy landlords known as 'snakeheads', renting them out for fees of up to $10,000 a night to familiar clients such as Hamas, Fatah and other militant groups.[19]

When I arrived in Rafiah on the Palestinian side, my mission was to find someone who would introduce me to the secret world of the tunnellers. This led me to the Al Shaaer family, widely known in Gaza as tunnel pioneers. They developed construction techniques, building up a store of knowledge about the geology of the graduating hard and soft sand stratum and, as a result, have become wealthy tunnel entrepreneurs. Nevertheless, even the family's expertise couldn't prevent the accident that had struck the Al Shaaers less than a year before. On Friday 2 November 2001, three young members of the family were killed inside one of their constructions when water from a damaged pipe seeped through the sandy tunnel walls, causing the foundations to collapse onto the young men. An Israeli patrol rushed to the area and scoured the tunnel for smuggled weapons, while the distraught family retrieved the bodies of Mohammed Salah Al Shaaer (aged twenty-four), Mohammed Abdullah Al Shaaer (twenty-one) and his twenty-year-old brother, Suleiman, for burial.

Karim Al Shaaer,[20] a tunneller of many years' experience, described the human warrens as 'pure oxygen for the Palestinians living in the Gaza Strip who are otherwise locked in a prison'. He explained how they have modified their designs to compensate for those they lose to Israeli bulldozers by producing low-cost models which he described as 'takeaway' tunnels. He put the cost of these at $15,000 to $20,000. They could be constructed in a relatively short space of time, and the cost recouped during one successful night's smuggling. But the ideal designer-model had an electricity supply, communication systems and basic elevators and cost up to $200,000 to build.

Karim entertained me with stories of brides-to-be taking the underground route from Egypt to Gaza to be married, accompanied by herds of confused sheep intended for the wedding feast. Many families were divided after Israel's withdrawal from Sinai when the border was redrawn, splitting the city of Rafiah into Palestinian Rafiah on one side and Egyptian Rafiah on the other.[21] The price of one sheep on the Egyptian side was $34 while over the border in Gaza it could reach $250 to $300. The tunnels were also used by Palestinians seeking hospital treatment having been refused permission to travel by the Israelis. Other users were avoiding arrest, like Sami Abu Samhadani, who was high-up on Israel's twenty-most-wanted list. When I met him in Cairo in 2001, Sami told me how he had been desperate to receive heart bypass surgery at a specialist hospital in Cairo, and he used the tunnel system to cross the border into Egypt. But when his wife tried to join him via the conventional route through the Israeli checkpoint at Rafiah crossing, the Israeli soldiers, Sami told me laughingly, 'refused to let her past and told my wife: "Why don't you just go back the way you came and start again through the same tunnel your husband took!"'

The existence of these tunnels provided justification for the Israeli forces to intensify their bulldozing programme. Between 29 September 2000 and 1 January 2004, the IDF discovered and destroyed ninety-four tunnels in the Rafiah region.[22] Within the same time-frame, 4,500 Palestinian homes were demolished.[23] Any home they suspected might conceal the entrance shaft or 'eye' to a tunnel was earmarked for demolition. Arbitrary explosions became a nightly occurrence in the hope of collapsing any one of the smugglers' rat-holes. The constant pounding from heavyweight Merkava tanks over the sand-packed foundations caused many to collapse, forcing the tunnel architects to rethink their blueprints and dig further, to depths of between twelve and twenty-five metres. Death in the tunnels is one of the many risks and it is given martyr status within the culture of Gaza as the tunnellers are considered to have died doing their duty for the Palestinian cause.

I was close to becoming a tunnel casualty myself, although, at the time, I was unaware of the existence of the tunnel culture. I visited Salah Al Din district, close to Block 'O' in Rafiah refugee camp, on the morning of 11 November 2002. The Israeli army were patrolling the 12.5 kilometre dirt-track buffer zone known as the Philadelphi Corridor, which demarcates Egypt from the Gaza Strip, a third of which runs alongside Rafiah. This narrow stretch of sand, approximately one hundred metres wide, was an Israeli creation to minimize the above-ground movement of drugs, weapons and people between Egypt and the Gaza Strip. That morning, Israeli troops had arrived with four tanks and three bulldozers and ordered the residents of two dwellings to evacuate their homes with barely enough time to retrieve their possessions. I crossed the waste-ground where local journalists, a CNN crew and residents of Salah El Din were gathered to watch the Israeli bulldozer, its engine screaming to a crescendo, as it advanced then reversed and advanced again, shuddering under the strain as it tore into one of the concrete-block houses, within 150 metres of an Egyptian military post. As I walked towards the retreating Israeli bulldozer and the homeless families who were escaping in panic clutching their few rescued belongings, a huge explosion threw me to the ground. My cameraman was filming the bulldozer scene a few metres away and captured a large pall of smoke, dust and sand which followed the unexpected blast. I survived thanks to my bullet-proof jacket and a helmet which I had fortunately borrowed from the CNN crew. My cameraman was unharmed. The Israeli army had planted explosives in a tunnel lying directly under our feet, but had neither alerted us nor given us any indication about their intended operation, despite the fact that they were aware of the presence of members of the press. As I wiped away the sand and dust from my otherwise unharmed body, I reflected on the recklessness of the Israeli soldiers, which has led to the deaths of so many locals, foreign aid workers, volunteers and journalists. I recall thanking God for our survival and the sandy environment.

If we had been amongst rocks and stones we would certainly have been injured, if not killed.

After incidents like this, the tunnel architects set about rectifying the damage. They were able to use the line of the former tunnel entrance as a guide and build a new shaft, running parallel to the original to eventually meet up with the undamaged section of the tunnel. The IDF could destroy the mouths of the tunnels but not their hearts.

The Rafiah crossing is the gateway to what Palestinians refer to as their open-air prison – the Gaza Strip. When I passed through the Rafiah checkpoint from Egypt on 18 January 2006, it was immediately apparent to me that both Egyptian and Palestinian officials were turning a blind eye in terms of normal border vigilance. Border guards on both sides appeared more sympathetic than officious. One offered to help an elderly woman across the frontier who had been on a shopping spree in Egypt. She was struggling under the weight of several parcels of household goods which were either unavailable or prohibitively expensive on the Gaza side of the border. Older women tended not to get searched out of respect and it was commonly known that many of them brought back several cartons full of cheap, black-market cigarettes for their men-folk, buried in the folds of their voluminous *gallbiyas*. This relative leniency on the part of the two Arab neighbours has prompted Israel to complain that the border has become a turnstile for terrorists.

As far back as December 2002, Israeli Prime Minister Ariel Sharon was making claims that Al Qaeda militants were operating in the Gaza Strip, promising that Israel would take 'all steps to protect itself from an attack': 'We know that they are there, we know that they are in Lebanon working closely with Hezbollah, we know that they are in the region.'[24] Yasser Arafat, in response to Sharon's statement that day, told an audience of reporters at his headquarters in the West Bank city of Ramallah: 'it is a big, big, big, big lie, to cover Sharon's attacks and his crimes against our people.'

When I interviewed him privately over dinner, Arafat explained: 'Osama Bin Laden has damaged the Palestinian cause more than any other being … If it wasn't for the September 11th terrorist attacks on the United States, the Palestinians would be closer than at any time in recent history of achieving our dream of an independent Palestinian State.' He went on to question the sincerity of Bin Laden's support for the Palestinian cause, highlighting the fact that 'not a single statement nor attack had been made against the occupying force in the West Bank and Gaza. Instead he has spent his fortune on bringing us Arabs and Muslims worldwide into disrepute by associating them with terrorism and hatred.'

Sharon's declaration that Al Qaeda cells were present in Gaza, coincided with a story in an Israeli daily newspaper, which appeared to reinforce his words.[25] The paper carried belated news of a planned Al Qaeda operation to attack the Israeli national football team during an away game in Malta. The match had taken place two months earlier, on 12 October 2002. A Tunisian man by the name of Hamadi Bawahia, with suspected links to Al Qaeda, was arrested in Italy where he lived, by Italian anti-terrorist forces, together with four other men. According to the Israeli newspaper, Italian police, tipped off by the Israeli security forces, had intercepted a call between alleged members of a terrorist cell in which one is reported to have said: 'Everything is ready for the game. The field is ready, we must play the game. We will win, we will always win.' Reuters News Agency reported that Italian police forces denied any knowledge of the alleged plot.[26]

The seeds for this story had already been planted in 2001 when Israeli agents from the Shabak adopted fake Arab identities and, claiming to work for Al Qaeda, set about making contact with Palestinians who could act as recruiters for bogus Al Qaeda cells to be established in Gaza. 'Ibrahim' from Gaza described himself as a 'key recruiter'. He responded to a carefully worded advertisement placed in a Jerusalem magazine in October 2001 and, as requested, forwarded his photograph and a mobile telephone number. He was contacted by a man using the alias 'Youssef' and nicknamed 'Abu Othman'. Youssef told the Palestinian that he reminded him of his son who had been killed, and sent him $2,000, urging him to become more observant and to continue performing his religious duties. Speaking in disguise at a press conference organized by the Preventive Security Agency on 10 December 2002, after the plot had been rumbled, Ibrahim described how, five months after their initial communication, the bogus Arab told him: 'You are a good candidate to work for us in the company of Osama Bin Laden and the Al Qaeda group,' and claimed that he had already established an Al Qaeda cell inside Israel. At that point, Ibrahim alerted the Palestinian security services, who began to monitor the communications. When the Israeli agent began asking for more sensitive information about specific people in Gaza who were known members of Hamas, the Palestinian security services put a stop to the Ibrahim-Youssef relationship saying that it had become too dangerous.[27]

An Israeli agent using the same alias, 'Youssef', called a Palestinian citizen 'B.B.' from a Jordanian telephone number, 0096 277 670253, urging him to continue to perform his religious duties, to rent a house and purchase a fax machine. 'Youssef' then made money transfers to 'B.B.' and sent him mobile telephone cards for the Orange mobile network in return for information about likely Palestinians who could be recruited into Al Qaeda. He was also asked for instructions on how weapons could be smuggled into the Gaza Strip from Israel. 'B.B.' was given a local Israeli number, 055971295, on which to call 'Youssef'.

Another Shabak agent, using the pseudonym 'Abu Omar', made contact with Palestinian 'R.M.' using a Lebanon number, 0096 13868075. The agent claimed that he was formerly with Hamas but was now working under the leadership of Sheikh Osama Bin Laden and wanted to support the Intifada and maintain its momentum. Abu Omar then sent $1,000 to 'R.M.' to buy a computer and a fax machine. 'R.M.' was asked to nominate and recruit Palestinians who wished to become martyrs. Some contacts between the two were made via the Internet. The Israeli agent used different telephone numbers in his communication with 'R.M.'

'Abu Suhaib' courted a Palestinian with the initials 'A.M.', to whom he made several deposits of money, using drop points in the first instance and then through money transfers to an account at one of the Palestinian banks. 'A.M.' received approximately $7,500. The Shabak agent became nervous that the Palestinian Preventive Security Service was aware of their relationship and cautioned 'A.M.'

to hide the fax machine he was using for their communications; if he was arrested, he should confess that his contact was from Saudi Arabia.

Abu Omar, claiming to be calling from Lebanon, telephoned two other Palestinians, 'A.S.' and 'H.S.' and told them they would be going to Turkey under cover of a business trip, for training in advanced weaponry. They were told that money would be sent in the form of a wire transfer from East Jerusalem in the name of Khalid Jabir for the sum of 200 Jordanian dinars, and another bank transfer of 340 dinars in the name of Imad Younis from the Arab town of Um Al Fahem inside the Green Line in Galilee. Abu Omar's second contact with the pair was via the Internet using the email address Omar3500@unicum.de on 25 June 2002. In it, he informed the two Palestinians that he worked for Sheikh Osama Bin Laden and that they had carried out 'large operations against the enemy'. The oil tanker *Cole*[28] was mentioned in this communication saying: 'After we destroyed [it] … our enemies surrounded the organization but definitely we shall beat them.'[29]

The Shabak enlisted at least eleven potential Al Qaeda recruiters in this manner, all eventually arrested by the Palestinian security services. According to Abu Shibak, seven of these provided useful information about their contacts and were released, while the remaining four would-be Al Qaeda recruiters, including 'Ibrahim', are in the custody of the Palestinian Preventive Security Service.

The USA, the UK and France were given concrete evidence by the Head of the Palestinian Preventive Security, Rachid Abu Shibak, that the Shabak, together with other Israeli intelligence agencies, had been involved in recruiting 'dummy' Al Qaeda cells into the Palestinian territories for over a year.[30] During an interview with Abu Shibak in Gaza on 18 February 2006, and a follow-up interview over the telephone from London, Abu Shibak told me that the reaction of western countries towards these revelations was one of great interest, 'but they couldn't promise anything or take action since they cannot be seen to take sides against Israel, despite the fact that they knew the whole story was an Israeli fabrication. But we kept them informed throughout the course of our six-month investigations until we had unravelled the whole truth.'

Abu Shibak accused Israel of 'playing dirty tricks' with the intention of undermining the Palestinian Authority and stirring up trouble between the USA and the Palestinians. Memories of the terror attacks of 11 September 2001 were still raw and the climate fearful, and the international community had declared its collective war against Al Qaeda. According to Shibak, the intended strategy was for Israel to take a frontline position alongside the USA in its 'war on terror' and be rewarded with a green light for its own anti-terror policies:

> Israel is attempting to justify assaults and military campaigns carried out by its forces by using the September 11th terrorist events to its own advantage ... The recruitment of phoney Al Qaeda cells to operate within Gaza was an attempt to 'Afghanize' the Palestinian territories as a pretext on which to launch a large-scale war against the Palestinian people after stigmatising them with terrorism. However, if current conditions such as poverty, misery, pain and unemployment persist, then we will have produced the perfect breeding ground in which extremist movements can flourish.[31]

A document sent out to all Israeli embassies contained a point-by-point guide for diplomats on how to gather support for Israel while reversing western sympathy towards the Palestinian situation by using every media opportunity to make a connection between Al Qaeda and the Palestinian leadership. It is clear from the document that it was irrelevant whether there was such a relationship. The diplomatic advice was to use these buzzwords as a strategy aimed not at informing but to give Israel the upper hand in the communications war with the Palestinians.

Israel has a long and sordid history of false-flag terrorism, most notably the Lavon Affair in 1954, codenamed 'Operation Susannah'. Israeli operatives planted bombs in various US and British facilities in Egypt and implicated the Muslim Brotherhood in order to create the impression that Arab terrorists had embarked on a campaign of sabotage of foreign interests in the country. Israel was strongly opposed to the planned withdrawal from control of the Suez Canal by Britain, which they saw as having a stabilizing effect on Egyptian

President Nasser's military ambitions. They calculated that by creating a climate of fear within the foreign business and diplomatic community, Britain would be forced to retain control of the vital maritime canal.[32]

Similarly, during the Six Day War of June 1967, Israel attacked the intelligence vessel USS *Liberty*, which was lying in international waters off the Sinai Peninsular. They claimed they believed the ship to be an Egyptian vessel, despite a large stars and stripes flag fluttering from the deck and other identifiable US insignia. Thirty-four American servicemen were killed and more than 170 wounded. Israel was accused of attempting to destroy the American spy ship to prevent it from intercepting Israeli communications of a planned attack on the Golan Heights to seize it from Syria, in advance of a ceasefire called by the United Nations.[33]

In another apparent case of false-flag trickery, the USA began receiving intelligence that Libya was responsible for the bombing of a Berlin nightclub in 1986, frequented by US soldiers. President Ronald Reagan reacted by ordering the bombing of the Libyan cities of Tripoli and Benghazi, specifically targeting Colonel Muammar Qaddafi's office and residence. Forty people were killed, including the Libyan President's adopted infant daughter. It was later revealed that Mossad had installed a six-foot-long communications device called a 'Trojan' on top of a five-storey apartment building in the Libyan capital, which was positioned to receive broadcasts from Mossad's disinformation service and relay them on frequencies used by the Libyan government. 'Using the Trojan, Mossad began to broadcast messages which appeared to be a long series of terrorist orders being conveyed to various Libyan embassies around the world'.[34] The broadcasts were intercepted by the Americans who interpreted them as proof that Libya was an active sponsor of terrorism. But while Israel's programme of dirty tricks was being performed, unbeknownst to the Israelis, the real Al Qaeda was operating below the radar to establish a serious network in the occupied Palestinian territories.

During their regular intercepts of telephone conversations, Israeli police became suspicious of cell-phone conversations between two nineteen-year-old Palestinians from Balata refugee camp near

Nablus, and began monitoring them. The two teenagers, Azzam Abu Al Adas and Bilal Hafnai, had met with Al Qaeda operatives in Jordan and arranged secret email communications. A bank account was opened for their use into which they received the equivalent of $4,240 in Jordanian dinars from Al Qaeda to fund a double suicide attack. The first was to target a pizzeria in the French Hill neighbourhood of Jerusalem. While curious onlookers arrived to gawp at the blown-up pizzeria, a car bomb would be detonated amongst the crowd which would inevitably form in the nearby street. This was the first time Israel legitimately linked West Bank Palestinians with Al Qaeda after a military court charged the two with receiving illegal funds.

The indictment gave a detailed account of how the teenagers came to be acquainted with the Al Qaeda operatives. The pair visited Jordan at least three times either together or separately to meet their handlers, Abdullah and Abu Talhah. The meetings took place in Irbid in the north of Jordan, starting in May 2005. The following month, the two young men were given a security briefing which included how to avoid detection, how to clandestinely recruit cells without anyone being aware of who else was a member, and how to behave if caught. When the two men returned to Nablus, they held meetings either in the cemetery of the refugee camp or in their homes, and began drafting others into their group to plan their double bombing. They got in touch with a bomb-maker from Tulkarem, the home town of the Queen of Jordan; the bomb-maker agreed to prepare and install a bomb into a car stolen from Israel, and smuggle it into Jordan. His fee was to be just under $10,000. In September of that year, Abu Adas travelled to Irbid and again met with the Al Qaeda operative Abdullah, who gave him a further $2,800 to plan the attack and told him that the bombings were to be carried out on 30 October, the twenty-seventh day of Ramadan. A final instalment of $1,400 was paid to Abu Adas. Another member of the cell, Maher Samara, was to get a payment of $7,000 from a woman named 'Naam' from the United Arab Emirates,[35] who was in contact with him via the Internet. Telephone intercepts by the Israelis foiled the attack, and the two youths were arrested by Israeli security forces while crossing the historic Allenby Bridge between Jordan and the West Bank in December 2005.[36]

Months after the discovery of the West Bank Al Qaeda activities, the Shabak began investigating the Jihad Brigade, another suspected Al Qaeda affiliate in Gaza. Acknowledging the presence of Al Qaeda-linked groups in Sinai, Shabak Director Yuval Diskin expressed concerns that they too could infiltrate the Gaza border. This claim of Al Qaeda's influence in Gaza was not limited to Israeli sources. Palestinians too spoke out about the rise in Al Qaeda entities within their territories, fuelling widespread anxiety and comment.

Palestinian Authority security forces told the *Jerusalem Post* that a new Al Qaeda group calling itself Jundallah ('Allah's Brigades') had become active in Gaza. Operating mostly out of southern Gaza, Jundallah was believed to have originated in Waziristan, a tribal, lawless, mountainous region of Pakistan where Osama Bin Laden was frequently reported to be hiding. Jundallah in Gaza was primarily composed of disillusioned members of Hamas and Islamic Jihad who felt that their own organizations had become too moderate. In May 2005, the organization carried out its first attack against IDF soldiers in Rafiah. A spokesman for the group, Abu Abdullah Al Khattab, warned of future attacks against America. 'Soon everyone will see operations [against the USA] that would make all the Muslims delighted,' he said.[37]

In a September 2005 interview, leading Hamas spokesman Dr Mahmoud Zahar confirmed that Al Qaeda was operating in Gaza. In addition to its physical infiltration, he warned that telephone contact from Gaza with other Al Qaeda centres in overseas countries existed as well. The Chairman of the Palestinian Authority, Mahmoud Abbas, aired his fears in an interview with the London-based *Al Hayat* newspaper on 2 March 2006, in which he admitted there was evidence of Al Qaeda's presence in the West Bank and Gaza and that its infiltration 'could ruin the entire region'. This was within a month of Hamas winning the Palestinian general elections. Without disclosing precise details, Abbas, known more familiarly as 'Abu Mazen', claimed that the terrorist organization was attempting to establish bases in the Palestinian territories. His words sent a chill through many, both within and outside Israel, raising fears that extremist elements were closing in on Tel Aviv and other Israeli settlements. Added weight was given to Abu Mazen's assertions via a videotaped message by Ayman Al Zawahiri. During the twenty-minute clip broadcast by Al Jazeera television on 3 March 2006, Al Zawahiri criticized Hamas for accepting seats alongside those in the Palestinian Authority, whom he described as having 'sold Palestine' through the peace agreements of Oslo and Madrid, and signed deals with Israel which he said were against the teachings of Islam.

'No one has the right, whether Palestinian or not, to abandon a grain of soil from Palestine which was a Muslim land that was occupied by infidels. It is the duty of every Muslim to work on getting it back,' Al Zawahiri pontificated. 'The secularists in the Palestinian Authority have sold out Palestine for crumbs.' He demanded that Hamas adhere to the armed struggle and reject all appeals to recognize peace deals with Israel. He also warned the organization to avoid becoming involved in what he described as 'the American game' by reaching a political settlement and legitimizing the existence of Israel.

The vehemence of Al Zawahiri's criticisms of Hamas' participation flagged up the differences that existed within the ranks of Islamism, divided between those, like the Muslim Brotherhood and Hamas, who were attempting 'Islamization from the ground up through the tactical support of the democratic process' and those, such as Al Qaeda, 'who refuse the western democratic political system altogether, enforcing a top-down transformation via the use of violence'. It is true that Hamas was quick to distance itself from Al Zawahiri's description of Islam and did not even comment on the way he categorized the Palestinian Islamic movement. Hamas leaders have always insisted that their struggle 'will never go beyond the borders or their country's occupiers', unlike Al Qaeda leaders who did not hesitate to strike in western and Islamic capitals in pursuit of their goals.

Zawahiri changed his mind and, in his second statement, appeared more conciliatory towards the world's newest Islamic government as it came under pressure from the West for its political ambitions, and the movement's continued refusal to recognize Israel and ongoing peace agreements proved unacceptable.

The timing of Bin Laden's top commander's statements took the Hamas leadership by surprise. The snub came as Hamas was making its debut on the international stage with a three-day visit to Moscow on 3 March 2006, at the invitation of President Vladimir Putin. This visit even received a back-handed blessing from the American administration in the form of a White House statement, in which it approved the Russian initiative. The compliment was tempered by a subtle threat to the Hamas leadership, suggesting that it should be worldly enough to look beyond its constrained beginnings and realize it had to court the international big guns if it was to achieve its wider ambitions. The leader of Al Qaeda himself jumped into the fray, showing that, whatever cave he was living in, he was able to access the latest developments in the world's news.

A smiling, relaxed-looking Bin Laden, with a greying beard and a loose white head-covering framing his face, delivered one of his now-familiar videotaped messages which was aired by Al Jazeera TV on 23 April 2006. Despite the fact that the new Hamas government was fresh in office, Bin Laden gave it only a cursory mention, saving most of his diatribe for what he believed to be the American-Zionist conspiracy. He claimed the decision by western governments to halt aid and impose other sanctions on the Hamas-led government, proved the West was in a 'crusader war' on Islam. The term 'crusader' is frequently used by Bin Laden and other Al Qaeda figures in reference to Christians. Bin Laden added: 'I say this war is the joint responsibility of the people and their governments. While the war continues, the people renew their allegiance to their rulers and politicians, and continue to send their sons to our countries to fight us.' Hamas Prime Minister Ismail Haniyeh reacted swiftly to distance Hamas from Bin Laden's comments. Speaking in Gaza he said there was an 'unjust blockade imposed on the Palestinian people which is pushing parties and individuals to express their solidarity'.

On the final day of the Moscow visit, Khalid Mishal, the exiled political bureau head of Hamas, based in Damascus, commented that his organization did not need Al Qaeda's guidance: 'Hamas has its own vision and always acts in the interests of the Palestinian people.[38]

Sami Abu Zehri, Hamas' spokesperson in Gaza, made a

distinction between his organization and that of Al Qaeda. He said that the group's ideology 'is vastly different from that of Bin Laden and Al Qaeda'.[39] Increased awareness of Al Qaeda's presence in Palestine had begun to surface in January 2006, following Hamas' sweeping victory in the parliamentary elections. Videotapes, CDs and pamphlets purportedly bearing the signature of Al Qaeda began circulating throughout the West Bank and Gaza. One pamphlet, claiming to be from Jaish Al Jihad ('Army of God') included the following message: 'All foreigners who are not Muslims [should] leave our Holy Islamic land.'[40]

I was shown a similar statement issued by Al Tawhid Wa Al Jihad in the Gaza Strip, which warned that Iraq's Al Qaeda leader, Zarqawi, would 'soon reveal himself in the Palestinian territories and orchestrate local and global jihad from the area'. The statement went on to say: 'Is there now among us a person like Saladin, like Sheikh Osama Bin Laden, like Abu Musab Zarqawi? The answer is yes. We have this man and he will appear with the help of Allah very soon on the land of Palestine.' Moreover, the tract declared, 'We will fight all the corrupted and unbelieving politicians. It will be a great war for the purity of the land of Islam and Palestine.' Referring to its longer organizational name, Al Tawhid Wa Al Jihad in Greater Syria[41] and the Land of Kananah (Egypt), the statement went on to promise 'to cut the throats of the infidels from Fatah organization' and named senior members such as Nabil Amr, Abu Ali Shahine, Mohammed Dahlan, Yasser Abed Rabbo and Samir Mishhrawi. The new extremist organization praised 'our sheikh Abu Musab Al Zarqawi' and announced the launch of their activities in Palestine 'to avoid a Palestinian civil war'.[42]

Further activities emerging in Gaza created deeper anxieties. Small cells of around ten members sympathetic to Al Qaeda were organizing money collections and training. An attack planned by this group was foiled before targeting various sensitive facilities in Gaza such as the offices belonging to the Palestinian Authority, Palestinian leaders and members of the Fatah organization.

The tradition amongst Palestinians of joining global jihadist movements such as Al Qaeda was not new. Amongst the most notable Palestinians to do just that was Sheikh Abdullah Azzam, who became Bin Laden's spiritual leader. Born in Jenin in the West Bank in 1941, Azzam was an eminent scholar and mujahid and was integral to the development of contemporary Islamic radicalism, particularly in the formation of Al Qaeda. Azzam obtained his Ph.D. in Fiqh (Islamic Jurisprudence) at the renowned Al Azhar University in Cairo, where he befriended Sayyed Qotub, an eminent Egyptian scholar, Sheikh Omar Abdul Rahman, a blind Egyptian cleric who was convicted of trying to blow up the World Trade Center in 1993, and Ayman Zawahiri. Azzam became a member of the Palestinian Muslim Brotherhood before he had even come of age. When the Russians invaded Afghanistan in December 1979, Azzam issued a fatwa declaring that both the Afghan and Palestinian struggles were legitimate jihads and killing infidels from those countries was a personal obligation for all Muslims.

After a lecturing stint at the King Abdul Aziz University in Jeddah, Azzam travelled to Pakistan and established a guesthouse in Peshawar, the ancient capital of the North West Frontier Province from where the Khyber Pass winds steeply through the Tribal Areas into Afghanistan. The guesthouse, known as Bait Al Ansar, alias the Mujahideen Services Bureau, became the focal point for Arabs heading for jihad in Afghanistan to receive advice and military training. Sheikh Abdullah Azzam first established ties with Osama Bin Laden in the early 1980s, while Azzam was living in one of Bin Laden's homes in Saudi Arabia. In 1985, Bin Laden visited Pakistan and became heavily embroiled in the Afghan cause. In May 2006, during a telephone conversation with Abdullah Azzaz, the influential sheikh's son-in-law, I learned that Azzam had hosted a lunch in honour of Bin Laden in Peshawer during his three-day visit in the 1980s. The two men had strengthened their bond over this mutual cause. Years later, Azzam's notions and ideology were mirrored in the rhetoric expressed by Bin Laden through his videotape messages, which have been broadcast worldwide since 9/11.

There is a mysterious coda to the story which to this day remains unsolved. Sheikh Abdullah Azzam – who was responsible for writing the constitution for Hamas – was killed in Peshawar along with two of his sons on 24 November 1989. Three roadside bombs exploded as their car travelled along its regular route to the mosque.

No one claimed responsibility for this, one of many assassinations of Hamas' leaders.

Despite his untimely death, the teachings Azzam left behind gave him the posthumous distinction of becoming the spiritual leader for many Arabs and Muslims who felt compelled to follow his path into the battlefields of Afghanistan. Those of Palestinian or Jordanian origin who ventured to Afghanistan and Pakistan looked to Azzam's writings. They sought justification for the fact that it was too difficult to perform jihad in Palestine because of the relatively strict border controls, unlike the porous borders which led to the frontlines of Afghanistan, Bosnia, Chechnya and, most recently, Iraq. Omar Mohammed Othman (Abu Qatada), who for the last few years has been labelled Bin Laden's operative in Europe, Abu Mohammed Al Maqdisi, mentor and spiritual leader to Al Zarqawi, and Abu Anas Al Shami are the most notorious Palestinians within international jihadist circles. They are known as 'the Palestinian Afghanis'.

Al Shami was born in a Palestinian refugee camp in Jordan. As a religious scholar, his knowledge of Islamic jurisprudence became useful to Al Zarqawi in seeking legal fatwas to support his condoning of kidnapping and killing hostages as a legitimate religious duty. Al Shami was killed in Iraq by a US missile, which hit his car during a 'successful precision strike' on Al Zarqawi supporters.[43]

In a letter sent to Al Zarqawi dated August 2004 from Qafqafa jail in Jordan,[44] Al Maqdisi urged Iraq's Al Qaeda leader to expand his activities to 'the west of the river' – a reference to the West Bank and Gaza. Many followers interpreted this as confirmation that Al Maqdisi was not happy to see his 'pupil', Al Zarqawi, concentrate his terrorist activities solely in Iraq. The two men had shared a prison cell in the mid 1990s, when Al Maqdisi, a Salafi spiritual leader,[45] was influential in introducing Al Zarqawi to a highly politicized form of Islam. On their release from prison, the two men became involved with a Salafi jihadist group, which plotted to attack American tourists in the Jordanian capital of Amman in late 1998. The plot was thwarted and the two men were re-imprisoned,[46] only to be freed less than a year later in an amnesty by King Abdullah of Jordan. Al Zarqawi used his freedom to go to Afghanistan and then on to Iraq from where he waged his deadly campaign of car bombings, attacks and kidnappings. Al Maqdisi soon found himself back in jail.

The Palestinian camps in Jordan, Lebanon and Gaza provided a fertile environment for cultivating potential Al Qaeda members, due to the economic situation and the despair many of them had experienced. It took very little encouragement for this despair to spill over into violent anger at the lack of a just solution to their long dispute with Israel. Al Qaeda has not yet reached the stage of broad popular support where it would become necessary to appoint an 'emir' responsible for Palestine, as Bin Laden has done in Iraq, Syria and Lebanon. Many of his followers in Jordan, however, believed that the message sent by Abu Mohammed Al Maqdisi from prison in early 2006, to Al Qaeda's late emir in Iraq, Al Zarqawi,[47] should be interpreted as a signal that their murderous operations were imminent in the theatre of the West Bank and Gaza.

As a result of the pamphlet statements made by Al Tawhid Wa Al Jihad and distributed in Gaza and the bombing campaigns of the Egyptian Sinai resorts, many in the Middle East intelligence community cautioned that it was a case of 'when and not if' a more threatening relationship would be forged between jihadist groups in Gaza and their counterparts in the Sinai to target the very heart of Israel. Many Palestinian militants attached to Hamas' military wing enjoyed a warm relationship with their Bedouin comrades across the border in the Sinai desert and were already flexing their muscles against the post-election ceasefire ordered by their government.

For many years, Al Qaeda has exploited the Palestinian cause, using it as a tool with which to recruit its fighters by offering sympathy for the injustices, the double standards and the refusal of the world's superpowers to implement UN resolutions calling for Israeli withdrawal from occupied Palestinian territories. Al Qaeda has employed this emotive issue to justify attacks against foreign 'infidels' and divert attention from the reality which is that most casualties of Bin Laden's organization have been Arabs and Muslims in Saudi Arabia, Morocco, Egypt, Yemen, Iraq, Tunisia, Pakistan and Indonesia. Whatever remains of the sympathetic masses who demonstrated so vociferously in the streets of western capitals in defence of the crimes committed against Palestinians must surely be eroded by the unwelcome arrival of Al Qaeda into Gaza and the West Bank.

The interests of both the mainstream Palestinian population and the more extreme groups including Hamas are very simple: the return of their land and the formation of their own state. Al Qaeda, on the other hand, has a more nebulous interest which includes the unlikely re-establishment of the Caliphate,[48] the elimination of western interests from all Muslim lands and a full-blown conflict of civilizations. Therefore, theoretically, Al Qaeda and the Palestinians should not make easy partners. But with the tension in the Middle East showing no sign of abating, Al Qaeda's potential to recruit the most disaffected Palestinian elements has remained strong, as was the case with the three Hamas members arrested by Egyptian security services in the aftermath of the series of suicide bomb attacks on resorts in the Sinai over the last few years. Any future alliance between Palestinian militants and Al Qaeda is likely to harm the more focused cause of the Palestinian nation by tainting it with wanton and random violence and hatred that the wider world has come to associate with Al Qaeda.

9

The Future
of Hamas

It was a small cell by anyone's standards. Beyond the row of four tightly packed, grubby and malodorous sponge mattresses reared a half-metre-high wall, too low for modesty's sake, to conceal the roughly hewn hole which formed the basis of the prisoners' bathroom. The area of confinement was lit by a depressing light, barely one candle flame in strength. In this gloomy environment, engineer Wasfi Kabaha, ironically the appointed Palestinian Minister of Prisoners' Affairs, was to spend one month as a prisoner. In a similar cell, a further five democratically elected government ministers, arrested together less than six months into their term of office,[1] were tossing up for the relative privacy of the outside mattresses. The dignitaries had been detained following the abduction of Corporal Gilad Shalit on the Gaza-Israeli border.[2] In the space of two months, Israel had arrested no fewer than ten ministers, two dozen members of parliament and a handful of heads of municipalities, as well as a large contingent of Hamas' senior figures in the West Bank. Aziz Duwaik, head of the Palestinian Legislative Council, and Nasser Al Shaer, the Palestinian Deputy Prime Minister, were just two of the high-profile detainees. With many of its government in hiding fearing assassination and a similar number in prison, the joke circulating amongst the Palestinian electorate was that Hamas had cleverly dreamed up a cunning formula to provide a safe environment in which to discuss their parliamentary business.

Wasfi described how he and his cell-mates had been treated, both mentally and physically. From the moment they were forced from their family apartments in Ramallah city, their hands and legs were tied then, blindfolded, they were led to a military HQ in Beit El settlement close to the West Bank town of Ramallah. After spending five hours seated on the ground, trussed and sightless, they moved to Ofer Prison, where they were held in a number of small cells for two weeks before being dispersed to various Israeli prisons. Wasfi was interrogated about his membership of Hamas and about money which had been transferred to charities in Jenin city in the West Bank. He was also questioned about statements inciting violence it was claimed he had made. He reminded his interrogator that he was a minister in an independent government and 'Israel should treat me with respect', demanding that the intelligence officer address him by his government title rather than his given name which, according to Wasfi, 'used to drive the Israeli officer mad'.[3] The public prosecutor tried to force him to sign an indictment listing three alleged crimes: membership of a 'terrorist organization'; taking a job in the said 'terrorist organization' as a minister; and offering the services of a 'terrorist organization'. After eleven days of investigations, a military judge decided to release him, finding no substance to the accusations.

The decision to jail the Hamas government and destroy the movement's infrastructure was decided at a Cabinet meeting chaired by Prime Minister Ehud Olmert and Minister of Defense Amir Peretz.[4] A spate of bombing raids began on 2 July 2006, lasting days and pounding the Prime Minister's offices in Ramallah, Gaza and Nablus and the Ministries of the Interior and Foreign Affairs in Gaza. As part of the same offensive, bombs destroyed the empty offices of the Prime Minister in Gaza.[5] A few hours afterwards, Ismail Haniyeh made a night-time sojourn to inspect the burned-out buildings. At around 3.30 a.m., as he was about to rejoin his security convoy, his bodyguards were alerted to the deadly sound of Israeli planes overhead. Haniyeh signalled to the drivers of his protection squad to leave without him and, protected by two of his bodyguards, he made for the residence of the Palestinian President, Mahmoud Abbas, four hundred metres away. Abu Mazen was roused by his own bodyguards and, dressed in his *galabiyah*, he offered sanctuary to the Palestinian Prime Minister until he felt safe to leave. Despite the supposed animosity between the two leaders, Abu Mazen would always protect Haniyeh. In the weeks following his appointment, there was more than one occasion when Haniyeh called Abu Mazen in distress to say that Israeli planes were following him, whereby Abu Mazen would immediately send his presidential convoy to provide a moving shield.

The arrest of Hamas government ministers and members of parliament was an unprecedented act in Israeli-Palestinian modern history. It left a political void and increasing chaos at a time when the Palestinian leadership had been attempting to find a compromise and move forward. But there were no concessions from the Israeli side. Their government tried to open a dialogue with the imprisoned West Bank's frontbench Hamas ministers and MPs. According to Wasfi, 'The prison authority would come round to our cells to tell us that there were Israeli researchers who wanted to interview us but it was obvious by their questioning they were government officials.' The high-ranking Israeli officials, who refused to disclose their names, held lengthy discussions with the imprisoned Palestinian government in order to delve into Hamas' views on many different issues with a view to divining its weak spots. None of the prisoners were in any mood to deal with representatives of the very government which was holding them captive in degrading circumstances.

By now, Ismail Haniyeh was a prime minister on the run. He hardly slept, furtively moving from one safe house to the next. His small two-storey house in Al Shati camp lay forsaken. Foreign Minister Mahmoud Zahar, who had survived a previous Israeli attempt on his life, was also shuttling between safe houses. This was a far cry from the heady times only a few months before when he had toured not just the Arab world but global capitals as an international diplomat.

A consensus was reached between the different political factions to form a coalition government. In these extraordinary circumstances, neither Haniyeh or Zahar, despite being the principal leaders of the Palestinian government, had effective control over the military wing which had abducted the Israeli soldier. Holding sway over the situation was Hamas leader Khalid Mishal, the head of the Hamas political bureau based in Damascus. He had quietly gathered up the reins of power following the assassinations of the movement's spiritual leader, Sheikh Ahmed Yassin, and his short-term successor, Abdul Aziz Al Rantisi. However weighty the titles of Haniyeh and Zahar might appear, it was Mishal who was running the show. The Al Qassam Brigades answered directly to him and any political move was agreed on between himself and the military wing irrespective of the Hamas politicians elected to govern, the Legislative Council, or Mahmoud Abbas. This situation was extremely frustrating for the worldly President of the Palestinian Authority who would try to mediate but, whenever talks reached crunch point, Hamas leaders would intone the phrase 'God will provide, God is with us.' Then they would call Mishal, report on the situation and be totally reliant on his decision.

Even the Hamas leadership was reconciled to the fact that it would be impossible for one party to manage the political crisis single-handedly and that only a coalition government would provide the way forward. In this instance, the Prime Minister would still be a representative from the Hamas movement as they held the majority in the parliament. According to Hamas, such a government would be formed on the basis of the National Reconciliation Document of the Prisoners, or the 'Prisoners' Document' as it became known, giving the Palestinian Authority overall power to negotiate on behalf of its people. The eighteen-point document, which was signed by a coalition of Palestinian prisoners on 26 May 2006, called for the establishment of an independent Palestinian state in the West Bank and Gaza Strip and East Jerusalem and the right of return for all refugees to their original homes. The signatories were Fatah leader Marwan Barghouthi, Hamas' Abdul Khaleq Al Natsheh, deputy head of the Popular Front for the Liberation of Palestine, Abdul Rahim Malouh, Mustafa Badarneh of the Democratic Front for the Liberation of Palestine and Sheikh Bassam Al Saida of Islamic Jihad. The document also laid down a framework to coordinate the different military factions under one umbrella. There was cautious mention, too, of Israel's right to exist – the most sensitive topic in the document. The PLO had already accepted this point and therefore Hamas, for now, found it politically expedient to go along with it.[6]

For Abu Mazen, the document fell far short of what he felt was the minimum required by the Palestinians to perform on the international stage, not to mention with the Israelis. He saw the process of getting Hamas to agree to the document as a first step in moderating the policies to something which would allow Palestinian representatives back into realistic negotiations with Israel for a Palestinian state. While Hamas might operate on a timescale of centuries and with Allah's will, Abu Mazen was more pragmatic, realizing that governments must be dealt with in the earthly and present world.

The Prisoners' Document laid down the groundwork for strengthening the relationship between Hamas and Fatah on a political level. Firstly, Hamas agreed to the Palestinian Authority being the legal and only representative of the Palestinian people. Secondly, the document recognized the decisions taken by Arab summits concerning the conflict with Israel. The most important of these was the one taken at the Beirut Arab Summit in 2002. So, in theory, when Hamas accepted the Prisoners' Document, they formally signed up to each and every one of the United Nations resolutions; in practice, they accepted nothing of the sort. The prisoners' pact came out of a showdown which exposed Hamas' worries. During the protracted negotiations, Abu Mazen forced everyone in the presidential office back to all-night Arafat-style hours, as he tried to coerce Hamas into complying in the knowledge that Hamas was not in a position to make an overnight volte-face. An unusually saturnine figure in the Arab world, Abu Mazen would uncharacteristically beat his forehead in frustration as tempers frayed, dark circles appeared under sleepless eyes, and stubble grew on defiant chins. Finally, Abu Mazen threw down the gauntlet and threatened to hold a referendum unless Hamas finally agreed to the Prisoners' Document. It was the first time an understanding on this level had been reached between Hamas and a faction belonging to the PLO.

It was a step forward, but not far enough to put an end to the boycott of its government and any future unity government. The Quartet had made it clear that any cooperation was subject to a total recognition of the State of Israel. If Hamas stood firm on this issue it would lead the movement into further political confrontations with the international community, leaving the Palestinian people to bear the crippling consequences.

Following its election win, statements issued by Islamic Jihad's military wing, the Al Quds Brigade, and Fatah's military wing, the Al Aqsa Brigades, had accused Hamas of preferring political power to being on the side of the resistance, which caused huge embarrassment to the Al Qassam Brigades and Hamas leadership. It forced Hamas into taking military risks as it did with the orchestrated abduction of an Israeli soldier. There was no political vision. During their first six months in government, there were no significant changes in services, salaries or reforms, and Hamas began repeating Fatah's mistakes by appointing more employees, who had no hope of being paid due to the international sanctions on the 'terrorist organization'. Before the kidnapping of the Israeli soldier, an opinion poll indicated that their popularity had waned to thirty-five per cent, yet, in a subsequent poll taken shortly after the abduction, opinion swung the other way, following a significant change in the mood of the Palestinian public, who sympathized with the prisoners' issue and were angered by the ferocity of Israel's attacks on Gaza. Hamas regained lost ground.

After the election, Hamas had announced their intention to form a national unity government comprising the whole political spectrum, opening the doors for all factions to join. The movement also declared it would undergo radical changes to fight corruption and introduce administrative reforms and promised to cooperate fully with President Abu Mazen on major issues, particularly the relationship with the PLO. Hamas' political strategy was clearly outlined in its election manifesto, and included the liberation of all Palestinian territory under occupation and the formation of their homeland as defined by 1967 borders and with Jerusalem as their capital. In public, Hamas avoided any mention of the destruction of Israel and, on paper, it began to look as if Hamas was not miles away from the PLO's agenda, which offered a two-state solution to achieve peace. In reality, though, Hamas' public concessions were just window-dressing. While it was happy to see unilateral withdrawals made by Israel, it would never relinquish its goal to create a Palestinian state encompassing the whole of Palestine. A Hamas senior told me: 'You will never find anyone in Hamas who will recognize Israel's right to exist. If you do, he is a liar.'

The first concession would be to agree to a ceasefire, but they will never consider a final settlement, as they believe they must leave the way open for future generations to fight for their ultimate goals. They consider the land of Palestine as indivisible and not something they can negotiate with. Nonetheless, with regard to the daily affairs of the Palestinians, Hamas would have no qualms about approaching Israel if it was to the benefit of their people. According to Dr Mahmoud Zahar, the Islamic movement has no objection to Palestinian technical teams liaising with their Israeli counterparts to solve day-to-day issues, while major problems should be tackled through a third party. Hamas opponents such as the Fatah faction claim this solution is impractical as the Palestinian population can't afford to wait for a third party to mediate in something like a medical emergency, for instance, where a patient needs to cross the border to hospitals in Egypt or Jerusalem. Similarly, the Palestinian population in Gaza relies heavily on the passage of goods via the Karni crossing between Israel and Gaza. This is the main day-to-day supply route for food and other perishable goods, as well as petrol and medical supplies.

In real terms, the closure of Gaza and the cutting off of international funds are hurting Fatah more than they are Hamas. While in opposition, Hamas relied on its own sources of funding, while Fatah and the Palestinian Authority institutions under the Fatah leadership had become reliant on international donors.

Turned down by other political parliamentary factions to form a coalition government, Hamas had no choice but to establish its own Cabinet. The movement's persistent refusal to recognize the PLO as the sole and legal representative of the Palestinian people had been a major setback in the course of its young political life. The following day, members of the newly formed Cabinet performed their duties under oath before the President in Gaza, while the rest of their Cabinet colleagues living in the West Bank followed suit via video-conferencing technology.

Hamas is faced with many challenges, not least if its fragile government fails to provide the minimum number of jobs for its followers. The loyal supporters who stood by the movement during the difficult days expect to be rewarded with jobs in the military or the civil administration. This would severely handicap the financially strapped government which is already incapable of paying the salaries of its civil servants and military service personnel.

The Palestinian Authority is suffering under the strained financial situation, as many countries have already cut their aid in response to a 'terrorist organization' coming to power. Hamas didn't take the threat seriously, refusing to believe that the USA and the European Union would turn their backs completely and risk the consequences of severe financial and economical hardship with its knock-on effect to the security situation.

There is a free-for-all state of security in the West Bank and Gaza with an uncontrolled amount of weapons being held by the armed militias attached to all the political factions. Although Hamas declared its intention was to resolve this situation, it has failed completely: the old conflicts between Hamas and the PLO based on family and personal feuds have re-emerged to exacerbate the situation which has culminated in Hamas assassinating some personnel from the Protective Security body. Even with his constitutional powers, Abu Mazen has been unable to make any progress in improving the security problem. Hamas has insisted on keeping its own armoured militia unless a National Army is formed, comprised of all the militias, something which would be difficult to achieve in view of the international boycott of the Authority.

Maintaining order and security without being undermined by the Ministry of the Interior is of major concern to Hamas, because the security organizations are mainly staffed by Fatah loyalists. The complexity of political affiliations in the community inhibits the smooth functioning of the police, so the major concern for Hamas is to bring under control the chaos rampaging throughout the Palestinian territories. The police are not operating alone. The

National Security Council and various Palestinian intelligence agencies also play their part. Although President Abu Mazen gave his approval for the National Security Council to be brought under the wing of the Ministry of the Interior as requested by Hamas, it was turned down by senior officers and executive leaders of Fatah. They were resolute that the President should retain his personal control on the national security system, and that the same procedure be applied to the intelligence agencies, the Headquarters' bodyguards as well as Force 17, established by Arafat in Beirut in the 1970s as a Presidential Guard and security force.

The Hamas electorate is unlikely to tolerate any diversion from the political and religious principles which Hamas has consistently advocated. By maintaining this rigid position, Hamas must realize that it risks losing a significant tranche of support unless it comes out and says categorically that it will accept UN resolutions and other agreements signed by the PA and the State of Israel. Hamas is further challenged by a range of public needs in every sector, whether it be health, education, the economy, commerce, the ports or the utilities. Most pressing is the question of manpower salaries, which cost the Treasury around US$175 million each month, much of which comes from the estimated US$50 million collected as an import tax by Israel. This is done on a monthly basis for the Palestinian Authority and normally transferred to its account. Payment of this tax, which was approved by the Oslo Agreement, was halted after Hamas came to office and dealt a major blow to the operation of the Palestinian Authority.

To add to the severe financial constraints, the Authority is clearly witnessing a perplexing economic plight caused by the blocking of free-trade channels with Israel and abroad, through the Karni commercial crossing between Gaza and Israel. It is not just business which is suffering. Israel is purposefully putting pressure on even the mundane activities of Palestinians, such as restricting the movement of health and medical supplies to and from Israel. Even the seemingly simple commute between Gaza and the West Bank has become an ordeal. All these conditions add up to a hellish daily life and create a bitter impression of the new Islamic government. To date, the Hamas government has had no available strategy for solving the overwhelming number of problems. Even partial solutions are unable to remedy the security situation while the social wounds which have been inflicted will persist like open sores.

Most members of the Palestinian Authority belong to Fatah and are completely reliant on their salaries. If they are fired from their jobs because there is no money to pay them, this could lead to a civil war. The Hamas movement and its parliamentary members have announced that they will not dismiss security personnel, no matter what faction they belong to. Hamas has openly declared its determination to eradicate all kinds of corruption but, understandably, since the bulk of the security systems belong to Fatah, Hamas realized from the outset how difficult taking disciplinary action and controlling the security organizations would be.

Both Israel's and Hamas' visions coincide in terms of postponing the 'final solution' issues and moving forward to a transitional, long-term solution such as a ceasefire. This interim solution would be crucial for Hamas, which desperately needs time and space to enable it to get a grip on power and convince the Palestinian people of its worth.

Hamas should expect a cocktail of financial, economic, security and political dilemmas. These difficulties will be similar to – if not worse than – what Fatah's last government encountered. The chances of overcoming these will be slim unless Hamas succeeds in convincing all armed factions of a genuine truce by opening up vital new channels of communications with the international community, including a serious political breakthrough with the European Union.

Despite Hamas' intentions to keep its military wing as an independent body, separate from the Palestinian Authority, it seems there has been a change of heart, as it has integrated some of its supporters and sympathizers to operate within both the military and political wings. Hamas, with the advantage of a parliamentary majority, challenged the authority of President Mahmoud Abbas, who objected from an early stage to Hamas' decision to allow a 3,500–strong militia consisting of Hamas supporters and other loyal factions as an Executive Force, functioning under the auspices of the Ministry of the Interior. To avoid heavy clashes in any military confrontation between Fatah and Hamas supporters, Abu Mazen embraced the new force as part of the military, receiving a salary from the Palestinian Authority. But he certainly did not let Hamas have it all its own way. He increased the number of his own Fatah-based force, putting them in charge of the crucial crossings into Israel and Egypt.

Said Siam, Hamas' Interior Minister, exasperated Abu Mazen and the security services by saying he would never arrest anyone from the resistance, even though Hamas had signed up to the *hudna* (ceasefire). Security officers were left wondering – 'Do we arrest Palestinians launching rockets into Israel or not?' Many just went home to wait for some clarity on orders.

I met Abu Yasser, the head of Preventive Security in Rafiah, and asked him: 'What is the change in your orders now Hamas is the government?'

He answered, 'As you see, I am drinking a nice tea and I am not wearing my uniform. We have no orders.' Weeks later, he was shot in the leg by Hamas in Gaza.

There is no underestimating the enmity that these internecine confrontations create for the future. But Hamas does appear to be beginning to understand the requirements and criteria needed for government and its tone has changed accordingly. It has become more moderate and is realizing how relatively easy it was to be in opposition with no responsibilities, when it could lob criticisms at Abu Mazen and, before him, Arafat and the Palestinian Authority. Now Hamas is in government, it is faced with the minefields any Palestinian government has to negotiate. The ever-present issue of the Intifada has been tactically replaced by the language of Palestinian rights. Although Hamas has always approved the continuation of the struggle, the Al Qassam military wing has remained totally silent since the elections, which confirms Hamas' new policy of freezing the Intifada's operations.

Reaction to the first suicide bomb attack to target Tel Aviv shortly after Hamas won the election was mixed. While President Mahmoud Abbas immediately condemned the attack, describing it as a cowardly act against Israeli civilians, the Hamas leadership in Gaza took its time before responding that the attack by Islamic

Jihad was the result of 'Israeli atrocities against our people'. Khalid Mishal in Damascus enraged Fatah supporters when he criticized Abbas' statement during a gathering in Al Yarmouk camp, the largest Palestinian camp in the Diaspora. He was forced to apologize to Abbas in order to avert a civil war between Fatah and Hamas as a result of his verbal attack.

The number of Al Qassam fighters in Gaza is estimated at 18,000. They are armed with machine guns and pistols as well as locally manufactured rocket launchers. The military wing's orders are received from the political leadership abroad through Khalid Mishal's office in Damascus. Within six months of its election victory, the movement was considering forming a national army which was not linked to any political faction. But the idea was ruled out for practical reasons. First of all, according to agreements with Israel, the Palestinian Authority is not allowed to have more than 76,000 military personnel, to be composed mainly of the police and the security agencies, which have been approved by the Palestinian Authority.

Alongside Hamas, there are small affiliated factions which are sympathetic to Hamas. When the Israeli solider was captured, for example, a number of cells were involved in the operation who were supporting Hamas. Many personalities in Hamas' military wing have come out of the shadows, although they remain secretive in their movements. Foremost of these is Mohammed Al Dayef, followed by Ahmed Al Jouabari.

Both have survived assassination attempts by Israel. Al Dayef and Al Jouabari, along with other senior leaders of Al Qassam, were attending a meeting on 12 July 2006 in a house belonging to Awad Selmi, a member of the Hamas political bureau in Gaza. Selmi, his wife, and seven of his children were killed when an F-16 targeted the house with three missiles, one of which contained a quarter-ton bomb. Israel was desperate to eliminate Al Dayef and Al Jouabari, who were instrumental in developing Al Qassam's not inconsiderable arsenal. Al Dayef was wounded in what was the fifth attempt on his life. Before becoming an explosives expert, Al Dayef flirted with acting, using the stage name Abu Khalid. His great sense of humour led him to his signature role as the fall guy in a play called *Al Moharrej*. One of his groups was called Al Aedoun ('The Returnee'), which was the first Islamic theatrical group in Khan Younis.

Al Qassam missiles have been upgraded and are capable of targeting Israeli settlements. According to Al Joubari and Al Dayef, who made a rare TV appearance only a few weeks before the attempt on their lives, it was only a matter of time before Hamas' military wing in the West Bank would have the ability to accumulate a similar arsenal. That means only one thing to Israelis who have experience of Iranian-supplied long-range missiles fired by Hezbollah. Hamas doesn't require such far-reaching rockets. A range of just a few kilometres is all that is needed to threaten Israel's main cities, including Tel Aviv.

One of the steps taken by Hamas after its victory was to partially legitimize its military forces. Because Fatah has its security organizations under preventive security and the general intelligence directorate, Hamas decided to establish its own security organization, loyal to its government, naming it the Intervention Force. Its military wing, the Al Qassam Brigades, was totally separate from the Intervention Force but would provide back-up if needed. It took two to three months of negotiations, during which time there were many confrontations between this force which was headed by Said Siam, Hamas' Interior Minister, and those forces loyal to Mahmoud Abbas. Many Fatah activists were assassinated or shot at by Al Qassam activists and whenever Abbas raised the issue with Ismail Haniyeh, the Hamas Prime Minister appeared taken aback and asked the Fatah leadership for patience until they brought things under control.

Although the Hamas leadership prepared the ground for its election success, most didn't anticipate the landslide win which forced Hamas to form the majority government. They were inexperienced politically, administratively, and technically. This complicated things from the outset and left them with two options, and even the better of these has, as we say in Arabic, 'a bitter taste'.

From day one of its inauguration, Hamas refused to accept the PLO as the *sole* representative of the Palestinian people. A decision was taken in early 1991, that the military wing should take instructions from its political bureau abroad, but influence remained with the leadership in Gaza until this recent development. Israel imposed restrictions on the movement of Hamas leaders to the extent that the government was unable to meet as a corps. Their meetings took place by video conference between Gaza and Ramallah. Their only exit route was to travel via the Rafiah crossing on the Egyptian border to Cairo and from there to other parts of the world.

Despite their victory and their ability to form their own government, Hamas still requires a transition period of around four years before it can get to grips with all aspects of power. Hamas remains outside the PLO umbrella, the most important body in the Authority. Hence, Hamas has invited Fatah and other factions within the PLO to join the government, not for the sake of unity and stability as Hamas leaders have indicated, but because Hamas is really unable to govern alone.

There are many indications that, in due course, the PLO would welcome power-sharing with Hamas to salvage the Authority and for the sake of national unity. Hamas leaders in the West Bank and Gaza are considered to be more pragmatic. They know the enemy. They've been in jail. They've experienced the dangers. Hamas' popularity amongst Palestinians hinges on the success or failure of the political process. When there is a breakthrough in the protracted peace negotiations with Israel with the promise of an end to their suffering brought about by changes to the economic situation, the Palestinians support the PA.

But neither Hamas nor the PLO exists in a vacuum. There are strong regional influences with sometimes contrasting goals. Jordan is nervous about the Hamas government even though it has a well-established relationship with the Muslim Brotherhood movement. In the 1970s, the Kingdom received considerable help from the Brotherhood when left-wing Palestinians tried to overthrow the monarchy in what was described to the world as the Black September confrontations. Jordan has demographic, security and economic interests in the West Bank, hence it is essential for the Kingdom to ensure its stability. They would like to see total conformity between the PLO and Hamas, preferably a joint, pragmatic Islamic government headed by the PLO.

Eygpt, as a leading power in the region, also has its interests. President Mubarak and his government persistently urged Hamas and the PLO to join together to save their country. There is self-interest as well as statesmanship in this position. Egypt does not want an impoverished and unstable entity on its border. Prime Minister Ismail Haniyeh is unlikely to enjoy the first-class treatment Cairo lavished on Arafat and, later on, Abu Mazen and his ministers, just as he no longer has the luxury of a helicopter to travel from Gaza to Ramallah, which was at the disposal of his predecessor. For example, a meeting was arranged in Gaza during the second week of August 2006, to discuss the fate of the abducted Israeli soldier, which was attended by Haniyeh and his Foreign Minister, Dr Mahmoud Zahar. In the epoch of Arafat, such a meeting would have been attended by Egyptian Cabinet ministers, but it was two, low-ranking intelligence officers who arrived in Gaza as the representatives of the Egyptian government. A precedent had already been set for this diplomatic brush-off. Shortly after Hamas came to power, its Foreign Minister embarked on a foreign mission which began and ended in the Egyptian capital, taking in Pakistan, China, Syria and several other Arab countries. Upon arrival in Cairo, Zahar was expecting to meet his Egyptian opposite number, but was told that Foreign Minister Abu Al Ghaith wasn't available. Foreign Ministry officials were evasive, opting for the excuse that the absence of their Foreign Minister was due to his hectic schedule. In truth, the Egyptian government was not prepared to deal with Hamas through normal diplomatic channels but through its Minister for Security and intelligence chief General Omar Suleiman.

Towards the end of his tour, Zahar returned to Cairo for a rescheduled meeting with the Egyptian Foreign Minister. Normally, visiting foreign ministers are seen at the Foreign Ministry but Zahar was diverted to the office of Osama Al Baz, President Hosni Mubarak's political adviser, a diminutive anglophile who has been the sage behind the throne for decades. Abu Al Ghaith told the Hamas Foreign Minister that Egypt has always supported the creation of an independent Palestinian state where its citizens would have the freedom of movement and the space to breathe. Since 1978, Egypt has chosen the path of negotiation and peace as the only way to stability in the region. Al Ghaith urged Dr Zahar to do whatever he could to maintain international support for their cause and to have the wisdom to create an environment which was open to negotiation. He also advised the Palestinian Foreign Minister to listen carefully to General Omar Suleiman: 'I know what the Hamas movement stands for but you should be tactful. Europe is prepared to deal with your government provided you react positively to their demands.' To which Zahar replied: 'We are willing to explore the Arab initiative because the Arab nation is our umbrella which shelters and guides us. All of Palestine belongs to us but we have agreed with other Palestinian factions to accept an independent Palestinian state within the 1967 borders.'[7]

The reason behind Egypt's diplomatic unease was twofold. First they were unhappy about the relationship Hamas shared with its opposition, the Muslim Brotherhood, a thorn in the side of the Egyptian government for many years. A future Islamic government headed by Hamas in neighbouring Palestine is eyed with suspicion by the Egyptian government. Second, incorporating religion into the legal system through sharia law conflicts with the Egyptian government's secular structure. Egypt has worked energetically to contain Hamas without success, and is now asking the PLO to do its utmost to persuade the movement from adopting a religious political system which could potentially inflame the tinderbox situation in the region.

Unlike Egypt and to some extent Jordan, Israel has had to bear the heaviest burden for allowing the situation on its borders to spiral out of control. Fingers of blame point towards previous Israeli prime ministers for not taking pre-emptive measures to nip the Hamas movement in the bud. Instead it was allowed it to flourish into such a robust foe against the Fatah movement, that it crushed its political rival, securing the largest majority in the Palestinian Legislative Council. Israel may have to live with this lapse in prescience for some time until a new election is held. Dovish Israeli politicians, and even hard-line military commanders, accuse the Israeli Civil Administration, which was responsible for running Palestinian civil affairs, of what they call a 'policy of tolerance' which allowed Hamas to enjoy a relatively easy rite of passage and mature so robustly.

Israel's approach to Hamas will be strongly influenced by its realization of the strength of Hezbollah. The repercussions of the capture of two Israeli soldiers by Hezbollah created mayhem on the Lebanese-Israeli border. For the first time in Israel's history, Hezbollah's rockets reached major cities in the north of Israel, forcing an exodus of more than one million people who evacuated towns, villages and settlements or bunkered down in shelters. More than one hundred Israelis and over a thousand Lebanese died in the six-week conflict. It ended when a ceasefire was agreed by both sides and a UN International Force was put in place as a buffer between the two fractious countries. A similar UN buffer zone should also be established to stabilize and secure the Syrian-Israeli border. Israel has exhausted all other means available and is left with one option, which is to reach a settlement with its neighbours with the support of the international community.

Shlomo Ben-Ami, the Israeli Foreign Minister during Ehud Barak's premiership, described Israel's war with Hezbollah and Hamas as a war fought on two fronts – Lebanon and Gaza – 'which has destroyed the agenda which Olmert's government and the Kadima party adopted for the West Bank'; by this he meant a unilateral withdrawal within three months of forming the government. Ben-Ami argued that a total withdrawal from the West Bank would be a much more complicated operation than Gaza, involving the dismantling of settlements and the evacuation of more than 80,000 settlers. Ariel Sharon's unilateral withdrawal from Gaza necessitated the evacuation of just 8,000 settlers. Gaza is a much simpler entity and its border with Israel has never been disputed, but nevertheless Israel felt compelled to invade Gaza, less than a year after its withdrawal, in an attempt to rescue their kidnapped soldier. 'So what are the long-term chances of such an operation in the West Bank?' asked Ben-Ami. 'The military operation to retrieve Corporal Shalit, called "Operation Summer Rain", highlighted the potential failure of such a strategy and Israel should be the first to realize it.' One lesson learned is that Al Qassam missiles fired from the new frontline in the West Bank are reaching Israel's cities. In the future, it's possible that these missiles will have the range to hit Ben Gurion Airport. According to Ben-Ami:

> If Olmert wants to save his unilateral plan, he should take a Palestinian faction as a partner, and I suggest that this faction should be the Hamas government led by Ismail Haniyeh. This would open up an opportunity to reach an agreement with Hamas which is more far-reaching than the exchange of the abducted soldier at a time when forty-five per cent of Israelis don't object to direct negotiation with Hamas.[8]

The Road Map, which has as its selling point the offer of a Palestinian state, could have new life breathed into it if Hamas would become more pragmatic in its government. Ben-Ami believes that if Hamas accepted such an offer, it would give the movement the opportunity to prove that 'it is united, has a vision and is capable of accepting ceasefires'. Doing a deal with Hamas would be in Israel's interest by creating stability in the West Bank and giving Hamas some satisfaction by putting an end to its isolation on the regional and international scene. It would also solve its ideological refusal to recognize Israel, while still allowing the movement to maintain its firm stand against the occupation.

As Ben-Ami and others point out, Israel has to deal with Syria, and to some extent with Hezbollah, to deal with Hamas. Many within Israel see it as imperative to begin such conversations, while America still has some authority left in the region to help broker terms that are acceptable to Israel. At the moment, America's credibility is draining rapidly and it appears to be in no hurry to engage in diplomacy.

Dennis Ross, who was asked to advise the administration during the 2006 Lebanon conflict, explained:

> I haven't seen them act on the advice in a way that would reflect they were serious. What I hear from them is that they are going to be much more active. I will believe it when I actually see them having a high-level presence with the Israelis on an ongoing basis. When someone is working on the issue publicly and visibly in the arena all the time, that's the manifestation of political investment. How they are working on the Lebanon case suggests a low profile. In the 1996 crisis between Israel and Lebanon, the President sent

me out that same day to the region, and Warren Christopher came
two days later. Christopher did an eight-and-a-half-day shuttle to
produce the ceasefire. And they agreed it. Where do you see the
administration now? David Welch has gone off to Lebanon but
keeping low visibility while Condi Rice leaves the area! Condi gets
there then she leaves the area![9]

In advance of the Secretary of State's arrival in the region at the
height of the Shalit abduction, Rice's Assistant Secretary for Near
Eastern Affairs, David Welch, prepared the ground by meeting the
Palestinian President, Mahmoud Abbas, in his West Bank office in
Ramallah. He asked Mr Abbas to relay a message to Hamas that it
should not make any links with developments between Hezbollah
and Israel. Welch reinforced the importance of keeping the issue
of Hezbollah separate from Hamas and repeated his government's
stance that it would not deal with a Hamas-led government
unless Hamas recognized Israel and accepted the conditions of the
international community. Welch asked Abbas, 'How can a recently
formed government ignore agreements signed by their predecessor
and expect us to deal with them?' Dr Rice saw first hand the
animosity that American foreign policy created in the Middle East
when her motorcade had to negotiate an angry crowd of placard-
waving Palestinian demonstrators chanting anti-American slogans
before reaching the embattled Palestinian President in Ramallah.
She repeated what Welch had told him earlier: she wanted to see 'a
government of technocrats without Hamas', adding that, if there
were any Hamas members in such a government, they would have
to publicly agree to abide by the conditions of the Quartet.

A group of Palestinian professionals, academics and
representatives of Palestinian civil society petitioned the American
Secretary of State to propose that a 'New Middle East', to use her
phrase, should involve a strong international force. This should
not be limited to the Israeli-Lebanese border but should extend to
the Palestinian Occupied territories of 1967 and the Israeli-Syrian
borders, 'to ensure security for all as a prerequisite step to final
status negotiations leading to the implementation of UN Security
Council resolutions'. They concluded that such forces would put

an end to the continuous clashes between conflicting parties and would indicate to the 'cohorts of peace' that there is a genuine drive towards the implementation of the guiding principles of the Middle East in the region, namely 'land for peace' and UN Security Council resolutions 242 and 338 and President Bush's vision for peace in the region.[10]

Two years before 'the New Middle East' was thrust onto the world stage, like some hapless actor who hadn't been given the script, the US administration unveiled its proposals for a 'Greater Middle East Initiative' (GMEI). These proposals were adopted by the industrialized nations which make up the Group of Eight (G8) at the Sea Island summer summit in Georgia.[11] The summit venue, a clutch of private islands just off the North Atlantic coastline of southern Georgia, was selected by President Bush for its natural setting and reputed southern hospitality. While journalists were housed on the mainland, the G8 leaders, under heavy protection from the US Secret Service, were put up on the exclusive Sea Island resort with its five miles of private beaches. Throughout the three days of talks, the delegates could be seen travelling sedately around the island in zero-emission electric vehicles, each one customized with a different flag according to the nationalities of the individual leaders.

I had a couple of discussions with Elliott Abrahams, architect of the GMEI who accompanied the G8 host President Bush to the three-day summit. Abrahams, a Harvard Law School graduate, is described as a 'neo-conservative and neo-Reaganite', mixing the soft and hard sides of the neo-conservative agenda.[12] The Deputy National Security Advisor and Special Assistant to George Bush served as Dr Rice's point man on Israel. As defined by his Initiative, the Greater Middle East stretches from Morocco to Pakistan and was a component of President Bush's 'forward strategy of freedom', by which the expansion of political rights and political participation in the Muslim world is meant to combat the appeal of Islamist extremism.[13] The day before the summit commenced, Abrahams was brimming with confidence in anticipation of the reception he would receive for his vision and enthusiastically explained to me how it was going to revolutionize the whole of the Middle East.

I told him that the main component for its success, a solution to the Arab-Israeli conflict, was missing and to talk about a 'Greater Middle East' without finding a lasting solution for this conflict was tantamount to failure. This fell on deaf ears. Whether through naivety or ignorance, Abrahams seemed not to consider the conflict to be of any great significance to the Arabs in the greater region. His so-called vision received virtually no comment from the Arab world, since Arab leaders and the masses alike felt that this latest design for a 'Greater Middle East' was only serving Israeli interests in the region without giving the Palestinians a fair solution to their dispute with the Jewish State. As I mentally re-ran the highlights of the day from the mainland, with its rush-hour traffic of eight-cylinder gasoline guzzlers, it occurred to me that Abraham's vision was aimed at as artificial a world as the one I saw buzzing with zero-emission electric vehicles on Sea Island.

Later in the summit, President Bush adopted another stance. During a meeting with the French President, Jacques Chirac, Bush was given a thorough briefing about the Middle East region. According to the minutes of that meeting, which were made available to me by French diplomats the following day, it was an interesting and thorough briefing by the European leader, who had just begun mending bridges with the White House after their falling out over the US decision to occupy Iraq. Following the Chirac-Bush private meeting and a similar briefing by the British Prime Minister, Tony Blair, another statement was adopted which called for a solution to the Palestinian-Israeli conflict. This was in line with the Quartet's two-state solution. The *entente cordiale* between Chirac and Bush stretched to the French President praising the cooking in the deep south, saying, 'The cuisine here in America was certainly on a par with French cuisine and I ask the President to convey my thanks to the chef during the summit.' Coming from the head of a nation which prides itself on its culinary tradition, this was praise indeed. Bush could barely conceal his pride when he announced to the people of Savannah and Sea Island, 'The French President liked your food.'

The Sea Island statement supported by the G8 leaders in Georgia never bore fruit, or even any new recipes. Mahmoud Abbas was left isolated and dangling with no firm framework for peace. He was subsequently faced with the Hamas victory of January 2006. Despite receiving verbal reassurances of support from the USA and Israel, Hamas' brothers-in-arms in Lebanon – Hezbollah – had the confidence to trigger a war with Israel which sent seismic shocks around the world.

Shortly after the announcement of the ceasefire between Hezbollah and Israel,[14] Bush described the region as standing 'at a pivotal moment in history'. He said that the recent fighting showed the determination of extremists to prevent 'modern societies from emerging' in the Middle East, and that his administration had sent a clear message to those opposed to the spread of democracy in the region. In an obvious reference to Hamas, Bush insisted: 'America will stay on the offense against Al Qaeda. Iran must stop its support for terror. And the leaders of these armed groups must make a choice. If they want to participate in the political life of their country, they must disarm. Elected leaders cannot have one foot in the camp of democracy and one foot in the camp of terror.'[15]

In many ways, the statement revealed America's refusal to deal with the subtleties of the Middle East and its impulse to simplify a complicated region by lumping two groups who have in some ways similar philosophies but very different roots under one label – 'terrorist'. That is not to say that there are not influential figures in Washington who are closely engaged, amongst them Martin Indyk, President Clinton's Middle East adviser at the National Security Council, who was responsible for handling the 1993 Oslo signing ceremony and for helping to negotiate the Israel-Jordan Peace Treaty. In Indyk's view, 'If Hamas were prepared to moderate its position then there would be a willingness to go along with Mahmoud Abbas. To co-opt them. But, there's no real expectation that that's going to happen. It's very hard to tell what will happen after the dust settles with Hezbollah.'[16]

Indyk defined the two Hamas entities, those inside the Palestinian-occupied territories of Gaza and those abroad, as having 'overall the same ultimate objectives; they share the same ideology.' But, as in any political movement, there are differences. 'Where you stand depends on where you sit. Those who are sitting in Gaza have a different stand to those sitting in Damascus. In the wake of the Lebanon crisis, the idea of trying to split off those in Gaza and those in Damascus began to evolve.' Indyk, who is a legend amongst American diplomats, sounded confident about his theory 'that it's not in the interests of Hamas in Gaza to have their cause hijacked by Hezbollah and Iran' in favour of choosing to side with Abbas and find a common front with him. If this were to happen, Indyk concluded, 'it would be regarded in Washington as an interesting development.'

What concerns not just Indyk and Ross but also many Arab and European leaders is that, in his last days in the White House, President Bush is unlikely to commit to tackling the real root cause, which is the Palestinian issue. For Bush and his Secretary of State, 'the root cause' is Hezbollah and Iran. Only leaders like Blair and Chirac could persuade Bush to say something positive about the Palestinian situation in the wake of the Lebanon crisis. But to get the American President to actually engage in an effort to move that process towards a Palestinian state is highly unlikely during the dying days of his administration. It remains to be seen if Haniyeh and Abbas can present a united front in a practical partnership that Israel can deal with. Olmert's ambition is to get Israel out of the West Bank, which he mistakenly believes has been made easier post-Lebanon. But to convince the Israeli public that Israel should pull its troops out of the West Bank after its catastrophic battle against Hezbollah in Lebanon is going to be determined by whether Israel feels it has a capable and responsible partner on the Palestinian side. Indyk predicts:

> If it's just a unilateral withdrawal, as was the case in Gaza, nobody's going to support it, because that means there's going to be rockets falling on Tel Aviv from the West Bank. So, after the lesson of Lebanon, unilateralism is not a realistic idea. Even within Olmert's government there were warnings that you can't just pull out and toss the keys over the fence. We have to have a partner on the other side, to handle the withdrawal from the West Bank.

Indyk did not believe that the Prisoners' Document would provide a way out of the stalemate. 'Neither the Americans nor the Israelis were convinced that the document signed by Haniyeh would make any difference. The answer would be an emergency government which doesn't have either Hamas or Fatah in it as a way of creating a kind of neutral base on which you can resume the system.'

Internationally, Hamas would naturally try to woo the European Union to prevent the fate of the area lying in the hands of the USA alone. Russia and other European countries are considered good friends in Hamas' book as it struggles to win acceptance from the international community and to clear its name, which has become synonymous with 'terrorism'. The movement believes it would benefit from strengthening its ties to Arab countries, particularly neighbouring Jordan, Syria and Egypt, which maintain good relations with the West. This would further reinforce its legitimacy. Iran is also a vital element in Hamas' sights on both a financial and ideological level. The Arab Gulf States, in particular Qatar, which embraces the Muslim Brotherhood, also inject a potent dose of moral and political support for Hamas. Its success in these manoeuvres will be determined by Hamas' leadership ability to moderate to some extent its more unachievable aims.

Conclusion

Ephraim Sneh was Head of the Civil Administration in the West Bank between 1985 and 1987 under the Labour government of Yitzhak Rabin, just as the nascent Hamas movement was about to emerge onto the world stage. According to Sneh,[1] his role at that time 'was to encourage moderate Palestinians in the West Bank and Gaza to come out against the hardliners. I had an open door to those whom I would describe as the pragmatic elements of Fatah.' In this camp, Sneh placed people like Helmi Hanoun, known as Abu Youssuf, the Mayor of Tulkarem, Palestinian academic Sari Nusseibah, Hannah Saniora, editor of *Al Fajer* newspaper, lawyer Jameel Al Tarifi and intellectual Faisal Husseini, who eventually became a minister, in charge of Jerusalem affairs, for the Palestinian Authority. All were identified as Fatah moderates who later became key political figures in the PLO.

Sneh, who believed he was one of those closest to the late Rabin, didn't recall any alarm bells ringing at the mention of Hamas. At that time, he said, 'it was not considered a dangerous movement. It was a rising force. They were neither prominent nor important politically, nor considered a significant military organization.' Elected to the Knesset in 1992, where he represented the Labour Party, Sneh has served as a member of the Foreign Affairs and Defence Committee.

He believes that the problem in the Middle East 'is not between Israel and the Palestinians but between the moderates and the fanatics'. He would like to see the moderates joining hands as soon as possible to implement a permanent agreement on a two-state solution and to build a new Middle East 'of modernity, of progress and of economic development'. In doing so, he cautioned, 'we must contain the hardliners who want to turn all of the Middle East into a Mogadishu. I don't know if [Olmert] is willing, but he has to. The alternative is horrifying. Compromise and moderation are the only answer.'

Sneh was resolute that:

> Hamas will not change. I have no illusions about that. But sooner or later I would like to see that the majority of Palestinian people will be represented in the government. It is not my business but I care about it. I think the only way to defeat Hamas which is as dangerous, or almost as dangerous as Hezbollah, is to give hope of a political future to the Palestinian people through the implementation and fulfilment of their vision of an independent Palestinian state. Without this prospect, Hamas cannot be defeated because Hamas is building on despair and poverty.

Sneh's opinion is not shared throughout the Israeli establishment. Politician and Knesset member Israel Hasson participated in many of the peace negotiations, including Wye River, Taba and Ehud Barak's Camp David negotiations. The former deputy director of the Shabak had an altogether different perspective from Ephraim Sneh's. The Civil Administration in Gaza's attitude towards the Islamic movement which nurtured Hamas in the early 1980s was 'to turn a blind eye'. This remained until 1983 when Sheikh Ahmed Yassin was arrested for possessing weapons.

In fluent Arabic, Hasson, who was born in Damascus before emigrating to Israel, told me that Hamas first became a significant blip on the political radar around 1992. At that time, Shabak and other intelligence agencies were warning both the Israeli government and the Civil Administration that the movement should be treated as a terrorist organization. Hasson went on to say that, after the signing of the Oslo Agreement in 1993:

We advised the government to pressure the Palestinian Authority to take action against Hamas, but not only would Arafat not cooperate with us, he even allowed Hamas' military wing to take revenge for the assassination of their leader, Yehia Ayyash. It was only when Netanyahu was elected, that Arafat began carrying out mass arrests of Hamas members. Around 2,400 were rounded up and incarcerated in Palestinian jails.

Hasson suggested that the general feeling within the intelligence community was that the Israeli government would only establish contact or negotiate with Hamas if the movement changed its charter and abandoned its threats to destroy Israel. He believed there was a strong feeling inside Israel that Hamas' 2006 election win was merely a temporary victory, adding that the Palestinians in general 'are not militant and prefer to live peacefully. We don't know what the future will reveal. Hamas will take into consideration the outcome of Israel's war in Lebanon against Hezbollah, and whatever steps Israel might take in the future concerning Syria and Iran.'[2]

It is not just in Israel that Hamas is seen as an implacable force, almost a force of nature, which came out of nowhere. Dennis Ross was the first to tell me of America's fears about the new movement in the Palestinian territories which, he said, 'first rang anxiety bells' at the time of the kidnapping by Palestinians of the nineteen-year-old Israeli-American Corporal Nachson Waxman in 1994. Ross shuttled between the region's capitals to alert Arab and Israeli leaders to 'the danger ahead', as he described Hamas. Ross gave the same message to every leader, from President Mubarak of Egypt and the late Hafez Al Assad of Syria to Arafat and Rabin: his peace plan had to remain on track. When he visited Damascus in the early 1990s, there was no one from Hamas who was seriously operational. According to Ross:

The late Hafez Al Assad told me that he was giving them [Hamas] refuge 'because I owe it to the Palestinians', but that he kept them on a tight leash. In '96, we couldn't even get the Syrians to condemn the suicide bombings at a time when we had these agreements going on at Wye River. I tried to say to Farouk Al Sharraa, the Syrian Foreign Minister at that time, that at the end of the day these people will subvert what you say, so you really must get them out. But Damascus didn't want them out.[3]

In late 1995, following the assassination of the Israeli Prime Minister, Yitzhak Rabin, and the series of suicide bomb attacks which brought Netanyahu to power, Ross recalled Mohammed Dahlan, who was head of the Preventive Security Services and Fatah at that time, telling him that, out of concern about Hamas, 'he went to Arafat saying to him: "Look, let me go after Hamas because they are building themselves up too much." He wanted written instructions from Arafat, but the Palestinian leader wouldn't give him written instructions, he said, "Yeah, you can do it, but I'm not going to say so in writing".'

Looking back, it is possible to trace the shift in strategy from the desire to promote Islamic resistance to the desire to knock the PLO off its perch to 1993, when Hamas announced its rejection of the Oslo Accords and began the campaign of 'martyrdom operations' in the region to impede any consensus between the two sides. The period between 1994 and 2002 witnessed the climax of Hamas' suicide missions, preventing any possibility of a reconciliation with Israel. The impact of those operations eventually resulted in the humiliating Israeli siege of President Arafat inside his headquarters in Ramallah and a thorough destruction of the national infrastructure in the territory, including the newly built international airport.

Although Mahmoud Abbas was democratically elected on the strength of his programme of peace with Israel and the demilitarization of the Intifada, Israel, with US support, not only isolated him, but also suppressed his efforts and ignored his opinions and suggestions for peace, leaving him incapable of solving his people's problems.

As the Palestinian Authority became weakened politically, economically and socially, the way was paved for Hamas to show its mettle. The movement had been energetic in its benevolent works in the West Bank and Gaza, earning significant popularity and moral strength in the region. Not only did Hamas defy the Legislative Council, it also had the gall to ask for a share of office, claiming the movement had sacrificed considerable blood in its struggle against the enemy.

Conclusion

Hamas is not a gang. Hamas is part of an Islamic society and the USA has committed a grave error in writing it off as a terrorist organization with whom there can be no negotiation. The movement will not change its Islamic dimension, which is a constant. This is not to say that a Hamas government is the future; simply that attacking and isolating Hamas, as has been done, is merely making the movement more popular.

Fatah is still influential in Palestinian society, its roots firmly entrenched in the Palestinians' recent history. Its political profile suffered a knock when it proved incapable of protecting its own leader when Yasser Arafat was under siege; it suffered another when it failed to call for an open and serious investigation into his death. Fatah's only hope is for Hamas to fail to make headway while in government, giving Fatah the chance to retrieve its powerbase. The powerlessness of Mahmoud Abbas is undermining Fatah. It still has a powerful grassroots network, which could help it to recover majority support for its policies in the future, if it reforms its structure.

The Palestinian Authority itself, meanwhile, has weakened under Abbas, because neither the Israelis nor the Americans have helped him to implement reforms to improve the appalling security situation and standard of living for its citizens. Moreover, the Authority was not given the opportunity to act as a negotiator in the final legal framework. Unlike his predecessor Arafat, Abbas was elected by the people with unlimited American and Israeli support. The momentum was there for him to reach a deal with Israel which was welcomed by both George Bush and Ariel Sharon at their Jordan summit at the Dead Sea in June 2003. But Israel delivered nothing in exchange for Abbas' concessions; instead, the Israeli government dithered and stalled on the details. The momentum was lost and, ultimately, the concessions delivered nothing. A deadly cycle resumed.

Sharon then shifted his tactics to unilateral solutions on the grounds that the Palestinians provided 'no real partner'. Eventually, Sharon withdrew Israeli occupation forces from Gaza and dismantled the Jewish settlements. Sharon's new political party, Kadima, continues but, with Sharon out of the frame, his real agenda was lost by his successors.

The two countries with the lowest profile but the most influence in the current stand-off are Iran and Syria. Neither has ever recognized Israel. Both have openly voiced their support for Hamas, but they are playing an even stronger hand behind the scenes. Khalid Mishal, the real leader of Hamas, is based in Syria. Any actions he takes will be influenced by the policies of Bashar Al Assad and his government. Even the futures of Ismail Haniyeh, the Palestinian Prime Minister, and his successors are more likely to be decided in Syria than Gaza.

Hamas cannot turn back the clock to its former days of championing a military struggle and encouraging suicide bombing. As Mishal sits in his apartment in a Damascus suburb, guarded by undercover Syrian intelligence agents who do their best to blend in with the locals, he will be mentally juggling his goals with Hamas and those of his allies and foes in the Middle East. Hamas' acceptance of a coalition government would give the movement the breathing space to assess what's going on in the region. It is clear that the Americans are not , for now, going to launch a new initiative and it's difficult to see Mahmoud Abbas reaching an understanding with a Damascus-based Mishal. For Mishal, the best option for the time being would be to stick to the Syrian position, allied with Iran. There are behind-the-scenes plans by Arab moderates to bring Syria into the fold by tempting Damascus with economic incentives and the guarantee of stability in exchange for breaking its alliance with Iran. If those plans succeed, Mishal may well have to reconsider his options.

The Syrian-Iranian alliance succeeded in challenging Washington in the playground of Lebanon in the summer of 2006. The strength of this partnership will no doubt be further tested in future confrontations. During the brief war between Israel and Hezbollah, Hamas was instrumental in galvanizing the Sunni Arab world to support the Shia Hezbollah, which deepened the alliance between Syria, Hamas, Iran and Hezbollah. There is certainly still a good chance that this alliance will not dominate Palestinian political life, but if Israel wants to put an end to its conflict with the Palestinians, which could take Iran and Syria out of what is essentially a conflict between two peoples, the price will be to withdraw from the West Bank and reach an agreement on Jerusalem.

mic Jihad Publications.

Maktura Incident took place in Jabaliya refugee camp on 8 December
7.

rview with author on 21 November 1992 by telephone from London to his
se in Gaza.

ra is an Arabic word for 'consultation'. It is the method by which pre-Islamic
bian tribes selected leaders and made major decisions. The role of the Shura
ncil in Hamas was to make sure all its decisions adhered to the sources of
nic legislation, the interests of the public and the unity of the community.

Qur'an, Sura 17, Verse 1.

Islam Online, 7 April 2004.

nel 1, Israeli Television, 3 April 2004.

Islam Online, 7 April 2004.

3. Ez Ed Din Al Qassam Brigades

sm describes a movement that seeks to return to what its adherents see as
urest form of Islam – that practised by the Prophet Mohammed and the
enerations that followed him.

Jarrar, *Sheikh Ezz Al Din Al Qassam: Movement Leader and Martyr to the*
(Al Dia'a House for Publishing, 1989).

l-defined domain extending into the upper Euphrates region with a
ation consisting mainly of Armenians and Syrians.' From 'Crusades',
opaedia Britannica (2006).

fantry Weapons, 1999–2000, Jane's Publications.

ne 1992.

ha-Bitachon ha-Klali (Shabak) is also known as Shin Bet, the Israeli
r-intelligence and internal security service.

ds Al Arabi, 9 August 1992.

ment Expansion: Ariel and Ariel Bloc', *Peace Now*, May 2005, quoting
Central Bureau of Statistics.

d on *Islam Online*.

rabic for 'the Mosque of Abraham in Hebron', which is how the
ians refer to the massacre which was committed by Dr Baruch Goldstein
ebruary 1994, for which there was the traditional forty-day mourning

w with Asrar Ayyash, www.albareek.com, 14 February 2005.

w with Adnan Al Ghoul, *Islam Today*, 27 October 2004, a few days
is assassination.

Defense Forces (IDF) – Qassam Rocket Models, 1, 2 and 3.

w with Salah Shehada, the Hamas Commander of the Al Qassam
, May 2002, *Islam Online*, 29 May 2002. Shehada was assassinated two
later.

The facts on the ground are that, whatever Hamas' political fortunes, they are not just going to melt into the background, nor will any military action succeed in eradicating them. The idea that the Israeli army could destroy Hamas by rolling in the tanks and raining down the missiles brings to mind a chilling American comment during the Vietnam War: 'We destroyed that village in order to save it.' This strategy did not work in Vietnam and it will not work with Hamas. Hamas is not some alien guerrilla force. It is someone's brother, neighbour, or the guy who gives your son money for his education. For as long as these people represent the Palestinian people at the ballot box, the West and any future Palestinian Authority will have to accept it for what it is – a leopard that is unlikely to change its spots – and negotiate with Hamas.

Note

1. Choreograph

1. 29 January 2006.
2. In the *New York Times*, 30 January 2006
3. Ibid.
4. Figures from Hanna Nasser, President
   representing seventy-seven per cent of r
5. In *Yedioth Ahronoth*, 30 January 2006.
6. PSR is an independent, non-profit insti
   and academic research.
7. Figures from the Central Elections Co
8. In the *Washington Post*, 27 January 20
9. Netanyahu, Cohen and Ascherman
   (PBS), 2 February 2006.

2. Hama

1. 1948 refugee figures provided by UN
2. Ahmed Bin Yousif, Islamic Resistanc
3. Bernard Lewis, *Islam and The West*.
4. The war against the newly independ
   the First Arab-Israeli War in which
   were defeated, and Israel went on
   been Palestinian territory under the
5. A bloodless military coup d'état, wh
   corrupt rule of King Farouk I was o
   of his infant son.
6. Yassin was arrested for carrying we
7. Interview with the author, January
8. For further details, see Ze'ev Schiff
   1989).

9. Isla
10. The
    198
11. Inte
    hou
12. Shu
    Ara
    Cou
    Islar
13. Holl
14. On
15. Ibid
16. Chal
17. On /

1. Salaf
   the p
   two g
2. Hosn
   Caus
3. 'An i
   popul
   Encyc
4. See *In*
5. 22 Jun
6. Sheru
   counte
7. *Al Qu*
8. 'Settle
   Israel
9. Quote
10. The A
    Palesti
    on 25
    period.
11. Intervi
12. Intervi
    before
13. Ibid.
14. Israeli I
15. Intervie
    Brigade
    months

Notes

4. The Informers

1. Interview with Shimon Peres, CNN, 24 July 2002.
2. Reuters, 23 July 2002.
3. The names of the dead come from the press release issued by the Palestinian Red Crescent, 23 July 2002.
4. White House spokesman Ari Fleischer.
5. Interviewed in prison by the author, 8 November 2002.
6. 8 November 2002, Gaza City.
7. The *Eid Al Adha* ('Feast of Sacrifice') falls on the tenth day of the Hajj pilgrimage to Mecca, one of the five pillars of Islam which faithful Muslims aspire to perform during their lifetimes.
8. See *Al Wasat* magazine, 20 July 1992.
9. On 13 October 1987.
10. During the Holy month of Ramadan, *Iftar* is the breaking of fast at sunset.

5. The Martyrs

1. On 27 January 2002.
2. On 14 January 2004.
3. Video posted on Hamas website, January 2004.
4. 23 October 2003.
5. Interview with author, Rafiah, February 2005.
6. One *dunum* is approximately a quarter of an acre, or 1,000 square metres.
7. Figures from the UNRWA website, www.un.org/unrwa.
8. The Qur'an, Sura 8:17, Al Anfal, 'The Spoils of War'.
9. Figures from UNRWA for Palestinian Refugees in the Near East, based on assessments by its social workers, Human Rights Watch Report: Rafiah 2004.

6. The Politics of the Sheikh

1. Sheikh Ahmed Yassin interview by the author for *Al Wasat* magazine, 18 January 1999.
2. Sura 5, 'The Table', Verse 20.
3. Sura 5, 'The Table', Verse 24.
4. Copy of text written by Sheikh Yassin about his meeting with Talab Al Sana'a, reproduced in *Al Wasat*, 1 November 1993.
5. An inalienable religious endowment in Islam, typically devoting a building or plot of land for Muslim religious or charitable purposes.
6. On release from prison in 1998, Sheikh Yassin embarked on a tour of several Arab countries, South Africa and Tehran.
7. The Wye River Memorandum was signed in Maryland, USA by Prime Minister Netanyahu and Chairman Arafat on 23 October 1998, in a ceremony attended also by King Hussein of Jordan. It claimed to revive the peace process between Palestinians and Israelis after the collapse of the Oslo and Gaza-Jericho Agreements.
8. 2 November 1998.

9. A copy of the letter was obtained by the author.
10. Quotations from Sheikh Yassin's letters, *Al Wasat*, 1 November 1993.
11. Public statement issued by Hamas and seen by author.
12. 21 August 2003.
13. Interview with author for *Al Wasat* magazine, 18 January 1999.
14. Interview with author, 27 July 1998.
15. Israel signed several commitments to withdraw from the West Bank, which it subsequently reneged on.
16. Interview with *Al Hayat*, 4 December 2003.
17. 25– 27 September 1997.
18. The Hajj, the fifth of the five pillars of Islam, is represented by a pilgrimage to Mecca in Saudi Arabia. This takes place annually between the eighth and tenth days of the twelfth month of the Muslim lunar calendar.
19. Dawn prayer *fajr* takes place between dawn and sunrise.
20. Israeli Ministry of Foreign Affairs, Sunday 14 March 2004.
21. Reuters, 22 March 2004.
22. The Maktura incident sparked off the first Intifada on 7 December 1987.
23. Agence France Presse (AFP).

7. International Relations

1. Of the sixteen original refugee camps in Lebanon, three were destroyed during the civil war, while one was closed down and the refugees transferred to another camp. There are currently twelve registered by UNRWA.
2. 2 August 1990.
3. The Hamas office was closed down the day following the statement, on 30 August 1999.
4. Qatar has been ruled by the Al Thani family since the Ottomans departed in 1915 and is the only state apart from Saudi Arabia whose population subscribes to the fundamentalist Wahabi form of Islam.
5. The Shah of Iran fled the country on 16 January 1979. Ayatollah Khomeini returned on Thursday 1 February 1979.
6. 5 May 1974.
7. 17 March 1974.
8. Lebanon's civil war spanned 1975– 1990.
9. The Israeli-Iranian Strategic Rivalry Middle East Report Online: 'Under the Veil of Ideology', 9 June 2006.
10. From 'Yasser Arafat and the Islamic Republic of Iran', IranianVoice.org, 2 May 2002.
11. The photo, by UPI, was reproduced in *Newsweek*, 5 March 1979.
12. Quoted on *The New Republic Online*.
13. The Israeli-Iranian Strategic Rivalry Middle East Report Online: 'Under the Veil of Ideology', 9 June 2006.
14. Afshin Molavi and Karim Sadjadpour, 'Tehran Dispatch: Change Up', *The New Republic Online*, 10 November 2003.

15. Ibid.
16. Wording from a Judgment given by the Revolutionary Islamic Court of Tehran to transfer title deeds of abandoned property to Bonyad-e Mostazafan za Janbazan, Appendix 1 DGAM 29640 Case No 60/TA/2745/1, 22 August 1972.
17. Iran Free Press Service, Paris, 24 September 1998.
18. The Iran Revolutionary Guard Corps (IRGC), identified by the British government in February 1998 as 'a military force', was created following the 1979 Revolution and originally entrusted with internal security. It was considered separate from the regular armed forces; it includes ground forces, air forces, navy, Quds Force (special operations) and Basij (Popular Mobilization Army). See 'Iranian Entity: Iran Revolutionary Guard Corps', *Iran Watch*, 10 April 2004.
19. An association of fifty-six Islamic states, the conference aims at promoting Islamic solidarity by coordinating social, economic, scientific and cultural activities. Under the banner of strengthening the struggle of Muslims, the conference pledges to eliminate racial segregation and discrimination, especially in regard to the PLO.
20. Telephone interview with the author, 1 December 1994.
21. Telephone interview with author, 5 December 1994.
22. Ibrahim Goshi's trip to Tehran, October 1992.
23. Interview with author, 5 December 1994.
24. Abu Moussa, Abu Saleh and Kadri are all *noms de guerre*.
25. An alliance opposed to the peace process as defined by the Oslo Accords.
26. Alawites are a Shi'ite sect representing fifteen per cent of the population and are the ruling minority in Syria. Figures from Washington Institute of Near East Policy, March 2005.
27. Carré, Olivier and Gérard Michaud, *Les Frères Musulmans: Egypte et Syrie, 1928– 1982* (Paris: Gallimard, 1983).
28. In *Al Hayat*, 4 August 2006.
29. DEBKAFile attributed the nickname to Yitzhak Rabin, 27 September 2004.
30. Channel 2, Israel, 26 September 2004.
31. Al Jazeera, 27 September 2004.
32. Hamas statement, 27 September 2004.
33. In *Al Hayat*, 26 September 2004.
34. 31 August 2004.
35. 25 June 2006.
36. See *Jerusalem Post*, 28 June 2006.
37. Israeli Army Radio, 28 June 2006.
38. Jean Shaoul, 'The Political Failure of the PLO and the Origins of Hamas', Part Two, *World Socialist* website, 6 July 2002.
39. US Department of Justice press release, 20 August 2004.
40. See *Ha'aretz*, 25 March 2005.
41. US Office of Public Affairs, 21 August 2003.
42. 22 December 2005.

43. 9 January 2006.
44. 2 July 2006.
45. White House press release, 4 December 2001.
46. Al Jazeera.net, 12 April 2002.
47. *New York Post*, 13 February 2002.
48. Sky Television, 17 July 2002.
49. See *Ha'aretz*, 3 July 2003.
50. US State Department, Thursday 24 July 2003.
51. Sean McCormack, State Department spokesperson.
52. 'US and Israelis are said to talk of Hamas ouster', *New York Times*, 14 February 2006.
53. 'Distance Learning: Hamas's US Education', *Washington Post*, 30 April 2006.
54. Interview with Abu Marzouk, *Al Wasat*, 19 May 1997.
55. See *Al Wasat*, 19 May 1997.
56. Cited by Associated Press.
57. White House press release, 24 June 2002.
58. White House press conference, 26 January 2006.
59. Interview with Dennis Ross, BBC News, 26 January 2006.
60. Martin Indyk, telephone interview with author, August 2004.
61. Mark Perry and Alastair Crooke (co-directors of Conflicts Forum), 'How to lose the "War on Terror", Part 2: Handing Victory to the Extremists', reproduced in *Asia Times Online*, April 2006.
62. Intelligence and Terrorism Information Center, 29 November 2004.
63. Jeffrey Godlberg, 'The Martyr Strategy', *New Yorker*, 9 July 2001.
64. Ibid.
65. Weapons list from *Ha'aretz*, 8 May 2001.
66. Israel Ministry of Foreign Affairs, 'Iran and Syria as Strategic Support for Palestinian Terrorism', 30 September 2002.
67. Reported in *Al Hayat* (London), 10 May 2001.
68. One of the terms in the Gaza-Jericho Agreement of 4 May 1994 under 'External Security' states that: 'Israel maintains security control and supervision over the entry of persons, vehicles and weapons at all points of entry. Israel retains security control of the sea as well as control and supervision over all air space.'
69. In *Ha'aretz*, 17 July 2001.

8. Fiction Precedes Fact: The Al Qaeda Connection

1. The Coptic Christians of Egypt follow the Orthodox Christian calendar.
2. Ministry of Health figures quoted in *Al-Ahram Weekly*, 4– 10 May 2006.
3. Emanuel Marx, *Nomads and Cities: The Development of a Conception* (2003).
4. See *Al-Ahram Weekly*, 1– 7 September 2005.
5. See *Al-Ahram Weekly*, 4– 10 May, quoting a Ministry of the Interior statement.
6. Marx, *Nomads and Cities*.
7. Press release, Egyptian Ministry of the Interior, 30 April 2006.
8. MFO press release, Rome, 27 April 2006.

Notes

9. See *Al Hayat*, 1 May 2006.
10. See *Asharq al Awsat*, 7 May 2006.
11. According to Associated Press, 9 May 2006.
12. Horn of Africa countries include Sudan, Kenya, Somalia and Ethiopia.
13. Under the pact, Israel agreed to return Sinai to Egypt, a transfer that was completed in 1982.
14. See the *Sunday Times*, 17 July 2005.
15. In *The Guardian*, 22 May 2004.
16. AFP/AP/Reuters.
17. Interview with Mohammed Juma, *Human Rights Watch*, Rafiah, 13 July 2004.
18. Marie Colvin, *Sunday Times*, 17 July 2005.
19. See *Sunday Times*, 17 July 2005.
20. Not his real name.
21. In April 1982, when Israel withdrew from the Sinai, Egypt refused to take Gaza and Israel insisted on creating a security buffer between Egypt and occupied Gaza.
22. According to *Middle East Quarterly*, Summer 2004.
23. Palestinian Centre for Human Rights figures September 2000–2004, quoted in *Al Haram Weekly*, 30 September– 6 October 2004.
24. Ariel Sharon, press briefing, 5 December 2002.
25. In *Yediot Ahronot*.
26. Reuters News Agency, 9 December 2002.
27. Executive Intelligence Review, 20 December 2002.
28. USS *Cole*, a guided missile destroyer, was attacked on 12 October 2000 in the Port of Aden, Arabian Peninsular, by a small inflatable boat carrying explosives, in a suicide attack which killed seventeen Americans and seriously injured more than thirty-six.
29. The above case studies appeared in a document produced by the Palestinian Preventive Security in 2002, from information provided by the arrested Palestinians, and shown to the author.
30. BBC News, 5 December 2002.
31. Secret document obtained by the author from Palestinian Preventive Security, 2002.
32. For further reading, see Ian Black and Benny Morris, *Israel's Secret Wars: A History of Israel's Intelligence Services*.
33. See *International Journal of Intelligence and Counterintelligence*, Vol. 8, No. 3 (1995).
34. See *Washington Report on Middle East Affairs*, October/November 1999, quoting former Mossad case worker Victor Ostrovsky in his book, *The Other Side of Deception*.
35. Reported by Associated Press/BBC News, March 2006.
36. Washington Institute, *Al Qaeda Infiltration of Gaza: A Post-Disengagement Assessment*, 16 December 2005.
37. Al Jazeera, 4 March 2006.

38. BBC World News, Sunday 5 March 2006.
39. Press statement by Sami Abu Zehri, 4 March 2006.
40. Palestinian General Intelligence, March 2006.
41. Referring to ancient geographical Syria which includes Syria, Lebanon and Palestine and settled areas of Jordan.
42. 28 April 2006.
43. See Stephen Ulph in *Terrorism Focus*, Vol. 1, No. 5, 1 October 2004.
44. Available on Al Tawhed wa Al Jihad website, www.Tawhed.ws/r?=2971.
45. Salafism describes a movement that seeks to return to what its adherents see as the purest form of Islam – that practised by the Prophet Mohammed and the two generations that followed him.
46. Zaki Chehab, *Iraq Ablaze: Inside the Insurgency.*
47. Abu Musab Al Zarqawi was killed on 7 June 2006 in a US air strike.
48. An Islamic state governed by sharia law that would stretch across all formerly Muslim lands.

9. The Future of Hamas

1. 29 June 2006.
2. 26 June 2006.
3. In *Al Hayat*, 3 August 2006.
4. According to Israel Radio, 5 July 2006.
5. Also on Sunday 2 July 2006.
6. Interview by telephone with the author, 6 August 2006.
7. Office summary of Foreign Minister Al Zahar's trip to ten Arab countries, April– May 2006.
8. Shlomo Ben-Ami interviewed by *Le Monde*, 12 August 2006.
9. Interview with author, 8 August 2006.
10. Al Quds Administration Office, 23 July 2006.
11. 8– 10 June 2004. The purpose of the G8 Summit is for the leaders of the world's major industrial nations to meet to discuss the issues facing the world in an informal setting.
12. International Relations Center Right web profile of Elliott Abrahams.
13. 'The New US Proposal for a Greater Middle East Initiative: An Evaluation', Saban Center Middle East Memo, 10 May 2004.
14. 14 August 2006.
15. White House transcript, 14 August 2004.
16. Telephone interview with author, 18 July 2006.

Conclusion

1. Telephone interview with author, 18 August 2006.
2. Telephone interview with author, 18 August 2006.
3. Telephone interview with author, 8 August 2006.

Index

Index

Index